To Gladly Learn, and Gladly Teach

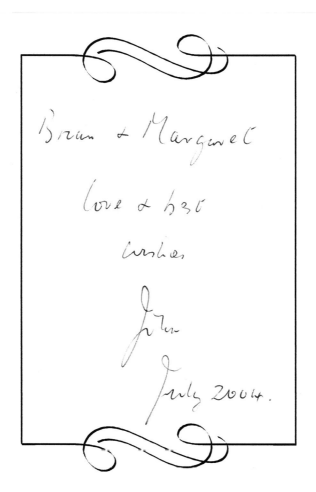

Brian & Margaret

love & best

wishes

John

July 2004.

To Gladly Learn, and Gladly Teach

by

JOHN MANN

The Memoir Club

First published in 2004 by
The Memoir Club
Stanhope Old Hall
Stanhope
Weardale
County Durham

British Library Cataloguing in
Publication Data.
A catalogue record for this book
is available from the
British Library.

ISBN: 1 84104 056 8

Typeset by George Wishart & Associates, Whitley Bay.
Printed by CPI Bath.

To Margaret, who encouraged me to embark on this enterprise, hoping she says only that this would make time and space for her gardening, and whose sympathetic critiques of the rough drafts have helped to bring the barque safely to port.

Contents

Soap and education are not as sudden as a massacre,
but they are more deadly in the long run.

Mark Twain

Illustrations

Acknowledgements

Hundreds of lively pupils and countless committed, talented and stimulating colleagues have nourished and enriched every stage of my life and work. I treasure happy memories of innumerable exchanges and our shared interests and aspirations. It's impossible to mention everyone by name but I was singularly fortunate that Jack Elam at Colchester, George Taylor in Leeds, Michael Harrison in Sheffield, and John Tomlinson at the Schools Council all gave me ample space in which to flourish. I was equally fortunate in my personal assistants, of whom Jennifer Ruttley and Christine Poole in Sheffield, and Irene Hall at the Schools Council were unstintingly supportive colleagues. Julia Wenham, Chair of Governors, and Sue Mogg, Head of Broadstone First School, Sarah Morgan and Lynn Miall of the National Westminster Bank, Broadstone, the staff of the Local Studies Centre at Poole's Waterfront Museum and Clare Hopkins, Archivist of Trinity College, Oxford, were all most generous in the help they gave me in refreshing my memories.

Introduction

O UR CULTURE went through a remarkable transformation over the last half
of the twentieth-century. By the end of the period the pre-war deferential
society had disappeared, heavy industry had given way to what has been called
a 'weightless' economy, a relatively innocent population became deluged in
information by mass media, the 'Long Revolution' of an educated and
discerning people predicated by Raymond Williams was well on its way to
reality. But manifold change was a complex process; so it is a rare treat to have
the story of a leader's career in the public education service throw a light on
social change from the inside track. John Mann demonstrates how professionals and ordinary citizens, vocal and questioning, were well attuned to the
background of an age suddenly modern – because they were an organic part
of it.

He shows us vividly the depth and width of the continuous debate that took
place among teachers, administrators, citizens and parents, and elected
members of local education authorities, at a time when the ideals of the 1944
Education Act were reaching their first stage of fulfilment. Born a dissenter, as
he says, he shows how provocative exploration of issues and a demand for
clarity of aims with systematic pursuit of ends was achieving through hard-
won consensus a promising unity of endeavour. This was then shattered by a
government, it has to be said, ignorant of the temper of its own people – who
were busy at ground level, fruitfully shaping their own destiny. But instead of
building on success already achieved locally, government used education as a
scapegoat at a time of economic turmoil, devising artificial, State-driven
machinery to back its charges of educational underperformance. The measures
were counter-modern; they smacked of a Stalinist centralism and they were
just as hopeless. It was all bitterly ironical coming from a government that
declared itself opposed to ideas of intervention and planning.

If only central government could have lifted its game and put superior
minds to developing the vision and strategies appropriate to the coming
twenty-first century, what a valid and strong position national education now
might occupy, with intelligence and commitment of legions of hardened
practitioners and supporters behind it!

Telling a story full of sharp observation and wit, John Mann delivers a piece
of essential and entertaining reading for those who want to know the truth of
how affairs in public education were dealt with in the half century before 2000.
It will probably take another half-century before the neglect and mistakes of

the past are put right. His tale gives vital clues as to how education's future might be managed more effectively and led more intelligently during the next stage to 2050.

Michael Harrison
Rigmaden, Kirkby Lonsdale
February 2004

CHAPTER 1

East Dorset

First the infant

'Founded 1890'. Like some American prairie township, Broadstone can claim a pretty firm date for its foundation. In the nineteenth century farms, quarries, and a large brickworks provided steady and growing employment on this part of the Dorset heath. In 1871 the local magnate funded a new school, and in 1872 the railway decided to build a station at the junction of its main line to Dorchester and a new branch line to Poole. School and station formed the nucleus of a new village. By the time village and station adopted Broadstone as their name in 1890, there were several houses near the new parish church, and a clutch of shops and houses on either side of the old turnpike road from Gravel Hill to Blandford. Prominent among them were five substantial red-brick villas between Ridgeway and Church (now Macauley) Road.

We lived in one of these villas, a handsome double-fronted house standing in about a third of an acre. It had extensive attics on the second floor, a drawing room, three large double bedrooms and a sizeable single room off the first floor landings, and four large rooms opening off front and back halls on the ground floor. In one of these, an all-purpose room for cooking and laundry which we always called the scullery, was a mysterious square patch of tiles which was said to cover a well. There was no mains water in Broadstone when these houses were built. A projecting wing at the back held pantry, bathroom and assorted boxrooms. At one side of the house there was an elegant conservatory, and in the back garden an even larger greenhouse, both heatable and both equipped with large water tanks, much used for watersports later on when we acquired stirrup pumps for wartime firefighting. The garden was well stocked with black currant, loganberry and gooseberry bushes, raspberries, strawberries, and damson, apple, plum and pear trees. There were well-groomed lawns and privet hedges at the front, with plenty of grass at the back for playing whatever games were in season.

Some of these villas had gone down in the world by the time they celebrated their golden jubilee in 1938. One was Hadfield where Dr Norman lived and practised. Then came Lindisfarne, a children's home run by Miss Eva Muriel Oldfield and Miss Violet Oldfield. Mr Wilson's gentlemen's outfitters had grown to fill the ground floor of a third, and when Mrs Scutt died, a year or two after giving me a handsome Victorian child's chair, lock-up

The fifth villa retained some of its aura.

shops replaced her house. The gardens in front of all these shops had gone, their place taken by a new service road. This road came to an abruptly menacing end at our garden fence. On our side of the fence the fifth villa retained some of its aura even though its downstairs windows advertised the National Provincial Bank, who opened their doors on three days a week from 1921. The Bank used just the front door and one of the front rooms. When my father came there in 1928 to open a full-time branch, the rest of the house went with the job. We lived as it were in a tied cottage, rather grand but tied all the same.

I've often wondered how the Bank came to be there. Did National Provincial wait patiently until they could buy the premises immediately opposite their arch rivals, the former Wilts and Dorset Bank, now Lloyds? Or did it fall into their hands by chance? Mysteriously vacated because of some financial mishap, a common enough event between the wars when gentlemen, and even ladies, sometimes fled Broadstone precipitately, leaving behind an assortment of unpaid bills? Perhaps their fate shaped Dad's thinking. He was of the Polonius school, 'neither a borrower nor a lender be, for loan oft loses both itself and friend'. It was an odd doctrine for a banker, and later on he took great pride in having helped to fund several successful businesses.

By that time Broadstone was its own place. Fresh heathland air, a renowned golf course, and good rail services to London and the Midlands brought in people with business interests and waves of retired servicemen. By 1931 there was a veritable corps of commanders, captains, majors, and colonels. There were at least two dozen retired officers, headed by General Tyndale-Biscoe and Admiral D'Oyly whose names Dad mentioned always in most reverential tones. 'For a long time,' says one anonymous authority quoted in Nona Bowring's *History of Broadstone*, 'the principal residents of Broadstone were golfers, retired Army and Navy men, Bank Managers, and Clergy. Life was very peaceful and everyone knew everyone else.' It must have been their big houses which put the two local Bank Managers in this league. And it may explain why an old school friend with whom I spoke for the first time some sixty years after leaving the area said immediately I gave my name, 'Ah, the bank manager's son.'

The job and the house evidently carried a certain cachet. They might have given my parents an entree to Broadstone society. Their status would have been amply confirmed the day two Rollers parked outside our house, one in the morning and another in the afternoon. No one else was to know that one of my uncles worked for Rolls Royce, and that his duties included delivering a courtesy car whenever an owner's car had to be taken to Derby for servicing. But it was not to be: my mother was bewildered when ladies called and left their cards. That was a refinement for which her upbringing in Derby had not prepared her. She was more at ease playing tennis, preparing cricket teas, immersing herself in the varied activities of the Methodist Chapel, and becoming a housewife and mother.

The baby she bore on 4 June 1930 shares my birthday and my name. It was nine months to the day after a tiny tremor on Wall Street, the first portent of the Great Crash. Amy Johnson had just flown in from Australia, and in that year Marks and Spencer opened their Oxford Street store, the English Folk Dance Society established itself near Regents Park, and the *Daily Worker* went on sale. That same 4 June *The Times* reported 'the usual services from Paddington to Windsor will be strengthened' to carry parents to the annual celebration of George III's birthday by the boys of Eton College. And at the bottom of the same column *The Times* reported that the Australian High Commissioner had told fifty young Barnardo's boys who were setting off to a training farm near Sydney that he didn't much care for boys who were too 'goody goody'.

The new baby fell somewhere between these two extremes. He and I have the same birth certificate, and quite possibly the same DNA code. But he's a stranger, and so too are his young parents. I can remember little that he did in his first five or six years, and even less of what he felt about the world around him. Screams of delight and terror when out of banking hours Dad would lift him on to one of the five-foot high safes in his office. But no recollection of the railway journey to Derby for a longish stay when his brother Derrick was born in early 1933. By that time he was said to be house trained, speaking

The photographer won a prize for this collage.

clearly and beginning to show a mulish independence, 'I can do it mine own self.' His children relish the phrase, relayed to them by their grandmother.

The journey north could hardly have been more straightforward. In those days the Pines Express from Bournemouth to the Midlands stopped most conveniently at Broadstone and after a meandering journey through Templecombe arrived eventually at Cheltenham where Dad's family lived and then at Derby where Mum's family lived. Until first one and then another pater familias acquired his first car, the Pines Express was the lifeline which held our dispersed family together. Seasonal family gatherings in Cheltenham or Derby were feasible, and even when the adults had cars the railway guards were happy to keep an eye on unaccompanied minors, so that we and our cousins could sometimes exchange visits. The station itself was always a delight with its signs advertising Marmite, Players Please, Cerebos Salt, Lifebuoy Soap, Mazawattee Tea, Reckitt's Blue, Virol, Wills Cigarettes, Heinz 57 Varieties and other staples.

Dad must have bought his first car, a little red Singer 8, in about 1934 or 35. When we went on holiday, heavily laden, to hillier parts of England or Wales, the radiator used to boil, and we had to stop while it cooled down and fresh water was brought. But its most remarkable contribution to my happiness was at Christmas 1935 when we stayed with my grandmother in Cheltenham. That year Father Christmas brought me a sturdy pedal car which must have travelled with us secretly from Broadstone. It certainly went back to

Broadstone, where it travelled many miles up and down the garden path until I transferred my affections first to three and then to two wheels.

The garden was huge, and safe. I used to play there with John Alexander, a well-mannered boy from the home along the road, and with Vera Richardson, a pretty girl who was said to be Kathleen Loveless's younger sister. Kathleen used to help in the house. The Bank paid for someone to clean the office, and Kathleen went on then to help Mum in the house. There were grates to clean, stone floors to scrub, lino to polish, bedding and clothes to launder, and children to nourish: there was lots to do in a large house, and perhaps even more important for Mum, there was someone else in the house for a few hours each day. There don't seem to have been any other young marrieds in our part of Broadstone, and in those early years Hilda often felt rather lonely.

Life in a cavernous bank house was very different from her previous life. Off duty, she'd been one of the young 'flappers' of the twenties, loved dancing, and all her life sang and hummed WW1 hits and the pop tunes of the twenties, 'Tipperary', 'Pack up your troubles', 'If you were the only girl in the world, and I were the only boy', 'Daisy, daisy, give me your answer, do...', 'Tea for two, and two for tea' and a whole repertory of songs and hymns from the News Chronicle Song Book or the Methodist Hymn Book. Isaac Watts was a great favourite:

> How doth the little busy bee
> Improve each shining hour,
> And gather honey all the day
> From every opening flower.
>
> For Satan finds some mischief still
> For idle hands to do.

She was in truth a closet follower of Thomas Carlyle's Victorian doctrine, 'work is the grand cure for all the maladies and miseries that beset mankind', but she was far more likely to be heard reciting W.H. Davies,

> What is this life if, full of care
> We have no time to stop and stare.

Like Don Quixote's servant Sancho Panza she had too an inexhaustible fund of homely proverbs for every occasion: 'take care of the pence, and the pounds will take care of themselves', but too many people were 'penny wise and pound foolish'. 'Many hands make light work' when she needs help, but 'too many cooks spoil the broth' if she is in '"I'll do it myself" said the little red hen' mode. 'You'll eat a peck of dirt before you die' was a useful line at any sign of undue fussiness, but 'cleanliness is next to godliness' was her creed, inherited from a maternal grandmother who may have been 'in service'. 'Dirt is the natural emblem and consequence of vice' the *Servants' Magazine* had proclaimed in 1839.

After leaving school Mum had worked for six years at one of Derby's most prestigious firms, the Midland Railway, as it was about to disappear in the newly formed London Midland and Scottish Railway. She was soon promoted head of the typing pool and then secretary to various senior managers, including the general manager. In May 1926 she was at the centre of things during the General Strike when ASLEF and the Railway Clerical Association decreed that 'no trains of any kind must be worked by our members'. When the strike ended on 12 May the LMS was running only one in eight of its passenger trains, and only 3 per cent of its goods trains. Hilda's sympathies lay with the strikers.

Life at home in Broadstone was a good deal less exciting for her. But for Fred, busy with Banking Institute exams and establishing a new branch, there were no such problems. He struck rich seams in billiards and snooker tournaments at the Liberal Club in York Road and in their whist drives; and he was too a useful village cricket batsman. One week an errant cricket ball hit him in the mouth. From then on he wore a one-tooth plate which he could manoeuvre to make the most horrifying grimaces. Like Bradbury's History Man he must have practised in the mirror. On Saturdays, after the Bank closed at midday there was a family outing, to the cricket field in season, sometimes to see the Quarter Jack strike the quarter hours at Wimborne Minister, but most often to Poole. John wanted only to see the boats unloading coal and clay on Poole Quay and go on to feed the mute and haughty swans in Poole Park. You daren't go too near because, it was said, they could break an arm or leg with one flap of their wings. In the evenings Mum or Dad would read aloud: nursery rhymes, Hans Andersen, the *Arabian Nights*, Pooh, and above all, Peter Pan. Peter was my hero. There was no better name. My little reddish rubber doll was named Peter, and our new cat, and in due course my second brother. Long before I could read I was reckoned to know *Peter Pan and Wendy* off by heart, would correct the slightest (deliberate?) error in their reading, and lie panting with excitement as the climax approached, 'AND THE FIGHT BEGAN!'

It was a long time before I realized that this was a different fight from the good one we all promised to fight with all our might on Sundays. Sundays were special. The Methodist Chapel was next door, which could not have been handier. There was a little Sunday School before the morning service at 11, a cold lunch to save work on Sunday, Sunday School in the afternoon at 2.30, and an evening service at 6.30. John usually managed the morning and afternoon sessions from quite an early age, and Dad the morning and evening services where his light tenor was valued in Mr Chivers' choir. In these early years Mum managed only the morning service because there was always a baby to look after and in any case she was active at the chapel during the week. Gradually she and Fred found kindred spirits in the small Methodist congregation: the Coles, the Wilsons, the Greens, and the Sharlands became lifelong friends though I never heard my mother refer to even the closest among them by first name. It was always Mr Cole and Mrs Cole, even after they were dead. She joined the Good Templar Lodge founded by Ernest Green a few years earlier and got her father to address a couple of its meetings, founded and led a Girls' League, and began to speak at Women's Meetings in that and other chapels even though at first she was almost sick with fright. Her father and his father had been crusaders and evangelists all their lives; nature and nurture now propelled her in the same direction. Life, her example taught, is a battle to be fought.

Not that there were any great battles to be fought at school. Broadstone School looked old when I went there in September 1935, a neat stone building funded by Sir Ivor Bertie Guest in 1871. The school bell was said to be 3,000 years old and to have come from Assyrian Nineveh or Nimrud, excavated by Sir Henry Layard and given to his cousin Ivor Guest. Perhaps this story encouraged my lifelong dilettante interest in ancient history, in no way diminished when I heard that the story was disproved when the bell had to be repaired in 1999. The school building doubled as an Anglican church until the late 1880s when Sir Ivor, now ennobled as Lord Wimborne, provided funds for a parish church. Having started life as a church school run by the National Society the school itself became a council school in the early 1900s. Its job was to provide an elementary education for children of five to fourteen. When I went to school in 1935 Broadstone School had 236 children in its five classes, so mixed age and mixed ability classes were the order of the day. On my first day Mum and I walked from the playground straight into Miss Stevens's class. I dimly recall a trim grey-suited woman with short steely hair, a room packed with double desks, individual slates, an abacus, and a small blackboard and easel. 'The curriculum,' said the official guidance then current, 'is to be thought of in terms of activity and experience rather than of knowledge to be acquired and facts to be stored.' As there wasn't a great deal of space our most active pursuit was chanting our multiplication tables singsong, all the way from once two is two to twelve twelves are one hundred and forty four. Dad thought we ought to learn our guzintas too, two guzinta two once, two guzinta four twice, and so on, but Broadstone School was less ambitious. At the end of every day we sang

> We plough the fields and scatter
> The good seed on the ground,
> But it is fed and watered
> By God's Almighty hand.
> He sends the snow in winter,
> The warmth to swell the grain,
> The breezes and the sunshine,
> And soft refreshing rain.

Then our reedy trebles rose to a crescendo as we gabbled the chorus,

> All good things around us
> Are sent from heaven above,
> Then thank the Lord, oh, thank the Lord,
> For all His love.

And rushed off home.

My second term was a time of troubles. My second brother Peter was born on 13 January 1936. By that time the school log was already recording measles. By 2 February one in four of the children were away with measles, chicken-pox or heavy colds. By 21 February more than two in five were away. I had measles, recovered, and went back to school. By mid March the epidemic had subsided, but not before the measles had caught Derrick. When I got home from school on Wednesday 18 March Mum was sitting downstairs in our dining (family) room in one of our brass-studded, leather-covered armchairs, crying. 'What's the matter, Mummy?' 'Derrick's gone to Jesus.'

I was slightly puzzled even then that she should be crying about someone going to heaven. Wasn't this what we were all working and struggling for? I'm even more puzzled now that I've never had any recollection of the little boy who must have been my companion and playmate for three years. Perhaps I needed to suppress some sense of responsibility for having brought measles into the house. Perhaps it's partly because I had a new and entertaining baby brother. The need to look after the baby Peter, Dad would say much later, was what saved Mum from total despair at losing Derrick.

I can only marvel now that they saved me from any sense of gloom then and in the following year when Mum's mother died in our house. Life went on. I had the usual ailments. For most of these Mum's standbys were Thermogene, Milk of Magnesia, worm powders and Virol. My Saturday penny was an opportunity to go across the road to buy a small bag of peardrops, while Dad bought himself a packet of Wills Cigarettes and me a cigarette card. We began to explore the Dorset countryside, long walks on the local heathland and along the Roman road, the Blue Pool, seasonal visits to Bournemouth to see Father Christmas arrive with sleigh and reindeer before settling down to his work at Beale's (or was it Bealeson's or Bobby's?), Studland, the Globe at Swanage, the red squirrels in the Bournemouth chines, the cinema at Poole with Sandy Macpherson playing the cinema organ as he rose from the pit, and Shirley Temple, just about my own age and already a starlet. Whenever we were in Poole Dad would search the High Street for quality doughnuts, a field in which he reckoned to be a connoisseur. Very often we would have tea 'out', usually at Poole's new department store, the Bon Marche. On one splendid occasion we saw *Peter Pan and Wendy* at the Pavilion in Bournemouth.

At home there were always lots of games, Ludo, Snakes and Ladders, and another dice game called Touring Europe which involved planning routes to all the major cities. Mum had never played cards before she married, but we played strip jack naked, sevens, the fashionable memory game called pelmanism, cribbage, and three-handed whist. Chinese Chequers was another favourite and Dad also taught me to play draughts, at which I never ever beat him, and chess, at which I sometimes did. Soon after it came out one of Dad's brothers gave us a Monopoly set. You win some and you lose some, but I learned early on that a keen match gives enormous pleasure and satisfaction whoever wins.

Every summer we had a seaside holiday. In those days the brochures listed innumerable landladies who offered bedrooms, a separate family dining room, and meals. Mum and Dad used to pore over these brochures as they tried to weigh the rival attractions offered by Mrs Evans, Mrs Jones and Mrs Williams. Three years running after Derrick's death we stayed in the same town as my Uncle Edgar and his family, the Dye family and the Knee family who were friends of theirs, and sometimes other uncles, grandparents and friends. There were always sixteen or eighteen of us for enormous games of cricket on the sands at Tenby, Bude or Westward Ho, and lots of fun and laughter. We swam and surfed and searched the salt rock pools for sea anemones to feed. One year when I was seven or eight as we changed in the warm sun after swimming I wondered why my aunt covered my eleven year old cousin Rosemary so hastily with towels.

There must have been girls in my class at school But they did not play conkers or any of our weird games which involved flicking cigarette cards and other larger cards across the playground. They indulged in skipping and hopscotch and other girly pastimes. They could safely be ignored.

When the inspectors came in 1935 there were two classes with over fifty children. I think Miss Stevens's must have been one of these because I can only remember having three teachers in my four years there, and I've a feeling I stayed with her for two years. I can vaguely remember sitting near the door at first, and then graduating by stages to the far end of the room. That was where I learned to knit. Mum was amazed when I went home with a couple of misshapen kettle holders. Perhaps we also had occasional lessons with Arthur Shaft who taught woodwork. It was probably under his guidance that I once fashioned some sort of wooden penholder. This experience may have been useful a few years later when I tried to make a machine to write multiple copies of the lines which were doled out so generously at Poole Grammar School. I also undertook some very modest craft work at the little pottery which used to stand near Darby's Corner on the way to Poole.

And I began to learn joined-up writing, with guide lines for the upward and downward loops on certain letters. I like to think I was moved up to the next class before I'd really learned cursive writing. That might excuse my adult scrawl. But the evidence is against me. Both in 1938 and 1939 I scored nine

out of ten for 'penmanship', though I'm sure every one of the typists and
secretaries who kept me going for thirty years will die laughing if they ever
read this paragraph.

After a couple of years I moved up to Mrs Hart's class, which was in the
new wooden hut in the playground. This hut served most helpfully to enclose
the playground, providing a shield against the wind which threatened our
games. Mrs Mary Hart was the wife of Mr Percy Hart, the Headmaster, but no
one would have presumed to use their first names. She left an indelible
impression, once giving me a penny for excelling in a spelling bee. I rushed out
of school, heading for Waterman's dairy some thirty yards down the road.
Somewhere between school and dairy that penny disappeared. I stood sobbing
on the pavement. And then a fairy materialized, touched a grown up on the
shoulder, and the grown up gave me another penny for an icecream.

The Board of Education gave up inspecting school timetables in the mid
1920s, and in those days, says A.J.P. Taylor, 'politicians never raised the great
question of what should be taught...we know little of what (the pupils) were
taught and virtually nothing of its underlying character...anarchy prevailed, a
last great bastion of English freedom.' I don't recall what I was taught but I do
know what was tested when I was seven. Mrs Hart gave marks for four
branches of English: Reading, Spelling, Penmanship and Recitation; and three
branches of Mathematics: Mental, Accuracy and Problems. English was worth
70 marks in all, Arithmetic 50, and Geography and History together a paltry
10. I don't remember ever being taught to read though by this time I was an
avid and omnivorous reader. R.L. Stevenson, Walter Scott, the *Pears Cyclopedia*
we had at home, Arthur Mee's *Children's Newspaper* which my teacher aunt
gave me for Christmas, Dickens' *Christmas Carol*, *Oliver Twist* and *David
Copperfield*, G.A. Henty, Richmal Crompton, all were swallowed whole.
Deciding which books to taste and selecting a few to chew and inwardly digest
came much later.

Mrs Hart seems to have thought quite highly of me. 'John', she wrote, 'has
been working very well indeed and deserves his position at the top of the class.
He is keen on his work and very anxious to help the outside work of the
school.' For the life of me I cannot remember any outside work, but it must
have been an outward-looking school even to think of it. Perhaps she was
thinking of 28 May 1936 when the school took part in the Borough's Empire
Day celebrations. All the schools in the district assembled in an enormous
arena and we children marched to and fro making intricate patterns like some
early corn circles. These occasional days out of school are far more vivid
memories than the days spent in school, so perhaps I earned my mention in
despatches for taking an interest in the Empire.

Mrs Hart also had cheering words about my behaviour: 'His conduct has
improved a great deal.' Perhaps it was only naughtiness. I don't remember ever
being punished though the school log records frequent canings for G. and

Michael Lawrence. What teasing imp was it which prompted me to tell my mother again and again that I'd been caned four or five times that day?

The following year I was in Mr Kirkpatrick's class. We occupied the upright part of a large T-shaped hall which made three separate classrooms when its two folding partitions were in place. The partitions were drawn back each day for an act of corporate worship by those three classes. When we were all ready Mr Hart would emerge importantly from his study roughly in the middle of the top of the T, and mount a small dais to conduct our little service. Then the partitions were drawn, and we settled down to work. The curriculum seems, if my report is reliable evidence, to have been even more focused than in the previous year. English was much the same, though Composition had replaced Spelling; but Mathematics now comprised only Arithmetic and Mental. Although the Education Committee's printed report form had lines for Geography, History and Art, Mr Kirkpatrick, a tetchy little man, awarded no marks in these esoteric subjects to anyone in Class II.

Our house was of course the centre of my world. We always kept a cat, either Fluff or Peter, to wage an unending war against the rats and mice. When the cats could not cope, Dad would bait a cage and leave it overnight. We took no prisoners; any found in the cage went to a watery grave in the great tank in the conservatory. And so I fear did most of Fluff's innumerable litters. The sycamore tree contributed bows and arrows, and laurel clippings made a noxious gas for any hapless butterfly I caught and prisoned in a jam jar. From time to time I dug a pit and sometimes caught a hedgehog; they seemed safe in a hole two or three feet deep, but to my amazement they always disappeared overnight. I learned to ride on two wheels by cycling round and round the damson tree on a small patch of grass behind the house. I was never allowed to play in the front garden. This was most emphatically Bank territory, watched over from opening time at 10 till closing time at 3 by Mr Billett. He looked like an ex-policeman, or possibly a soldier, just the man to stand guard outside a one-man office. On wet days he used to retreat inside the front door, taking cover in the bank's foyer, which took a small corner from our front hall.

Ours was a well-ordered household. The seasons were clearly marked. Marmalade came early in the year when Seville oranges were in season. Bottling and jam-making ran seriatim through the summer. Christmas cakes and puddings were usually made quite early and left to mature. The days were equally well marked. Monday was wash day. There was a copper dolly tub and blue for the whites, a posser, a hand-turned wringer, an enormous bag of clothes pegs, and a long clothes line running from one tree to another with a forked stick to keep the line aloft and stop sheets especially from trailing on the ground. By Wednesday the clothes were dry and ready for ironing. Two or three flat irons were warmed up on the gas stove rings, ready for use in turn. Thursdays was often a day for making cakes and pastries. I was always on hand then to help scrape the bowls. In the evenings there were socks to be darned with a mushroom, clothes to be mended, buttons to be sewn on, sheets to be turned edge to middle, socks and pullovers to be knitted. Friday was bath night. Mum used to light a great coal-fired range in what we called the kitchen though it was never used for cooking. This heated a tank of water, plenty for one bath if it was really hot, but not enough for two. Keeping the range going to provide a series of baths was a tricky job. On Saturdays, to greet Dad as he closed the office, there was almost always a roast and a wonderfully rich and creamy rice pudding. I've never met its equal. In those days pork came with crackling, and beef with its own crispy fat; so there was no need for extra fat to baste a joint. For Sunday breakfast, the week's greatest treat, bread and dripping, pork or beef, rich and tasty, with perhaps a touch of 'too much spoils the flavour' Marmite. Cold roast meat on Sunday, cottage pie on Monday, and some sort of made-up dish on Tuesday followed as surely as night and day.

Dad's working conditions were pretty antediluvian even for the 1930s. He stood alone all day behind a huge mahogany counter with fine pewter inkwells, steel-nibbed pens and huge blotting pads for the customers. There were no protective screens in those days. He ate his midday dinner in the office, snatching a bite as and when he had a moment between customers. It must often have been cold by the time he was able to get to it, but I remember Mum and Dad getting a plate-sized bain marie with an under-plate container for hot water. This must have helped. Loo stops were a problem too. There was no separate loo for the office. The only one was in the household bathroom upstairs. In extremity Dad had to wait for a customer-free moment and get Mr Billett to drop the catch and close the office for a few seconds while he scampered upstairs.

I must have been a difficult child to feed. Breakfasts, of cornflakes and a tasty fry, were fine. So too were teas, of wafer-thin bread and butter, jam, scones, and little cakes and pastries. When Dad was in charge at teatime he sometimes offered a special treat, a little sugar sprinkled on top of a mashed banana sandwich.

But dinner could be a nightmare. 'Eat your greens!' 'You can't *taste* the greens in bubble and squeak.' 'Do eat your fish, John.'

Mum was a brilliant cook. Her shortbreads and pastries melted. Her sponges and fruit cakes were a joy. But when it came to boiled cabbage, brussels sprouts and cod, she had a gift for bringing out vapours that turned my stomach. And of course it wasn't just that greens are good for you, that carrots help you see in the dark, and that fish of all nutrients is the best for growing brain cells. It was your duty to eat up. There were many starving children in other parts of England, and in Asia and other distant places, so it was wrong not to eat what was put in front of you. 'There's no pudding until your plate is clean.' But no amount of ketchup would help the cod go down. And when confronted with boiled cabbage or brussels, my sensitive nostrils echoed the French WW1 generals as they faced the Huns at Verdun, 'ils ne passeront pas', 'they shall not pass'. I found out how to retch on demand, and learned at my mother's table the art of peaceful protest. As an admirer of the suffragettes she may have been secretly pleased by my Gandhian grasp of the tactics of protest. If so, she kept her feelings well hidden.

We were strong on duty in those days. It wasn't just greens and cod. It was a duty to go to Sunday School and chapel, to clear the bowels first thing every day, to put one's toys and games away on Sunday, to listen when grown ups were talking, to take the pledge, to give surplus fruit from our garden to the orphanage across the road, to avoid gambling, and to love all our relatives regardless of their age, sex or likeability. It wasn't easy to understand why one should love relatives who were more remote than any of one's friends as much as those who were kind and affectionate. Since gambling made the bookies rich it seemed a silly way to spend one's Saturday penny, though I wasn't so clear about why it was morally wrong.

Was the confusion in my own mind, or was there some mixing and mingling of categories? There could be no doubting the selfless impulses which led missionaries to the South Seas, no doubting the social concern of those who deplored the addiction of some wage-earners to pay-day drinking and gambling. But were these concerns of the same kind as eating one's greens, doing one's 'duty' in the bathroom, and loving one's gloomily black-gowned great aunt and having to find a way round her ear trumpet to kiss her good night? Some of these things seemed to have more to do with good housekeeping or physical well-being than morality. My mother was never much at ease when I started asking why. Why must I eat my greens? Why must I make myself sick eating fish? Why must I kiss everyone good night? Dad was the one who loved discussion and debate. Mum was more practical, what the French call a bricoleuse, with a remarkable ability to improvise and make do with whatever materials or tools happened to be handy.

I never thought of asking how and where they first met or how their friendship grew. But it's not too hard to guess. Fred was seventeen and still at Cheltenham Grammar School when WW1 ended on 11 November 1918. He had his Oxford local, was in the first XV, kept wicket for the first XI, swam in the water polo team, and was drum major in the OTC. In the Debating Society he moved in 1917 that 'the franchise should be extended to women' and in the following year he spoke in debates on the navy, daylight saving, the relative merits of scouting and military training, a republic for England, and several more. This love of debating lasted all his life. He was a great practitioner of 'creative tension' and even those who knew him best did not always know whether he was using debating techniques to stimulate discussion or to take a rise from an unsuspecting victim.

Fred was expected to apply for Sandhurst. His father had done very well. From next to nothing Alfred Mann had become a prosperous coal merchant and an active Tory councillor and grammar school governor. Known always as 'the working man's Conservative', and a bit rough spoken, he mocked his radical opponents as 'jokers'. On hearing of the Armistice Alf swung into action. Two weeks later on 25 November Fred started work as a temporary clerk at the National Provincial Bank branch where his father banked. Four months later he became an 'Apprentice' on £75 a year. The Bank's records of Fred's appointment include oddly detailed notes about Alf's financial standing. He usually kept £300 to £400 in his current account, owned his own house which had cost £700 and ten other houses worth almost £4,000. His wife owned more houses worth £600. 'Safe as houses' ran the saying, and buying to let was even more in vogue then than it is in the twenty-first century. Fred's brothers used to say their father could and should easily have afforded to send Fred to 'the' university.

The Manns had a century's commitment to Methodism. Fred's great grandparents were active Methodists by the time William Mann left the army after twenty-five years as a Light Dragoon farrier with an enhanced pension for service at Waterloo. Their two farrier sons maintained the link. The elder, John, became a minister and president of his United Methodist connexion. When the younger son, William, moved to Cheltenham in the early 1860s, he and his family joined the Royal Well Methodist Chapel. In due course William's son Alfred became a lifelong member and generous benefactor, once giving the Chapel a grand piano. When his first wife died leaving him with two young sons Alf married the minister's daughter, Emily Pennell. Fred was the elder of their two sons. Like his forebears Fred was always most at ease in Methodist circles.

Three years after he joined the bank Fred was appointed Clerk at a new branch in Dudley, only to be moved a few months later to Derby. When he went to Derby in 1923 Fred must soon have found his way to Dairy House Road Methodist Church. The congregation there included the Johnson family, Ebenezer Josiah, Eliza Jane, and three of their four surviving daughters. The second oldest, Gertie, had recently sailed to Australia to marry an Australian cousin who'd seen service in England during WW1. The girls' grandfather was a successful tinsmith and ironmonger whose growing commitment to Methodism and part-time evangelical missionary work led him to bankruptcy. Ebenezer shared both the bankruptcy and the fervour. He had served his time in the railway engine sheds at Clapham but left once he qualified. His interests lay elsewhere. He preached his first sermon at fourteen and became an accredited local preacher at sixteen. He was drawn more and more into political and social campaigning, was associated with the Clapham League, had a hand in organizing the crowds which rioted in Trafalgar Square in the 1880s and then worked for a couple of years as agent for John Burns, who was later to become the first working-class Cabinet Minister. Ebenezer claimed later that he learnt to speak at Speakers' Corner in Hyde Park. Then in about 1896 he was moved to become a full-time temperance agent. For over thirty years he travelled the country addressing thirty or forty meetings a month, in chapels and temperance halls, and above all in the open air, in dockyards, at factory gates and in innumerable market squares. When he eventually cleared his and his father's debts he stood twice for parliament as 'The People's Friend', but it was too late for Liberals to have much hope.

Eb's third daughter Hilda was two years younger than Fred Mann, like him had continued her secondary education well beyond sixteen and had held increasingly responsible jobs. They were a good match. But they married in haste.

In October 1927 Fred was moved to Wimborne in Dorset. Six months later came the appointment to take sole charge of a satellite office in Broadstone, complete with Bank House. Fred and Hilda decided to bring forward their intended marriage to Easter 1928. He was twenty-six, and she was twenty-four.

The Broadstone into which they moved was still quite tiny, with fewer than 2,000 people. Houses were being built in Clarendon and Springfield Roads and there was a growing number of big houses on the Upper and Lower Golf Links Roads. But the arrival of shops and banks meant that the Broadway was now the commercial centre of this new community. Our house was not just the centre of my world. It was not so very far from being the centre of the village too. The outer limits of the village included the Roman Road and Darby's Corner, less than a mile away; but pine woods, heaths and recreation ground were much nearer. Shops, post office, library and school were no more than two or three hundred yards away. The chapel was next door. In those almost car-less days I could safely take myself to Sunday School and school and go alone on little errands from an early age. The grocer French's was just along the road, and I was sometimes sent to buy one or two specific items there. The fine wire cheese- and butter-slicers were always a fascination. More often Mum went in with an order, and before long the ever cheerful, ever whistling Bill would come along on his sturdy bike to deliver the order to our back door. Bill seemed at least as old as Mum and Dad, and he probably wouldn't have been a delivery boy if he hadn't had special educational needs. But he was perhaps the most familiar figure in the village, better loved than even the postman, Mr Jonier. Later on we sometimes bought groceries from Mr Finlayson, who had one of half a dozen newish shops in Wimborne (now Dunyeats) Road, just below the school. In the same block, as well as Mr Joiner the cobbler, Mr Higgs had his fancy goods shop and Mr Waterman his dairy. Round the corner occupied by Rumsey and Rumsey the estate agents, Station Road offered a lively cockney greengrocer, Mr Fudge the butcher, and Mr Haynes the chemist. Next door to his pharmacy was the old Lavender factory which went up in flames one night in 1935. Dad and I were among the milling crowd who went to watch the fun. In the Broadway itself there was another butcher, Mr Cobb, Mr Yard the newsagent, stationer and haberdasher, and the diminutive Daisy Brown, darting about amidst her wonderful array of pots and pans and household bits and pieces. Nearby lived a one-legged man who was darkly reputed to have lost his leg while fighting as a Black and Tan to impose order in Ireland. We might have established some sort of rapport if only I had known then that a century earlier my own great great grandfather William Mann had also been one of the occupying English soldiery in Ireland. On the corner of York Road just opposite our house was another grocer, Mr Victor Watkins, who had won fame as England's first King's Scout and was Captain of the local fire brigade. Since his shop was so handy and always looked well ordered I sometimes wondered why we never shopped there. Perhaps it was because he banked at Lloyd's, or because he had an off-licence. Next to Lloyd's Miss Amelia Street ran a small children's orphanage, and beyond that there was a little petrol service station and my Saturday sweet shop. On our side of the road, three or four lock-up shops replaced the house next door just before WW2. Some were still unoccupied when war broke out in 1939 and one was taken over by Dad and his fellow firewatchers. Next door but one, Miss Wilson and Mr Wilson, who had served with the Royal Flying Corps in WW1, refurbished their gentlemen's outfitters and made it one of Broadstone's smartest stores. This was one of my most valued resources. Among all my books and games and jigsaws there were never any toy soldiers but Mr Wilson gave me hundreds of redundant display cards and labels which I used to represent battalions, corps, divisions, and indeed whole contesting armies. Not very sophisticated, but very satisfying. Beyond the Wilson's shop was Lindisfarne, where the Misses Oldfield looked after a few young children, perhaps children whose parents were abroad. My mother was much embarrassed when our dog came home one day with a joint of meat he'd stolen from Lindisfarne. Beyond Lindisfarne lay Dr Norman's surgery.

Broadstone offered a calm, untroubled haven for a young lad growing up in the 1930s. The climax came in 1939. That summer we spent our holiday in Bembridge in the Isle of Wight. My father was a cautious man, not at all given to bold flamboyant gestures. But on that occasion we flew. He always took a keen interest in public affairs and throughout the 1930s he and Mr Cole traipsed in to Poole or Bournemouth to hear many of the country's leading politicians. In those days he took the *News Chronicle* of course, and like many non-conformists supported the League of Nations and the Peace Pledge Union. Soon after he bought a piano in about 1937 or 1938 he came home with a Moral Rearmament song book and for a while our eaves rang with their choruses, 'harbingers of a brave new world are we…'

Perhaps he read the runes well enough to realize there would be no more seaside holidays for several years, and determined to make the last one truly memorable. I can't remember how we travelled to the airport at Christchurch, or what kind of seven- or eight-seater plane we flew in. What I do remember is that once aloft we seemed to lurch from one air pocket to another, holding our stomachs each time as we dropped like a brick some thirty or forty feet. But that was a small price to pay for an idyllic sundrenched fortnight on the Bembridge sands, with the white sails of countless yachts cutting through the waves, silver seaplanes silhouetted against a blue sky, and the greatest liners ever built, the *Normandie* and the *Queens, Mary* and *Elizabeth*, cruising up and down the Solent.

This comfortable world of mine had already suffered one disruption. A few weeks earlier I'd been standing in the school playground when one of the Lawrence boys, a few years older than me, suddenly said 'Fuck!' I knew immediately that he would go to hell. Since I wasn't aware that I'd ever heard the word before, and hell was no part of my family's cosmology, it's a bit of a mystery how I came to be so certain about his fate. Perhaps much earlier we'd heard his father, the general factotum at Broadstone station, using similar language. 'Just an ordinary railwayman' is how I remember my mother once making plain that he and we moved in different circles.

There was worse to come. As the war clouds gathered, arrangements were made to evacuate children from the great cities. Many from Southampton came to Poole and Broadstone on 2 September. The authorities billeted three brothers of round about my age in our large house. They represented a fearsome challenge to my mother's sense of propriety. They seemed never to have seen a bath, did not undress to go to bed, were clearly unused to sitting down for meals, and found it hard to handle knives and forks. They must have found my mother's ordered regime a great burden, though I found their company most stimulating. Best of all was when we got together to chew the cud, sitting side by side on the roadside kerbstones outside the Bank. Mum was horrified. After three weeks of purgatory they all ran away, back to Southampton.

CHAPTER 2

'We Have Refrained'

The not-so-whining schoolboy

SEPTEMBER 1939 SPELT WAR. It was also a most significant threshold in John's life, the moment when he donned the green blazer with gold trimmings and dolphin crest that identified a Poole Grammar School boy. The choice of secondary school was a conundrum for his father. Broadstone was roughly halfway between Poole and Wimborne. Wimborne had a Grammar School with hundreds of years of history behind it. Its main winter sport was Rugby Football, the cad's game played by gentlemen, whose aficionados had no doubts about its character-building properties. Poole was a twentieth-century foundation, had a more distinguished academic record (in one famous year its pupils won three of the 360 State Scholarships awarded for the whole country) and had just become a single-sex school; but its winter sport was Association Football, the game played by cads. After an inner tussle Dad opted for Poole. Early in the summer I went to Poole to take a simple entrance examination, and was offered a place in Form 1.

Form 1 was a preparatory class for little boys under eleven. We were all feepayers. So too were many of those in the main school. A lucky few who passed the scholarship exam had free places, but only if their parents had low incomes. Parents who were a little better off had to pay fees related to their income even if their sons had won a scholarship. In my case Dad paid £57 in the year when I was a feepayer in Form 1, and £104 in the following year when I was a scholarship boy in Form 2A. It was a sizeable chunk of his disposable income.

Once the die was cast there was little contact between those who stayed at Broadstone School and those who went to the grammar schools; few of those who went to Wimborne fraternized with those who went to Poole. From then on most of my friends were fellow Poole Grammarians. Dad must have had a word with Mr Hart to see if there was any slightly older boy from Broadstone School who would keep a protective eye on me when we started at Poole. This thankless task was assumed by Ken Smith, a retired policeman's son who lived on the Ridgeway about ten minutes' walk from us and was two years older, and who soon became my best friend. The Broadstone contingent consisted of about ten or a dozen boys, some of them very grand and almost twice as old as me. At first we all travelled together by train to Poole with a fair amount of badinage to while away the journey. From time to time when our seniors thought we'd stepped out of line we little boys were forced to eat the Southern Railway's green and nauseating soap. On a separate occasion in a fit of pique the Congregational minister's son fired his air rifle in my direction. To my surprise Mum never asked about the resulting indentation in my brand new blazer. Once when we got back to Broadstone station after school two of us were frogmarched a few yards up the road to a little pine tree copse off Moor Road and threatened with having our trousers removed and placed high up on a nearby pine tree. I was terrified. I was a chubby little fellow and with or without trousers tree-climbing was not for me. Fortunately our torturers thought better of their jape, and we were allowed to escape.

One of the great advantages of travelling by train was that on the way to and from the station I used to pass Poole's handsome Free Library and got into the way of dropping in there. Even better was the small secondhand book stall near the station at Poole. I often had time to kill before my train arrived, and spent many happy hours browsing quietly and spending little. In those days booksellers were rather more relaxed about browsing than they are now, or perhaps they took a very long view about creating a market for their wares. By this time I'd graduated from the *Children's Newspaper* to the *Boys' Own Paper*, to Captain W.E. Johns and Percy F. Westerman, to Ballantyne's *Young Fur Traders* and *Coral Island*, Bulwer Lytton's *Harold, Last of the Saxon Kings*, Fennimore Cooper's *Last of the Mohicans*, and *From Log Cabin to White House*, the life of President Garfield. My diet was rich and varied but William and the Outlaws remained firm favourites. Only a few miles away in Salisbury William Golding was probably pondering already the teaching experience which enabled him to write *The Lord of the Flies* a few years later. We Poole Grammarians were not as naively effervescent as the Outlaws nor as savage as Golding's boys, but our lives during the war had something in common with both.

In 1939 the autumn term began late. This was because special arrangements had to be made for the Southampton evacuees. Among them were virtually the whole of another boys' grammar school, King Edward VI. King Edward's and Poole Grammar were to share the Poole Grammar School premises, working a two session day in a way I've now seen often enough in developing countries but which was most unusual in Britain before WW2. The buildings were used six days a week, with morning sessions from 8.35 to 12.45, and afternoon sessions from 1.05 to 5.15. The two schools worked either mornings or afternoons in alternate weeks. One week I had to finish my dinner by about twelve, the next week I arrived for a late meal at about 1.45; and Dad needed his at about 1 every day. Family activities on his half days were much curtailed because on alternate Saturdays I did not get home till after 6 o'clock. In the context of cataclysmic war these unsocial hours were a very minor inconvenience. I never heard anyone complain, but the alternating sessions must have imposed great strains on family life.

Form 1 was only loosely attached to the main school. Our form room was the one upstairs classroom in Seldown House, a mansion once commodious but now somewhat battered. Downstairs there were two more classrooms housing 2D and 2C. Their rooms were on either side of the front door and the main hall. The hall led directly to the main staircase. Though there was a back staircase it was not accessible from outside so we always had to pass their rooms en route to and from our own room. Whenever relations between Form 1 and Forms 2C and D reached a low we had to run a gauntlet of older boys armed with knotted handkerchiefs and rulers. Once installed on the first floor we had all the advantages of Leonidas at Thermopylae. We were few in number, but more than enough to defend the main stairs against assault from below and guard the narrower defile at the back. The noise of battle did not often reach the main school some two or three hundred yards away along Kingland Road. None of the teachers was based in Seldown House and they were not much in evidence except during lessons. But every now and again a prefect posse would march on Seldown House and impose martial law. It must have been they who handed out the three detentions I earned in the Summer Term, my last term in Form 1. These encounters with the prefects were a small but ominous cloud in an otherwise splendid year. In the spring I won a scholarship, of no great financial value at the time but it guaranteed a grammar school place anywhere in the country should we ever have to move. Once our form master Mr Clapham who taught maths, but not it seems psychology, was so put out by the mathematical obtuseness of Form 2A that he summoned the young prodigy from Form 1 to shame them. In the end of year exams I obtained almost twice the average marks in Form 1, and was top in four of the nine papers. One of these was Religious Knowledge, not so surprising a result as all that because I was already one of the Sunday School's star candidates in the annual Scripture Union exams.

The autumn and winter of 1939 passed quietly enough. Life in Poole was little disturbed during the Phoney War. This ended rudely in April 1940 when Hitler invaded Denmark and Norway. In May he invaded Holland and Belgium. Anglo-French forces driving forward to defend Belgium were cut off and forced back to the coast at Dunkirk. With the help of a myriad of small boats including some from Poole some 338,000 men were evacuated by 4 June. On that same day, my tenth birthday as it happened, Winston Churchill delivered one of the century's most celebrated speeches:

> Even though large tracts of Europe and many old and famous States have fallen or may fall into the grip of the Gestapo and all the odious apparatus of Nazi rule, we shall not flag or fail. We shall go on to the end. We shall fight in France, we shall fight on the seas and oceans, we shall fight with growing confidence and growing strength in the air, we shall defend our island whatever the cost may be. We shall fight on the beaches, we shall fight on the landing grounds, we shall fight in the fields and in the streets, we shall fight in the hills; we shall never surrender, and even if, which I do not for a moment believe, this island or a large

part of it were subjugated and starving, then our Empire beyond the seas, armed and guarded by the British Fleet, would carry on the struggle, until, in God's good time, the new world, with all its power and might, steps forth to the liberation of the old.

His inspiring oratory was a marked contrast to our humdrum lives in Broadstone. Our odd school hours meant that we boys had plenty of free time during the day. On cold damp days we gathered in each other's houses to play knock out whist or Monopoly, and on fine days we gathered in Broadstone Rec, a perfect adventure playground for games of tag and chasing among the pine trees which lined the sloping sides of the former brickyard. One day as Ian Case and I wrestled near the War Memorial on lawns above the slopes we suddenly rolled over the edge and I knew as we fell twenty feet that I had dreamed the whole event two or three weeks earlier. It was the first of two or three similar experiences in quite a short time, and came to mind five or six years later when I read *An Experiment with Time* by J.W. Dunne who describes exactly that kind of pre-cognition.

A prolonged and settled belt of high pressure in 1940 gave Britain one of the finest summers it ever enjoyed. The village cricket team must have drawn stumps for the duration because almost every day ten or a dozen of us young grammar school boys played happily on the square under the watchful eye of Mr Smith, Ken's Dad. In due course several of my fellow cricketers, people like Jack Fudge, Roy Hanham and Ken Smith, progressed to senior teams. Roy and Ken were village stalwarts for decades. My own cricketing career might so easily have been even more illustrious than theirs. I took to heart Dad's report that the great Don Bradman had learned to bat by hitting a ball against a wall, and spent hours with bat and ball and kitchen wall. It must have been the wrong kind of wall. 1940 was only the first of a series of splendid summers when we seemed to play cricket every day and fight fires on the nearby heath every month or two. My singed and yellowed eyebrows were for several years the outward evidence of days as a junior firefighter.

None of my weekday friends attended the same chapel. There my closest friends were Jim and Jack Griffin, the sturdy sons of a painter and decorator, one of the less eminent members of the ubiquitous Griffin clan who dominated the building and allied trades in Broadstone. The Sunday School Superintendent was Mr Condon whose two sons Stanley and Bert were a few years older than us and seemed to think they were Sunday School prefects. We led them a dance as they chased us round the trees and lawns which stood in front of the chapel as they tried to corral us in time for lessons to begin. Those in charge of the Sunday School evidently believed that a spoonful of sugar would help the medicine go down, There were prizes, parties and excursions. Our cards were stamped with a star each time we went to Sunday School, and my star-studded card won prizes year after year. British Bulldog, Pass the Parcel, and Musical Chairs were regular features of our annual party. One year

I had to pay a forfeit, a chaste and mutually embarrassing kiss for June Dicks, future GP and the first girl I ever kissed outside family. In the summer our annual excursion took us most often to Sandbanks or Studland, but all that ended in 1940.

The Dorset beaches were closed immediately after Dunkirk. A Local Defence Volunteer force was created, and almost every night vans went round calling 'LDV! LDV! To your posts. To your posts.' At home we blacked out all the windows and took delivery of an Anderson shelter which almost filled the kitchen. I slept in the Anderson shelter until it seemed that things were getting worse. Then Dad had wooden props installed to support the ceiling in our back hall which lay between the kitchen and the scullery. There was a door into the cupboard under the stairs and for a while I slept in the cupboard and the rest of the family slept in the hall. Gas masks were issued, a mixed blessing because we were supposed to keep them with us and I kept on losing mine. Mum had to trek into Poole time and time again to get a replacement. We got a stirrup pump in case of fire, and Dad was called for medical examination with a view to his being called up. He was graded C3 because of his varicose ulcers so he stayed at home and became a Fire Watcher, sharing overnight duties with other men. The rough, tough and licentious Canadian soldiery were stationed in the area, and for a while we wondered whether they or the Jerries were the more serious threat to rural peace. Dad sought expert advice from his gardening friends, and began to dig for victory. For the first time most of our huge back garden was cultivated. When rabbits came to share the crops he borrowed a shot gun, and sat for hours outside the back door, patiently waiting for Flopsy, Mopsy and Cottontail to appear and be blasted into eternity.

At school, air raid shelters were dug hastily in 1939 on waste land between the main school buildings and Seldown House. And the Battle of Britain began. Each time the air raid alarms sounded each form marched briskly to its allotted stretch in the underground trenches. These had been skilfully designed in lengths which could accommodate a class of about thirty-two boys. Each length ended with a short right-angle dog-leg connecting it with the next length of trench. By chance our neighbours when I was in 2A were 3A, and in the following year when I was in 3A our neighbours were 4 Science, many of whom had been in 3A the previous year.

In the twelve months from 25 July 1940 there were about fifty air raid alarms during school hours. In the following year there must have been as many, or more. Sometimes the all clear sounded in as little twenty or thirty minutes, but many raids lasted an hour or more, some as long as two or three hours, and at least one almost four hours. The trenches were too dimly lit for reading to be possible and although some of the teachers made sporadic efforts we were often left to devise our own amusement. What more natural than that we should contest the empty dog-legs with our neighbours? The trenches were too narrow for either side to bring all its forces to the front at the same time. We always had reserves waiting to take the place of any who fell at the front. We in 2A and then in 3A were always younger, smaller and weaker than our opponents. As we tussled and struggled we lived in constant fear of being captured and forced to walk the gauntlet of a whole class of hostile older boys.

On at least a couple of occasions we put aside these tribal feuds to unite against a common foe. In the great snows of 1941 hundreds of Poole Grammarians occupied a stretch of Kingland Road outside the school to fight pitched snowball battles against the barbarian hordes from King Edward's. On another occasion scores of boys rampaged across the surface of our air raid shelters. One unfortunate fell and caught his leg on a sharp metal projection which cut him to the bone. Summary retribution followed, a couple of sharpish cuts for almost every boy in half a dozen classes. To our surprise news of this debacle spread quickly in the Parkstone area. Bruce's mother had noticed her son's weals at bathtime. What humiliation! We could hardly credit that an eleven year old was still being bathed by his mother.

In warmer seasons we found other outlets for our surplus energy. The great summertime sport was 'horses and riders'. One boy would leap on another's back to scuffle and wrestle with another two-boy team until one of the riders was pulled off his horse. From time to time we even managed to assemble two or three dozen teams for a mini battle on the school playing field. Very rarely in the short interval between morning and afternoon sessions Poole and Southampton would joust amicably together.

You should not conclude that we were altogether oblivious to things of the mind. As I poured milk all over my corn flakes one morning cousin Keith observed challengingly 'if God had meant corn flakes to be soggy He would have made them that way'. It was an issue profound enough for Plato himself. I discovered the pleasures of 'Pitch and Toss' (aka 'Odds and Evens'), and spent happy hours playing with my friends, especially one named Clark who must have been the only Anglo-Indian and almost certainly the only dark-skinned boy in the school. I soon learned the valuable lesson that no matter how long the sequence of heads when you're tossing coins there is always an even chance that the next flip will deliver another head.

Even in those days some schools also provided opportunities for their pupils to gain experience of trade and commerce. One of the presents I received for my eleventh birthday was a Triumph Illustrated Stamp Album. It was soon lovingly inscribed:

> (Master) John Frederick Mann
> Bank House
> Broadway
> Broadstone
> Dorset

> (Master) John F Mann
> Form II A
> Poole Grammar School
> Kingland Road
> Poole
> Dorset

I found a shop in Poole High Street which sold packets of 500 or even 1,000 assorted stamps. Names like Abyssinia, Azerbaijan, Bosnia and Herzegovina, Danzig and Inhambane were no longer far-away places of which I knew little or nothing. They came alive through their stamps. And I became a dealer, buying from the shop and selling to my schoolmates. The turnover was modest, the margins low and the gains exiguous. But it was great fun and my own collection grew apace.

There was much else to do at school before and after the school day. Unknown in Form 1, homework came to fill my horizon in 2A. Like most Dads, mine took a keen interest in my progress. His forte was Latin. He loved Kennedy's *Latin Primer* and could recite all the mnemonic rhymes designed to help you find your way through the intricacies of Latin syntax. Latin is one of those languages, a bit like French today, where nouns are masculine, feminine or neuter. If you don't know which is which you may make all sorts of silly spelling mistakes. So Kennedy offers this helpful guide:

> The gender of a Latin Noun
> By meaning, form, or use is shown.
>
> A Man, a name of People and a Wind,
> River and Mountain, Masculine we find:…
>
> A Woman, Island, Country, Tree
> and City, Feminine we see:…
>
> To Nouns that cannot be declined
> The Neuter Gender is assigned…'

Kennedy also offered a couple of jingles to help you remember which prepositions take the accusative case, and which the ablative. This one lists the prepositions which take the ablative case:

> A, ab, absque, coram, de,
> Palam, cum, and ex, and e,
> Sine, tenus, pro, and prae:
> Add super, subter, sub, and in,
> When 'state', not 'motion', 'tis they mean.

These were, as it were, the 'starters for one'. There were many more such rhymes and I never managed to learn any of them. Despite this failing, Latin was my best subject and I was top of the class at the year end. And I was still pretty good at Maths. I was happy of course to share my expertise in these two subjects with class mates who were less comfortable with them. In return I looked increasingly for some modest support with my French, my Science and my English clause analysis. We ran a very efficient workers' co-operative on the time-honoured Marxist principle, 'From each according to his abilities, to each according to his needs.' There were however three problems. First, we could not manage to get to school early enough to pool our expertise before morning school, so the system only worked properly when we were on afternoon school. This meant we often had to find excuses for half our work being handed in a week late. Second, even in the afternoons we had to work at great speed in the fifteen or twenty minutes before school opened, and this meant unhappily that a good deal of what I handed in looked hurried and slapdash. Third, we were often hassled as we worked by marauding bands of prefects who took exception to our remonstrances. My work went steadily downhill until I was struggling to stay on our fortnightly mark lists. I wrote and rewrote the School Rules, a closely printed side of foolscap, more times than I can remember. I wrote hundreds of lines, 'I must pay attention all the time,' 'I must do what I'm told by a prefect,' and so on, and so on. The four-nibbed writing machine I made to help in this Herculean task was only a qualified success. On top of all this I may well have achieved a school record with twelve detentions in the autumn term, fifteen in the spring, and nine in the summer. When it became clear that I was unlikely to have time to serve all these sentences before my school career ended in a few years' time ('e'en all eternity's too short' I sang with feeling on Sundays) someone sent me off to the Headmaster, Mr A.W.M. Greenfield. He had served with great distinction in WW1, and was still an officer in appearance and bearing, so much so that his badge of office in school was still his officer's baton. Three light taps of the baton, and my sheet was cleared. It seemed like a bargain.

Detentions were usually scheduled for what would otherwise have been free mornings or afternoons when there were a few spare rooms because King Edward's had fewer boys than Poole. To explain these extra sessions at home I created imaginary extra lessons. Explaining a termly report brimming with phrases like 'rather lethargic in class', 'does not exert himself', 'could do better if he would rouse himself', 'erratic', 'often neglectful of homework', and 'has foolishly devoted himself to the evasion of work', was not as easy. I soon grasped the importance of focusing on the bottom line. Thanks to a good short-term memory, calm nerves, and surprisingly good results from my two 'bankers' in the end of term exams I always managed to end up comfortably in the top ten in the top stream. My termly apologia used to highlight this fairly creditable outcome, and also my relative youth, a good year less than the average of my form. All this Dad would concede, reluctantly. He was much more interested in the detail which I preferred to overlook. It became increasingly clear that erecting some sort of Chinese wall between home and school might be easier than trying to explain the ups and downs of school life to an uncomprehending audience at home.

When war broke out many teachers, including nine from Poole GS, joined the armed forces. The school was fortunate in keeping a cadre of old hands like Baldwin, Clapham, Cullingford, Sid Ewins, Froud, Doug Gould, Hicks, Lock, Murray, Oldman, Ovenall and Whitelock. I saw these begowned figures at assemblies though few of them taught the forms I was in. Heads must have had to scour the hedges and byways to find replacements for those who had gone to the war. Luckily we ended up with enough odd characters to make life interesting.

Monsieur Desages was the somewhat plumper Poirot who used to try to teach us French. Any minor blip on our part provoked an outburst. 'You appawlling arse' he would shout, 'Stand on the desk!' In a few minutes he might have half a dozen youths standing uncomfortably on the seats of their locker desks. We enjoyed his Gallic frenzy, but it did little for our French. Itchy Thomas, a fairly short-lived wartime teacher who taught us French the year after M. Desages, was an altogether different kettle of fish. A tiny bundle of energy, supercharged, his face and head twitched constantly as he hammered us into French, and French into us. He always seemed on the verge of exploding. I at least was terrified of what might happen, and worked hard to avoid catastrophe. My namesake Mr A. de L. Mann was another wartime appointment. He taught Geography with the help of a long wooden ruler which served as a pointer and always seemed ready to chastise some miscreant. He was a large man, tall and big with it. In the afternoons it was always clear when he'd lunched well in one of the local hostelries. Mr Lundie lasted only a term or two, a sad little man who never taught me. But we all knew that he paid boys, ostensibly to carry his small brief-case two or three hundred yards along Kingland Road to and from the High Street though we thought he really wanted company, We all knew too when by chance he passed within three or four yards. His tipple was gin.

I really regretted the loss of our two 2A form teachers. They both taught English. Mrs Joyce Crabbe was a pretty smiling woman who came in September and left at Christmas. Her place was taken by Miss M. Cuckson, a real poppet (had I but known the word in those days) who took me on one side more than once to try to find out why the system and I were so at odds with each other. She was amazed the next year to learn that I'd read *Jane Eyre* and enjoyed it, and it must have been for her that I read *Scott of the Antarctic* and wrote an extended essay about his expedition.

Our musical education was rudimentary. One of the classrooms off the hall was known as the music room. The only instrument was a piano, and the only kind of music-making was class singing. For one period a week ten year old trebles and thirteen year old bassos sang in unison such songs as *In Dublin's Fair City, Cherry Ripe, Die Lorelei, The Trout*, and *The Erl King*, and practised the hymns for the next week's school assemblies.

Science lessons were more exciting. We took General Science in Forms 2 and 3. I started well, fourth in my first term, but as taught then General Science consisted mainly of Biology, and Biology consisted mainly of stamens, sepals, pistils and petals. They made thin gruel for warm-blooded young men. Chemistry was even less nutritive. It seemed to consist mainly of writing down what should have happened when the teacher played about with test tubes and bunsen burners. Fortunately a few of us back-of-the-labs types found that the parquet wood block floors in the laboratories were ideal for experimental work of a much more active kind. In the course of a lesson we could lift a good many blocks from their bed, make interesting patterns in the floor, and build a few small castles. The trick was to get all the blocks back in place before the bell rang. Meanwhile an attractive young woman called Miss Thomas made unavailing efforts to engage our interest in her kind of science.

One of the teachers I most admired in those early days was Tusker Hicks. With enormous moustaches he looked far older than his thirty years. He talked quickly, covering the blackboard with writing as he spoke. Our job was to make rough notes of all we could catch of what he said and what he wrote. For homework we were expected to do a little extra background reading and turn our notes into elegant little essays. In practice the longest essays seemed to get the most marks. His methods would have won few plaudits thirty or forty years on. They were perfect examples of material passing from the teacher's to the pupil's notebook without necessarily passing through the mind of either. But I enjoyed the challenge of working at speed, trying to get it all down, and reconstituting the material in my own words. Tusker was also a keen Esperantist, and must have been the inspiration behind an exciting school lecture on Esperanto which left me an enthusiast for at least a week.

I was also stirred by one of the two or three thousand school assemblies I attended between the ages of five and eighteen. This was a day when Dicko was away for some reason and Mr Ovenall, who was Dicko's deputy throughout the war, took the assembly instead. I've forgotten the peg to which he attached his remarks. What he said was electrifying. Poverty was no barrier to a university education. Scholarships were readily available. We had only to win them. Sixty years on I still remember what he said. There is indeed a remote possibility that his words had some effect at the time.

After two years in the main school in Forms 2 and 3 about half the boys forged ahead in Forms 4 and 5, taking their School Certificate after four years. The other half spent a consolidating year in the Remove before progressing to Forms 4 and 5 and taking their School Certificate after five years. When we returned to school in September 1942 I found to my dismay that I'd been assigned to 4 Science. This meant being in the same form as my best Broadstone friend Ken Smith, who had taken the prettier route via the Remove. Working on the principle that it was a good idea to maintain a certain distance between school and village life, I asked to move to 4 Arts. This had the added advantage that I would go on studying Latin, at which I was still quite good, though I did not fully appreciate that it also meant going on with General Science for which I had little taste. The authorities were moved by my thirst for Latin, and agreed to my switching. This off-the-cuff decision to go on the Arts side turned out to be among the most far-reaching I ever made about my own life.

I had decided to turn over a new leaf, and got stuck in immediately. Tusker Hicks was now my form master and at the end of the first term he said I'd made an excellent beginning. It was unhappily no more than a beginning.

We Broadstone boys had abandoned Southern Rail some time before, preferring the buses. These stopped outside French's store in the centre of Broadstone and terminated at the George Hotel in Longfleet, relatively near the school. Going home at night the buses were always jam-packed. There was of course no queueing in those days. It was every man and every boy for himself when it came to fighting for a seat. Sometimes we little boys slipped through the heaving crowds and rushed for the front seat upstairs. Very occasionally we would stand to one side, doff our caps in at least a metaphorical way and allow our elders to board the bus in peace.

By this time however I had abandoned the buses too. I was a fairly proficient cyclist and three and a half miles each way was no great sweat. I could free wheel almost half way there, and coming home only the last half mile up Sharland's Hill was a real drag. Six weeks into the new school year I set out for school after an early lunch of egg and chips. An hour later the soldiers in an army lorry found me lying on the main road near Hatch Pond with my head embedded in the tarmac. Ten days later when I woke for the first time after this mishap I was astonished to hear wireless reports about fighting in Tunisia. While I was unconscious Montgomery had wrapped up the battle of El Alamein, Eisenhower had overseen landings in North West Africa, and the Russians had begun to turn the tide at Stalingrad. It was many years before I got these things sorted.

Mum dropped everything when she heard about my accident. Dad rejigged the office duties so that Mr Billet and the bank clerk Joyce could sit with and read to my six year old brother Peter. Mum sped to the hospital. For the next few weeks she was often there two or three times a day. It must have been a harrowing experience. For a few days the medics thought I'd fractured my skull but were too nervous to touch it to establish the full extent of the damage. They put a few stitches in a gash across my eyebrow, but these were so uncomfortable that I lay unconscious in my bed trying to pull them out. The one consolation for Mum was that in my delirium I sang one hymn after another. The other children's parents and visiting clergy could hardly find words for such a paragon. Then disaster struck. Dr Jekyll disappeared and Mr Hyde took over. To Mum's embarrassment, instead of hymns I began to recite long lists of expletives, every profanity and every obscenity a twelve year old could know. I was removed from the ward in disgrace and kept in a remote single room until this phase had passed.

Once I'd woken up properly, the ward was quite good fun. There were a dozen other youngsters there with strange names like Mervyn and Harvey, we had a wireless, and there was plenty to talk about. In spite of these attractions after another three or four weeks I was growing restive and the authorities decided, perhaps as much in their interests as mine, that I could safely spend Christmas at home. For a few weeks I lived quietly, discouraged from taxing my brain with too many jigsaws or too much reading, encouraged to build my strength by taking long walks in and around Broadstone. One day I met a lad of about my own age who said his name was Marmaduke. He was evidently neither fish nor fowl, not quite a Marquess, nor quite a Duke. I spent a long time with my Pears Cyclopedia trying to establish exactly where in the peerage a Marmaduke stood. On another day I was walking along the Broadway a few yards behind a military-looking type with glowing cheeks and plus fours. As we passed a couple of workmen digging a hole in the road one of them observed *sotto voce* of this military gentleman, 'Old lardy arse, I bet he don't eat 'alf what we do.' This I knew was very rude. I clearly had no recollection of Mr Hyde's behaviour a few weeks earlier.

By the end of January I was tiring of this regime. Although it was thought safest not to subject the brain to too much pressure after an accident like mine I was allowed to go back to school. But I carried with me the sort of letter every school boy would like to have. After describing my mishap, it went on to say, 'He must not be pressed.' I could have used an open cheque like this on a grand scale. But like Clive of India in a somewhat different context, 'I stand astonished at my own moderation.' I used it only once. For fear that I might bang my head I was not allowed to play football. This I regretted because I was well grown and sturdy for my age and in the autumn had contended seriously for a place in one of the school's junior teams. If I could not play football, I was certainly not going to climb ropes, hang from parallel bars, or leap over vaulting horses, for none of which had I any aptitude or liking. PE went out of the window with football. Otherwise I set to work with a will. Unfortunately the form had covered some difficult ground while I'd been away and it took me a long time to grasp the French subjunctive, simultaneous equations or Pythagoras' theorem and its extensions. When Tusker wrote enigmatically at the year end 'His accident has retarded his progress and we have refrained', perhaps it was Pythagoras and the subjunctive they had refrained from.

In August 1943 Dad was summoned to the Bank's Head Office and told he was to be accountant in their Tavistock branch. For a few months he commuted weekly, an arrangement which seemed satisfactory enough to me, but must have been trying for Mum and Dad. And we had in any case to leave our tied house. We stayed with Mr and Mrs Cole for a few weeks and left Dorset in December.

CHAPTER 3

Becoming a Devonian

And then the lover, sighing like a furnace

TAVISTOCK SEEMS HAPPY to shelter comfortably in its west-facing valley. To the east, Dartmoor's bulk protects the town from both easterly winds and trendy up-country fashions. The moor's grey granitic tors and treeless tops stand in amazing contrast to the town's soft green-tinged Hurdwick stone and rain-drenched meadows. Only the sparkling, darting River Tavy and its leaping salmon seem to challenge Tavistock's serenity. Perhaps this calm has something to do with a thousand years of stable government. Benedictine monks ruled the area from their abbey for almost six hundred years until Henry VIII gave their estates to John Russell whose family's estate office was to rule for almost another four hundred. Fertile ground it was not for innovative ideas. When a man of the north came to head the Grammar School he found not opposition but 'a bland and good natured disregard'. Perhaps a fellow feeling for that way of resisting alien ideas is why I somehow feel more a native of Tavistock than of anywhere else, even though I was a full-time resident for only five years and have never had the least wish to go back there to live.

When we moved in January 1944 Tavistock was enjoying a minor wartime boom. It had been the most important town in mid West Devon for centuries with its weekly markets, nine cattle fairs each year, and an annual Goosey Vair when the school had a day off, perhaps to give the quacks and cheapjacks a chance to widen our education as they tried to con the farmers into buying supposedly aphrodisiacal Spanish fly for themselves as well as their cattle. But the farmers had no need for Spanish fly; they had only to drink the local water with its traces of arsenic, a potent aphrodisiac if taken in small doses. From medieval times Tavistock had also had a significant role as a Stannary Town with some responsibility for regulating the tin industry. In the nineteenth century the exploitation of rich local deposits of tin, copper, lead and arsenic led to a phenomenal mid-century boom. Tavistock flourished as a mining town. Its population almost trebled between 1801 (3,420) and 1861 (8,912). The Duke of Bedford, grown even richer on mineral rights, funded astonishingly grand public buildings, a Town Hall, Guildhall, Pannier Market, Corn Market, schools and a new church. By the time they were in regular use the bubble had burst. The new Malaysian ores were more abundant and far cheaper. By 1911 Tavistock's population had fallen back to 4,392, less than half its peak. There it stayed until WW2. That led a few people from London and the Home Counties to trickle westwards to relative safety. Then in 1941 came the saturation bombing of English cities, few worse hit than Plymouth where 70,000 houses were damaged or destroyed. Before and after the blitz many Plymothians sought refuge in the surrounding countryside. Tavistock's population grew. Accommodation was at a premium. When Dad moved there in 1943 he could find nothing with vacant possession. When our time in Broadstone's Bank House ran out our furniture went into store and he settled for furnished rooms in Woburn Terrace, one of several handsome terraces in the Plymouth Road built for the burgeoning entrepreneurs of Victorian Tavistock. At Number 4 there were six or eight steps up to the front door which opened into a dignified hall. Our family room led off the hall. It was a magnificent room, thirty feet or more in length, looking on to both the front and back gardens. Upstairs we had two bedrooms and a bathroom. Downstairs in the semi-basement there was a kitchen with windows at grass-root level. Fortunately there was also a dumbwaiter on a pulley to carry food up to our own living room.

Mum shared this kitchen with Mother Pet, Little Ugly and Mrs Hart-Smith. Mother Pet was about thirteen years old, a much-cossetted old tabby whose one surviving daughter was the piebald twelve year old gnome known as Little Ugly. Mrs Hart-Smith indulged them both; on Little Ugly she doted. Their every whim took precedence, except perhaps on the relatively rare occasions when Dr Humphrey Moorhead Hart-Smith was also in residence. He, it seemed, had returned to the colours and was working as a naval doctor. He frightened us almost as much as he seemed to intimidate his unfortunate wife, a gentle, languid, saccharine kindly lady. His brusque impatient vigour was more than enough for two. He took a cold bath every morning, and as he towelled himself would fill the house with his harrumphing and trumpeting. Glowing with rude health, a seventy year old with all the self assurance of his Cambridge MA, London University Gold Medal, a mention in despatches as RAMC Captain, and a lifetime as GP, his domineering presence was never in doubt.

Mum could manage to smile wanly about having to give way in the kitchen to Mother Cat, Little Ugly, Mrs Hart-Smith and her foibles, but she froze when Dr Hart-Smith entered the house. Woburn Terrace might be handy for work and schools, shopping and chapels, but we had to find somewhere else to live. After six months Dad found a delightful period cottage at Whitchurch, a mile or two from Tavistock's hub in Bedford Square. It belonged to Norman Creber who ran, in so far as rationing and his own ill-health allowed, a fairly up-market grocery in Duke Street. The cottage had been made by adding kitchen and bathroom to two 'two up, two down' cottages and creating one or two inter-connecting doors downstairs. Upstairs there was no such link, and there were still two staircases, one to the grown ups' room, the other to a children's 'wing'. This was fine for Peter and me, but Mum and Dad were anxious to be re-united with their own furniture and the Bank's temporary rent allowance for relocated officers was running out.

So we moved again, to the only unfurnished house Dad could find to rent. Birchwood Terrace was at the town's western border, its three little blocks the last houses before the cemetery and the open road to Plymouth. Number 3 was a sad come-down for Mum, not to be compared with the Bank House, and well below the post-war Parker-Morris standard for council houses. Upstairs there were three bedrooms, one double and two small singles. Downstairs there was a small front parlour and a fair-sized family room. This led into a small kitchen about six or seven feet square. It was indeed our engine room. Sink, gas oven, and work top filled the right-hand wall. On the left, a tall cupboard housed an upright metal bath on a hinge. There was just enough room in the kitchen to let the bath down. Having a bath was not something to be lightly undertaken. First you had to clear space for the bath itself. Then some thought was needed to secure an adequate supply of water at the right temperature. This was because the kitchen sink had the only tap in the house, and kettles and sauce pans provided the only hot water. Opening off the kitchen as you took a couple of steps from kitchen to back door were a small pantry and our only loo. Co-ordinating the family's morning ablutions with toiletting and a cooked breakfast must have exercised Mum's managerial skills to the limit. Somehow or other Dad was sent off to work on his bike, Peter on his fifteen-minute walk and I on my five-minute walk to school.

Thanks to the scholarship I had won at Poole, Tavistock Grammar School was obliged to ignore my mixed record and find me a place. I had been in the fifth form in the middle of my School Certificate year but Tavistock used a different Examinations Board and I was young for my year, so the Head decided that I should revert to the fourth form. There was no disputing G. Newbold Whitfield's decisions. He had become Head the previous term, a lean and energetic thirty-four year old who went on to become Head of Hampton School, President of the Headmasters' Association, and General Secretary of the Church of England Board of Education. His mission at Tavistock was to animate a somewhat sleepy country grammar school whose Honours Board had mustered only a handful of university places and a couple of dockyard apprenticeships in some twenty-five years. There was a clear improvement in the sixth form results by the time Whitfield left in 1946. His successor, Major Kenneth Anderson, was no less ambitious and within a few years could claim for his own curriculum vitae that half a dozen of his Tavistock pupils had won places at Oxford. They owed much to the weekly discussions his wife Kathleen ran voluntarily at home for the small group of Oxbridge aspirants. My generation was lucky.

Tavistock differed most obviously from Poole in being co-educational. There were as many girls as boys, and women as well as men in senior posts. I soon learned that most of my keenest rivals in the fourth form were girls. I shared at times a double desk with Jeanne Bowman, a radiant Anglo-French nymphet at whom I barely dared to glance. But for the most part as far as I was aware there was little fraternization between us fourth and fifth form boys and girls. That came when we were a year or two older.

I settled in quickly enough. The work was not too hard, very largely a matter of consolidation and a much-needed opportunity to get to grips with simultaneous equations, Pythagoras and the French subjunctive. The subjunctive remains a mystery. A few risqué up-country jokes won me some immediate street cred among the dozen or fifteen boys in 4A. This compensated for the fact that I was an oddball. Almost every other boy in the upper school belonged to the Combined Cadet Force. I had never belonged to any uniformed organization and was not at all concerned now that Dad opted out of the CCF on my behalf. I rather suspect that this was at least as much because he felt his own time in the OTC had been abortive as because of any pacifist feelings or concern that I should concentrate on academic matters. As it was the cadets looked slightly ridiculous marching up and down in their uniforms, and I never found at all alluring either the smokers' den in their armoury or the laddish masturbatory stories which followed the annual summer camp. While the cadets played at being soldiers for a couple of periods a week we non-cadets had an agreeable alternative programme of playreading and discussion with Mr F.J. Dymond, a precise little man who had been Head of the private Hoe Grammar School in Plymouth until it was blitzed in 1941. He baffled us by talking 'Of shoes – and ships – and sealing wax – Of cabbages – and kings', and listened to every BBC news throughout the day. In the afternoon he came hotfoot from the one o'clock news and would bring us up to date on the latest developments. I suspect now that he thought we comfortable West Devonians needed to keep in touch with the real world. In most respects, apart from a large camp on nearby Plaisterdown whose American soldiers dispensed food, confectionery and cigarettes liberally to alleviate our wartime deprivations, by 1944 the war had little impact on every-day life in a dairying, fruit-farming community.

Tavistock was only about half the size of Poole Grammar School, and its curriculum correspondingly limited. When I changed schools I had to choose between General Science and Latin, and between Woodwork, which I had abandoned many years before, and Art for which I had little aptitude. Latin and Art won the day. I might have spent longer agonizing over the choice if I'd realized that dropping science would close more doors than it left open. That apart, fifty years later the curriculum would have been described as broad and balanced. I took English Language and Literature, French and Latin, History and Geography, Mathematics, Art and Physical Education. The teaching was good enough to get me a respectable School Certificate with exemption from the dreaded London Matric by the time I was fifteen.

In one respect at least the Bank had shown some astuteness in appointing

Dad to their Tavistock Branch. Their dossier must have included notes about his Methodism and the strength of nonconformity in Tavistock. On the religious census day of Sunday 30 March 1851 almost two in three of the worshippers had attended one of the town's six chapels. In the town's industrial heyday, in less than twenty years between 1838 and 1857, Tavistock's Methodists built three chapels, two of them still thriving in the 1940s. Dad and Mum were in their element sampling and tasting before they settled on the former United Methodist chapel in Russell Street in preference to its somewhat more aristocratic Wesleyan neighbour in Chapel Street. In one way or another the chapel was to fill a good deal of my time over the next five years. My parents evidently assumed that custom and practice were the best way of building a solid foundation for lifelong engagement.

They had an early warning that things might work out differently. After three months at Tavistock Grammar School, in summing up my first term's report Whitfield described me as 'a boy who thinks for himself'. I was obviously unfit already for some lucrative careers, as Ray Kroc, the founding father of McDonald's, made plain some years later when he observed, 'We have found out…that we cannot trust people who are nonconformists…We will make conformists out of them in a hurry…The organisation cannot trust the individual; the individual must trust the organisation.' In my case it's hard to know whether I carry a dissenting gene or learned dissent at home. Outside working and chapel hours, Dad was always ready to challenge assumptions and argue a case. As a young man in his twenties my grandfather had kept a diary which recorded his participation in a dozen or more debates in a single year. In his own schooldays Dad had been an active member of his school debating society. And as a thirteen year old member of the upper school at Poole one of my treats had been observing the cut and thrust of the debating society.

My first experience of debate with a purpose came in 1945. Following the surrender of German troops, first in Italy and then in Germany, Britain celebrated Victory in Europe on 8 May. In less than a fortnight the Labour Party compelled its leaders to withdraw from the wartime coalition government. Churchill became Prime Minister in a Conservative Government on 26 May, and a General Election campaign began immediately. Votes were cast on 5 July, and the results were declared on 26 July.

All this was arranged without any regard for the school examination timetable. Our School Certificate written papers were probably spread through June. They certainly came to an end in time for me to go to one or two election meetings. I heard the Conservative Henry Studholme and the Liberal Isaac Foot, father of several illustrious sons and a formidable orator himself. Clement Davies, the Liberal leader, came to support Foot on a rainy day. We were much taken with his wit and polish when he commented punningly that worst of all the weather that day was 'in-clement'. At the end of term the Head called three or four of us in and told us that the Returning Officer needed

John learns to paddle his own canoe.

some runners to help with the count. Were we available? Of course we were, and off we went to the offices of G.G. Pearce, Tavistock's most eminent solicitor and commissioner of oaths, to take a solemn oath not to engage in any hanky panky, nor betray the secrecy of the ballot. It was heady stuff for a fifteen year old, and great fun to be on the inside track on the big day. We may even have been paid as well.

It must surely have been that summer when the school debating society held its own mock election. There was no difficulty finding people willing to stand in the Conservative, Liberal, and Labour interests, and there may have been an Independent too. To add a little piquancy I stood as a Communist, drawing heavily for my election address on Bernard Pares' rose-tinted portrayals of Soviet Russia. To everyone's surprise, on the first past the post system then in favour I ran out the winner with seven or eight votes from an electorate of about twenty-four. I wonder still whether it's the only time the Communist candidate has won a political election in the West of England.

Elections were however of only passing importance that summer compared with the emotional turmoil I recorded some eight or nine months later. My jejune note says:

> I first noticed Brenda during the summer holidays of 1945…I however was still not un-infatuated with Christine…in addition to Christine I soon became attracted by Margaret (November) and Audrey (January 1946)…When on one or two occasions Brenda smiled at me etc I felt on top of the world. At a Bedford

Society meeting for the reading of *Richard of Bordeaux* (29 Jan) I again seriously noticed Brenda. It was not however until the next meeting of this society in February at which we read *Time and the Conways* in which I was cast as Brenda's husband that I fell – and fell pretty badly…A meeting of the Historical Society in which she and I were proposer and seconder of the motion was the next step…we had to co-operate and accordingly spent an hour together in the library talking. I found her interesting, intelligent, clever, witty and even prettier than I had thought her before.

When Brenda and I met briefly to arrange that discussion Taffy Davies muttered 'followers' when he came across us. Even that was a great stimulus, to me at least. There were opportunities to meet out of school as well. Mum must have marvelled at how willingly I ran errands for her on Saturday mornings. 'Having seen Brenda in town one Saturday I now go every Saturday and talk with her.' I usually went to queue for sausages and pies from Mr Friend the unsmiling pork butcher, to pick up a few groceries from Mr Barratt, the protoype for Snow White's Happy, and to browse in Boots' tiny book department for fifteen minutes or so. There were not many Saturdays when my inamorata did not have similar errands. She sent me a photo (she'll be surprised to know I still have it), she promised teasingly to look out for me on the school cross-country run, she gave me fudge. 'We kissed and it was heavenly. Her manner irritated me a wee bit – but still…it was Brenda.'

Then one of the oddest entries, since observing fast days had been no part of my upbringing: 'I'm pleased to see how she observes Lent – an excellent characteristic.' And perhaps the oddest of all: 'No thrillers etc is good.' 'I wish I were not going away. How am I to tell Mum and Dad?'

I found Dr Johnson's ode *To a young lady on her birthday* and inscribed it carefully at the other end of my notebook:

> This tributary verse receive, my fair
> Warm with an ardent lover's prayer.
> May this returning day for ever find
> Thy form more lovely, more adorned thy mind
> …
> So shall Belinda's charms improve mankind.

From time to time on Sunday evenings when Mum and Dad had gone to chapel and I was supposedly working on my latest essay I would sneak out to the parish church for the illicit pleasure of gazing distantly across the pews at my beloved.

In the interests of continuity I've omitted occasional references in that saga to Christine, Margaret and Mavis. When Mavis left Tavistock in 1946 and moved to Hampshire we corresponded regularly for several years, our fire refurbished by occasional meetings. On one occasion I cycled devotedly on an elderly upright bike from Oxford to Fareham to have lunch with Mavis and her parents. Meanwhile Christine and I found a secluded Sunday evening trysting place in the porch of a disused church. No wonder I liked the anonymous verse I found in the *English Book of Light Verse*:

Two Strings to a Bow

I don't want the one that I don't want to know
That I want the one that I want:
But the one that I want now wants me to go
And give up the one that I don't want.
Why I don't want the one that I don't want to know
That I want the one that I want
Is if I miss the one that I want (don't you know)
I might want the one that I don't want.

That was very much the story of the next few years: Chinese walls were an essential fitting, for my playtime at least.

There was of course much more serious business to be undertaken in the sixth form to which I had now graduated. A small school like Tavistock with about two dozen pupils in the sixth form could offer only a limited range of subjects. There were two set menus and no à la carte. I would have liked to take Mathematics, Geography, History and English but that was quite impossible. You could go on the science side and take, I believe, Mathematics, Physics and Chemistry, with Geography as an alternative to one of these subjects. On the arts side you took English and History with French and possibly Latin as subsidiary subjects. Having no science, it was Hobson's choice for me: the Arts menu. This ran against the grain of the school; at Tavistock, as in most co-educational schools at that time, there was a marked tendency for boys to choose the science and girls the arts programme.

Sixty years later this menu seems almost penally constrained. But those were the days when schools offered General Studies and technical colleges argued what to include in their Liberal Studies programmes. About a quarter of our time was assigned to a rich and varied programme of General Studies for the whole sixth form. We had a General English course which Whitfield inaugurated with his own *Introduction to Drama* and Michael Roberts' *Proper Study of Mankind*, courses in Art and Music, and the Post War Society. This Society was a consortium of about a dozen or fifteen sixth forms from schools in West Devon and East Cornwall. Each sixth form studied the term's chosen subject and then towards the end of term we all assembled for a grand plenary conference with keynote speakers. The subjects included Agriculture and Fisheries, Crime and Punishment, Town and Country Planning, and Entertainment. Our study of entertainment included a visit to Plymouth to see International Ballet perform Les Sylphides, Coppelia, and Dances from Aurora's Wedding. More memorably, our study of Agriculture made us experts on the innovative system of Artificial Insemination being developed in the model farm at Dartington, and gave us opportunities to propagate a few rural myths about the interestingly unbridled behaviour of pupils at Dartington's pioneering school. The Post War Society had of course a committee of teachers to do the strategic thinking, and a shadow committee of sixth formers concerned mostly with some of the more detailed arrangements for the termly conference.

A fish in a small pond has many opportunities. I became a pluralist: Post War Society representative, Prefect, Joint Editor of the School Magazine, Member of the Games Committee, just inside the hockey team, on the edge of the cricket team, 'a reliable member' of the choir, playreader and debater. We debated the need for radical reform of male costume and the case for voting at eighteen. I failed to persuade my friends that the House of Lords had outlived its utility or that a literary was preferable to a scientific education, but, relying heavily on Siegfried Sassoon's *Memoirs of a Fox-Hunting Man* did convince them that fox-hunting is a deplorable pursuit.

We were lucky in having a good mix of experienced and energetic teachers. The second master from 1929 until he died in 1955 was Cyril Hartley, dry, reticent and wry, always known as Spot because of his uncanny knack of detecting any misdemeanour, most often to be found in his stock cupboard doling out our limited ration of paper. Major W.C. Rawlings was rather more obviously in charge of the Cadet Corps than he was Head of Maths. Luckily *my* Maths was good enough to compensate for my absence from the Corps. My brother Peter was less fortunate, and was transferred to another maths teacher to save him from Rawling's impatient sarcasm. H.A. (Taffy) Davies had been at the school for more than twenty years, took a lively interest in our playreading and debating, and in due course got me reading Granville Barker's *Prefaces to Shakespeare*, Coleridge's *Notebooks*, and Maurice Morgann's splendidly eccentric defence of Sir John Falstaff's courage. Roy Gill took Miss Marsden's place as a French teacher. She, like one or two other young women teachers, was much admired by the fifth formers she met at Town Hall Saturday night hops. Even the quietest country town is a social hot house. Roy Gill encouraged me to read some of his Gollancz's pink-backed Left Book Club publications. One in particular developed the novel and disturbingly unMethodist proposition that wars are useful because they stimulate technological change and development. A year or two later another temporary French master arrived. He was, we understood, fairly recently retired from the army. He was a surprisingly effective teacher and soon introduced us to some lively colloquial French without fully explaining its provenance. On my first visit to France a few years later my Auxerre hosts were horrified when I aired my legionnaire's French in their drawing room. Another newcomer was D.S. (Charley) Charleston, who was both a former Head in India who came to teach Geography (if his pupils learned nothing else they all knew 'you muzt learrn zee text') and a former international hockey player whose stick work astonished us. As geographer he took the place of 'Smuggy' Smith who had moved to Kelly College, the local independent school, and to whom I once somewhat unfairly attributed some of my own ideas. In the Easter and summer holidays I usually signed on with the Devon War Agricultural Executive who used to arrange for little groups of workers to go to local farms in need of temporary short-term workers. We used to lift potatoes, hoe bulbs, trim hedges, pick strawberries, stook corn, and tackle whatever the farmers thought they could entrust to relatively unskilled bodies. My three or four fellow workers were women in, I suppose, their thirties or forties and not dangerously adventurous in their thinking. I was a bit radical for them, but much too young to be culpable, and when they asked where I'd picked up my strange ideas I could think of no one else to blame but Smuggy.

There were of course a number of teachers with whom I had little contact. Trevor Thomas came almost straight from North African tank battles to teaching woodwork, so highly charged that it was not an enormous surprise when he killed himself a good few years later. Young Rosemary Field lost her faith in the School Certificate when the art examiners allowed me through, and upbraided *me* when I laughed in amazement after someone else poured a supposedly solid pot of paste all over my head in one of her sixth form art lessons. J.C. Vickery was appointed for his cricket and also introduced us to Rugby football, an unexpectedly useful skill in one of my later incarnations. Freddy Wrench came in mid-career to take charge of chemistry. He seemed by all accounts to be good at his job, but he achieved lasting fame as a wag for his percipient advice to one of my contemporaries, 'keep it between your own legs'. That same young man was one of the two or three lusty choral basses whom the music mistress used to invite home for individual coaching in the evenings.

My own pastimes were surprisingly innocent. The school library doubled as the sixth form room, and when placed side by side the three or four library tables made a passable table tennis table until G. Newbold Whitfield dropped in on our sixth form tournament one Easter. For private study we often used a tiny room whose double locker desks were ideal for *Up Jenkins*, a simple guessing game with some resemblance to the fairman's *Find the Lady*. It made a pleasant interlude between demanding lessons. Since school matches were usually in the morning, on Saturday afternoons we could support Tavvy football in winter, or cricket in summer. Squire Kelly was always at first slip, too old and bulky to do more than struggle from one wicket to the other between overs. In the holidays I occasionally cycled to places like Plymouth and Launceston, tried to swim in the ice-cold Tavy, tramped over the moors, and played tennis endlessly.

Outside school Mum and Dad seemed to welcome my growing involvement in chapel-based activities. At thirteen attending morning and evening chapel services was part of the natural order. Afternoon Sunday School was part of the package, and so in due course was membership of the youth club and the choir. Inability to sight read music might have been thought a problem in the choir, but in those days choristers were scarce and I offered a passable baritone and enough savvy to follow the score and the rest of the basses at not too great a distance. It was good fun and gave me enough of a start to help out in the school choir.

The Methodist use of local preachers to take many of their services makes for a certain lack of continuity, some variations in quality, and an occasional mismatch between fervour and reason. Within a year or two I had learned the useful administrator's art of seeming wakeful while switching off during the sermons. As a family we usually sat in a central pew looking up to the preacher in the pulpit and at the choir in the gallery above the preacher. There were ample opportunities to watch and study, to admire and even fantasize about Margaret, Mavis, Molly and Muriel as they sat in pulpit or in choir. The Sunday afternoon class provided an opportunity for more purposeful activity. The little group of boys being tutored by Mrs Ivy Hancock was ill disposed to take anything at face value. On weekdays by this time I was reading Shaw and Renan and other freethinkers. We sharpened our talons and our minds on Mrs Hancock's well-intentioned presentations and went off with our doubts reinforced. We were also members, with perhaps two dozen other young people, of a lively youth club which met once a week on Saturdays in the chapel school room for table tennis, chess, discussion and other similar activities. In truly ecumenical spirit many of us used also to turn out on Fridays at the Brook Street Congregational Chapel where there was no ping-pong but better chess and more discussion. Our combined football team Wescon United began modestly enough like other church sides such as Aston Villa, Everton and Wolves. Fifty years on the Premiership remains a distant dream for Wescon players. In the fullness of time I became the Methodists' treasurer and was sent off to serve on the district youth council, which I later chaired. From time to time we met neighbouring districts for quizzes and debates.

Like Winston Churchill, who finally won a place at Sandhurst nearly four years after entering the Army Class at Harrow, I was well into my fourth year in the sixth form before I called it a day. My subsidiary subjects were translation from French and Latin, a process which tested my command of English without giving me any ability or confidence in either foreign language. For Latin we went to Miss Nichol, the Senior Mistress, a lady quiet, competent and middle-aged. We used to wonder why her face and neck flushed red whenever we read, as we often did, the story of Narcissus, the young man who is said to have fallen in love with his own reflection. What secret thoughts disturbed her? Why did we read the tale so often?

For three years in the sixth my chief mentor was Miss Dennis, a young history graduate who joined the school a term before I did. Tall, slender and sallow, with black hair and luminous black eyes Molly Dennis must surely, though she hailed from Somerset, have numbered among her forebears some West African traveller who had touched shore in Bristol or Bridgwater. Intensely committed, she must have spent hours preparing her detailed teaching notes. She ensured that we never lacked appropriate background reading material by ordering boxes of books from the County Library to fill the gaps in our own small library. It was hard to imagine that she might have a private life, but she certainly became friendly with Clifford and Ivy Hancock, who were also family friends of ours and whose radiogram seemed to me the acme of domestic luxury. It must have been Clifford Hancock, who tried a little later to lead me along the same path, who persuaded Miss Dennis to consider local preaching. Before long, more eloquent and even more intense than on weekdays. she was filling the pulpit at which I gazed on Sundays. What secret thoughts absorbed me?

I passed the Higher School Certificate with hardly a care in 1947, but I've rarely been as miserably concerned as I was in the run-up to my second attempt in 1948. At best, I feared, twelve months would have passed without any measurable improvement. Worse, I might even do less well than first time round. Fortunately Dad and Taffy Davies and Molly Dennis created a climate in which I did enough to satisfy the examiners. Her teaching helped me to end the year with a Scholarship at Exeter University College, a place at Oxford and a creditable Higher School Certificate.

Molly moved on that summer. We kept in touch for several years and met occasionally, in Salisbury when she was teaching there and again in Shropshire. There must always have been an eight or ten year age gap between us, and in my mid twenties I was quite unnerved to find her dolled up like a sixteen year old. Immediately she came in sight I wondered what construction she had placed on our meeting. We did not meet again. Molly prospered professionally and went on from one school headship to another in London. Like many others, as a single person and a head teacher she must have found life in London desperately lonely. When I heard she had taken her own life I could not help feeling a remorseful twinge. Only after that did I learn that in our Tavistock days she'd lived with the Hancocks for several months, recovering from depression and self-harm.

In the post-war years young men were liable for National Service but could defer their National Service to complete a course of study. I might have left school in 1948, deferred my National Service for three years, and taken an Exeter University course immediately. But the Oxford offer was of a place in two years' time after National Service. In the circumstances Dad and KDA, as Major Anderson was soon known, decided it was worth my staying at school for yet another term to try once more for one of the prestigious Oxford entrance scholarships. There would still be time for National Service, and then Oxford in two years' time.

That summer I persuaded Dad that a one-week sixth formers' residential conference at Truro School would add a certain *je ne sais quoi* to my education. Philosopher Olaf Stapledon was the most famous speaker, but what he said je ne sais pas. I signed on also for two weeks at a farm camp near Saltash. We all went hoeing and picking strawberries and new potatoes in Cornwall's Tamar Valley, and one afternoon when there was no work three or four of us went out with some of the local salmon fishermen in two or three boats with enormous nets with which we swept the river. My fellow workers included an alarming pair of fairground entertainers, a contortionist who could wrap his legs round his neck, and an ominously silent strong man, as well as the Lumb sisters from Pately Bridge. Betty Lumb and I corresponded affectionately for several years to come.

To my surprise, KDA called me in a day or two before the autumn term to announce his summer holiday decision. Whereas before the holiday he'd been talking about my becoming School Captain he had now decided to appoint Ken Sleep. Perhaps KDA judged that the extra line on Ken's c.v. would turn the balance for him. In the event Ken left school three weeks later on receiving a late offer of a university place and I found myself on top of the greasy pole after all. I enjoyed a private smile when KDA thanked me warmly later on for stepping in at short notice at some risk to my own studies. I was much helped in these by Bernard Wilkinson, the able Oxford historian who succeeded Molly Dennis. It was good and timely for me to experience a different perspective and a different challenge. He and Taffy Davies encouraged me to look into the growth of political and scientific and philosophical thinking in the seventeenth century and summarize my findings in a long essay, now lost. 'I did but prompt the age to quit their clogs' said the radical James Harrington. This struck a chord; 'prompting the age to quit their clogs' was what I admired George Bernard Shaw for doing in *Everybody's Political What's What* and his play prefaces. I also found my way to the Tavistock Subscription Library, one of only a dozen or two such libraries in England, which had splendid resources for exploring local history and archaeology.

Despite my concentration on history, my studies remained defective. No one brought English History to life by pointing out the Tavistock folk who had made a mark on national affairs: Aelred the Saxon Abbot of Tavistock who went on to become Archbishop of York and in that capacity crowned the Norman bastard William King of England on Christmas Day 1066; Sir John Glanville, Speaker of the Short Parliament where opposition to Charles I's despotic rule first took shape; John Pym, the MP for Tavistock who was for three critical years the leader of the parliamentary opposition to Charles I; William Russell, scion of the Russell family, who was arraigned for treason against James II; W.H. Smith, lampooned by W.S. Gilbert as 'Ruler of the Queen's navee' but of more lasting influence as founder of a chain of railway newsagents and a circulating library; and of course Francis Drake, the bowls player who shattered the Armada and singed the King of Spain's beard, who was the only one to have been born in the town's environs. Perhaps a budding historian might have been invited to assess the relative contributions of these six men to the making of England, but we knew little or nothing of their links with Tavistock. Drake alone we honoured. Someone had appropriated his prayer as the school prayer: 'It is not the beginning of any great matter, but the continuing unto the end until it be thoroughly finished which yields the true glory.'

My own quest ended for the time being in December 1948 when James Harrington's old college, Trinity, Oxford decided to make me one of their Minor Scholars. I was pleased, Dad jumped for joy. I rested over Christmas and went back to enjoy a few last weeks at school. When KDA arrived in January 1947 I had noted cautiously 'he's pretty good'. Two years later we old hands were not so sure The girls had a new uniform with fetching WRNS-like berets, but we boy prefects were expected to sport risible little scarlet caps. If we wore them we were clearly visible to malefactors, and if we didn't wear them Spot Hartley detected us. In October 1947 I'd had to speak to KDA about the need for him to provide a bit more backing for school societies, and now despite a reminder we'd gone a term or two without a school magazine. On Monday 17 January a few sixth formers decided to publish our own newsletter; we collected material, took the script to Ellams the printer on the 26th, agreed that three pence a copy would cover our costs and leave a small margin for charity, and went on sale in the lunch hour on Friday the 28th. By the time afternoon school began we had pretty well sold out, and when I went to invite KDA to buy a copy he insisted on buying all the rest 'for his friends'.

It was time for me to bow out in a flurry of hockey matches, table tennis, resignations and farewells. KDA managed to surprise me as we parted by asking, 'Have you ever thought of reading medicine and becoming a surgeon?' It was the first careers guidance I'd ever had. Instead of returning to school after half term, on Shrove Tuesday I set off to join the RAF. Dad looked as if he thought I was going down for a lengthy prison sentence.

CHAPTER 4

Wearing the King's Uniform

Then a soldier, full of strange oaths

I REPORTED TO Padgate on Ash Wednesday, ready to spend Lent in the service of King and Country. The Royal Air Force seemed a gentler, more gentlemanly service than the army, and there was no difficulty in securing my first choice. They had happily agreed to defer my medical for a couple of days so that I could play hockey for the school, and the call-up date a few weeks later coincided neatly with the school's half term. Off to Derby to stay overnight with my aunts and cousins, and then on to Padgate, the Lancashire reception camp known to generations of RAF recruits. We are Aircraftsmen Second Class, grappling with a new world of Identity Cards (Two four, two five, one five zero, Ssirrr), Ration Books, Ablutions, Kit Bags, Rain, and Off the Peg Uniforms trimmed to size overnight. I was to wear the King's Uniform for eighteen months but it never fitted well. Most of us are about eighteen; one, a bit older, has been in the merchant navy and has the scars to show that someone in a foreign port twisted a bottle round his stomach. Why should this make us scared of *him*? After forty-eight hours we're photographed in uniform. We begin to *look* a bit like airmen. 'Two four, two five, one five zero, Ssirrr.' Snow, Vaccinations, the Padre on the evils to which young airmen are exposed, the gentle art of 'Bulling' boots with a hot poker (which made more of a mark on my wrist than on the boots), Clothing Coupons, Stencil Name on all clothes, Pay Parades ('Two four, two five, one five zero, Ssirrr,' four shillings a day, a princely sum for someone straight from school). Cinema, more snow, Fatigues for seven hours, Brass Cleaning, lose skin from burnt wrist, send civilian clothes home. Write Christine. Write home. Play chess with Norfolk chess champion, or so he claims, and win. All this in a week. We spend only one week in the reception unit. Then what? Where are we going next?

Up at 6 a.m. on our eighth day. Fall over in the slush and mud. We're off by train to West Kirby, which is, we're told, a second Belsen. We're put to work cleaning the billets immediately. I have a stroke of fortune. I'm one of the first to enter our new billet. The veterans who've just passed out are leaving as we move in. Would I like to buy an electric iron at less than half price? It's a piece of vital equipment. I agree immediately, and become a monopolist, the only iron-owner in my new billet. For the next eight weeks other people borrow my iron and happily press my uniform and clean my rifle in return.

44

We meet Sergeant Benbow, Corporal Edwards and Corporal Burgess, the three NCOs who are going to turn us into airmen. We march, we halt, we stand to attention, we stand at ease, we stand easy. Their incredulity at our incompetence knows no limit, 'Chrriiist on a Bicycle!!' exclaims Corporal Burgess. 'Jeeesus Chrriist, and ranks descending,' adds Corporal Edwards. The Station Commander addresses us, the Education Officer tells us Japan is to be given the American blessings of democracy, birth control and Christianity; 'these Americans must be insufferable,' I write, 'thank God I don't know any.' We see Paul Temple at the cinema, we attend a Church Parade, the Medical Officer addresses us. I report sick and get an exemption from shaving. Fever, and I feel lousy. Four blokes fall out on parade. Wednesday night is bullshit night: lino polished, kit cleaned, brasses polished, kitbags squared improperly with bricks, blankets squared. Feel lousy. Films on how to engage in unarmed combat and how to avoid venereal disease. Corporal Burgess has lost his voice. Oh dear! Write Mavis, Christine, home, Dennis. Mess Orderly. Go to church in the morning and Hoylake Mission Hall for tea. See *Duel in the Sun*. We all take part in a boxing match, we march up and down for an hour, the squadron leader tells us off roundly, and the NCOs follow. Corporal Edwards has never seen such a shower. 'I'll have you in that guardroom so fast your feet don't touch the deck.' We whitewash coal. We're the worst flight they've ever seen. Confined to billets. We learn to crawl, literally. Several report sick. Ablutions orderly. Rifle drill. We shoulder arms, we present arms. Tea at National British Women's Total Abstinence Association canteen in West Kirby (my mother would be proud of me). Spend nearly all Sunday cleaning, polishing boots etc. Write home, aunts, Mavis, Bernard Wilkinson. Square bashing. Feel rotten at night. Diarrhoea. No food. Clothing Inspection. Fatigues in central veg. section. On guard. Road work with boots. Take trade tests, after which I'm a marked man, alone in the flight in being listed POM, Potential Officer Material! They must be desperate. Write home, Christine, Brian Leverton. Monday, on guard. Tuesday, cookhouse. Wednesday, Station Inspection by the Air Officer Commanding, a major event which stimulates expressions of proletarian democracy: 'Stand by your beds, here comes the air-vice marshal, He's got bags of rings…but he's only got one arsehole' like all the rest of us. NAAFI fatigues. Thursday, Officer says I should apply for a Regular Commission. Friday NCO says my kit isn't up to scratch. Saturday and Sunday bullshit all day and have my blues pressed for me. Write home. As long as my grandmother lived, religiously on Sunday afternoons in the interval between morning and evening services Dad wrote to her. For a while at least I too write home on Sundays. Monday, Tuesday, Wednesday, interviews with Flight Lieutenant (a flop), Squadron Leader (successful), Wing Commander, and Group Captain. Spend Easter in Derby, see Robert Morley in *Edward My Son*, Peter Finch in *Eureka Stockade*, *The Parradine Case* and *Badger's Green*. Watch Derby Tigers. Write Mavis. Go to Padgate for a Board Interview. My eyes are set only on Oxford. The Board evidently conclude eighteen months' national service is not enough to turn this low-grade ore into a fine blade. What if I'd been thinking a bit more laterally about a longer-term commitment? Their loss??

West Kirby beach, press best blues, obstacle course, firing practice. Sergeants Benbow and Harvey swap places. Corporal Burgess recoils in mock horror as he looks down my rifle barrel. 'Sergeant Harvey, come and look at this airman's rifle.' Sergeant Harvey comes, looks down the barrel, tut tuts sorrowfully and says something about the incongruity of anyone with a rifle like that ever thinking of becoming an officer. Films of various aircraft, bollocked for poor drill. But at least I've learned how to take at will a stride exactly 30 or 33 or 36 inches long. Asked to give a five-minute talk I bemuse my fellow airmen by talking about the excitement of history. Mess Orderly, Obstacle Course, Aircraft Recognition Test at which we all help each other or my score would have been zero, two and a half hour drill rehearsal, one and a half hour Ceremonial Rehearsal. Passing Out Parade, the band plays the RAF March, we're immaculate and sharp. Mr Kroc would applaud the way we've fallen into line. The Wing Commander presents us with an aspidistra, a reward for the best flight passing out that day. The Squadron Leader says we're the best flight ever. We believe him, proud to be highly polished cogs in a well-oiled machine.

We disperse, never to meet again. I sell my iron to the next flight at about 10 per cent below shop price. It's brought in a useful income in kind, and I've doubled my money in eight weeks. A career in commerce beckons.

Seven days' leave as reward for all our hard work. Meet Mavis at Exeter, see the *Yank at the Court of King Arthur*, home at 11.30 p.m. Swim and play tennis with Dennis, get soaked going to see Clare who wasn't there, write Mavis, and eventually meet Clare two days later.

Summer with the RAF passed most agreeably, a few weeks in Suffolk, two weeks in Norfolk and three in Sussex. Off first to Bawdsey Manor, Arthur Quiller-Couch's Suffolk home where the first experimental radar systems had been tested. There on a small promontory nestling between the River Deben and the coast we lived and slept in wooden billets scattered among the trees. Rabbits and squirrels played around our huts while our elite group of twenty were introduced to the mysteries of fighter plotting. There was Dick Macey, tall, seemingly unflappable, with a passion for cricket, Percy Cope, a sarf Londoner with the engrained pessimism of his tribe, Ben Brindle, a reflective, pipe-smoking countryman from the moors above Clitheroe, and John Dan, a cheery potter from Wivenhoe, the smugglers' haven on the River Colne, whose resemblance to me and the similarity of our names caused a good deal of confusion. George Edmundson was our natural leader, a blond Viking chieftain, Lancashire schoolboy cricketer, ballroom-dancing medallist, Blackburn's heart throb, and prospective Oxford undergraduate, a great guy

2425150: Britain's First Line of Defence, May 1949.

who knew instinctively how to play the system. While the others toiled one hot day to get things ready for the station sports, George and I spent a lazy afternoon finding a rope for the tug o' war. Then there was Jack Marsh the intending teacher from Durham, Sean McGrath who was going to read languages at Trinity College Dublin, Taffy Phillips who played rugby football for Swansea and the RAF, Frank, whose service was to be interrupted by a spell in the glass house, and Geoff Willetts, an epicene young mathematician who endured our taunts stoically before heading for Cambridge and the Bank of England. Roy Standbridge, Peter Jackson, Jim McCrimmon, Donald Thomson and Zach made up the billet. 'I don't know what effect these men will have on the enemy,' said Wellington, 'but by God they frighten me.' We were now an integral part of Fighter Command, Britain's first line of defence.

The demands of this prestigious role left little space to pursue our own interests. Luckily, in those post-war years the King's Uniform still had a certain aura. Anyone who was able to do so seemed happy to offer us impecunious airmen a lift, and as we were to find, the uniform excited a warm glow among both sexes. We explored the coast from Shingle Street to Felixstowe, walked to

Woodbridge on the Deben, celebrated the King's Birthday by hitchhiking to
Framlingham (castle and church) and Norwich (Anglican and RC cathedrals),
and travelled on the back of a lorry to London to spend a long weekend
discovering Westminster Abbey, Westminster Palace, Downing Street, Horse
Guards, St Martin's, Oxford Street, Lord's Cricket Ground, the Science
Museum and Trafalgar Square. As I stood innocently marvelling at the night
scene, an older man named Tom engaged me in conversation, and when he
heard I was heading for the Union Jack Club suggested that I might like to bed
down at his place in Philbeach Gardens. Neither Home, nor School, nor the
RAF Padre had warned me of this kind of danger. I escaped the next morning
with my virtue intact. As I regaled some of my almost equally innocent
colleagues with this story Zach got wind of what he took to be a heterosexual
adventure with a willing partner. I gave him my host's address, and never
heard which of them was the more discomfited when Zach was next in
London. Another long weekend at Whitsun saw me hitching home to Devon,
arriving shattered after crossing Dartmoor pillion on a motor bike. I saw
Humphrey Bogart in *The Treasure of the Sierre Madre*, and *Monsieur Hulot's
Holiday* at the cinema, and Emlyn William's *The Corn is Green* at a little theatre
in Felixstowe. Old habits were an unconscionable time a-dying, so on Sunday
evenings I walked into Felixstowe to the Methodist chapel for service and the
after-service fellowship. Despite this veneer of godliness, like the virtuous Job I
was smitten that summer with many sore boils and, though much inclined like
him to take me a potsherd to scrape myself withal, had to make do with a
noxious tonic and some vitamin pills. Boils on my face, and neck, and forehead
earned sympathy, exemption from shaving, and other benefits. Boils in more
private parts were equally debilitating but less rewarding.

After five weeks we were deemed to be fully fledged fighter plotters and
were whisked away to RAF Newton, the Nottinghamshire Headquarters of
Fighter Command's 12 Group. For two nights we shared an RAF station with
airworthy planes, for Newton was an aerodrome. That was as near as any of us
fighter plotters ever came to seeing a plane, let alone touching one. En route to
Neatishead in Norfolk we glimpsed Peterborough Cathedral and the Fens
through our railway carriage windows. Once there, a two-week exercise when
we worked round the clock for four hours on and four hours off introduced us
to the rigours to be expected on active service. Most of your four hours off
goes in snatching a meal, a couple of hours' sleep, and a quick wash. Somehow
there was time for a day at Wroxham canoeing on the Broads and another day
at Cromer and Sheringham. I damned them as 'stuffy' but was more than
compensated with a lift to Norwich in an open sports car.

Early in July we headed for Watnall, the small mining village just outside
Nottingham which was to be the base for my intelligence work for the next
fourteen months. We usually worked four-hour watches, on Monday
afternoons, and Tuesday, Thursday and Friday mornings, with a fatigues watch

on Wednesday morning, and occasional evening watches once or twice a week. These evening watches rarely went on much beyond midnight. We liked them because we were allowed to lie in the next morning and rise in time for an early lunch. On watch we wore headphones to receive the information which we then recorded on a large tote with metal tags or on a large map with metal arrows for the benefit of any supervising officer. This was long before the days of lightweight headphones, and was reckoned to be very demanding. Usually therefore when we were on watch we had an hour on duty and an hour off. As young men will, in our free time we debated art, literature, history, religion and women. For some now obscure reason I returned again and again to writing a long essay on the Commonwealth, a topic which had won me a sixth form county essay prize. Perhaps the new draft was required for one of the numerous courses I kept on applying for without success. We played some chess and I began to play contract bridge. My summer semester's reading included Voltaire's *Candide*, G.K. Chesterton's *Essays*, Hillaire Belloc's *The Man who Made Gold*, Arthur Conan Doyle's *The Brigadier General*, J.K. Jerome's *Three Men in a Boat*, C.S. Lewis's *Screwtape Letters*, Thornton Wilder's *Bridge of San Luis Rey*, Clive Bell's *Civilization*, Phillip Guedella's *Churchill*, Emlyn Williams' *Wind of Heaven*, Joseph Conrad's *Typhoon*, *The Rubayiat of Omar Khayyam*, D.H. Lawrence's *The Plumed Serpent*, and *I Did Penal Servitude*. My reading programme advanced rapidly in the week I spent as a Fire Picket and sole assistant to Corporal Catt, the station's Fire Officer. I was, as it were, on duty round the clock and obliged to stay in the fire section. On the first morning I carried six tins out, and brought them back again. On the second I filled five extinguishers. This took an hour and a half. On the third morning there were only three extinguishers to fill, and I was green enough to volunteer to do some entirely optional painting. There was still plenty of time for reading, and exploring Corporal Catt's philosophy of life. He was a man fullfilled. He had his own domain. Perhaps it wasn't very grand, but no one bothered him, his duties were far from onerous and he had in me and my colleagues enough modest help with the more demanding routine tasks. He'd achieved all he wanted of life and the RAF.

George Edmundson, John Dan and I talked often about going to Scotland. In the end we settled on a more economical alternative, visiting George's father in Blackburn. It was a new world to me. As our train approached Sheffield instead of the gloriously blue skies which covered the rest of the country there was just a shroud of industrial smog. In Lancashire, unlike the sprawling southern towns I knew, the towns seemed to crowd in on themselves in their valleys and had a visible edge. We watched Lancashire League cricketers score more than 400 runs in an afternoon, a game totally different from the few days of county cricket I'd seen. We toured George's Dad's brewery; his at least in the sense that he was the brewery's excise officer. By Monday morning we were well hung over.

Early in September the flight left Watnall for the south coast, for another intensive exercise. For three weeks we lived like real soldiers in tents somewhere on the Pevensey marshes, sharing a long trench latrine. In between our four hours on and four hours off we ventured into Hastings and Eastbourne, found a pub which matured its cider in old sherry casks, and explored the Martello Towers in Pevensey Bay. There were usually four of us, Sean, Dick, George and my self. We used to think of ourselves as the Three Musketeers with their faithful companion D'Artagnan. This was one of George's whimsies. He of course was the dashing, debonair D'Artagnan, but it was always harder to cast the rest of us in a particular role. As we strolled along the beach one evening with several friends, half a dozen of us launched a mock assault on one of these isolated Towers. We burst through the door and attacked the upper floors. Dick Macey, as steady a chap as one could hope to find, and one or two others drew back; there was something evil above us on the stairs. To their evident alarm two or three of us went on up. We returned unscathed, and I at least felt nothing. You can imagine the ensuing debate. Was the Tower haunted? And if so, why? Someone recalled the Crumbles Murders, and we wondered whether the Tower had been involved. The debate ran on for several days. I resolved to put the matter to the test. Well after dusk one evening I would spend an hour or so on the top floor and would shine a torch to let my passing colleagues know that all was well. Unfortunately our timing was faulty. When I shined my torch there was no one to see it. When my friends arrived there was no light and I'd gone off to find them. I went round the block, and eventually caught up with an extraordinarily agitated group of nineteen year olds, believing the worst, and about to call the Sussex police. Some of the gang are doubtless telling still the story of a haunted Tower, while I'm telling a tale of credulity and group hysteria.

Perhaps this was a defining moment. Only two or three weeks earlier I'd noted in my diary, 'other people continually impress me with their achievements'. A few days after the Tower epic I remember saying reflectively as we strolled in the gloaming that I felt there would be something one day which only I could do. Some thirty years later...

At about this time we learned a useful lesson about institutional competence. Of our little Bawdsey group ten had volunteered for service overseas and ten had not. Now the authorities announced that just two of the volunteers and all the other ten were to go to the Middle East. 'Nil illegitimi carborundum,' as we scholars used to say, 'don't let the bastards grind you down.'

The other eight who'd been hoping for El Dorado or Shangri La were destined to spend the rest of their National Service on the Nottinghamshire coalfield at Watnall a few miles from D.H. Lawrence's birthplace in Eastwood. We signed on for drama and dancing classes in Kimberley, met some local girls and soon realized that the sensuality of Lawrence's characters was in no way overdrawn. This was better than abroad. We visited Nottingham's famous *Trip to Jerusalem*, admired the prettiest girls in England, and ate out at the NAAFI Club. I played a lot of hockey and chess, and at weekends often stayed with my aunts in Derby, becoming a *de facto* Derby County supporter, marvelling at the skills of Billy Steele, Raich Carter, Tommy Docherty, Billy Bremner, Jack Stamp and such great men as those. In theory we were allowed a 48-hour pass once a month and a 36-hour pass at the other weekends. In practice, since our watch usually ended at midday on Friday and we were not needed again until Monday afternoon, most of us helped to cut down red tape, did without passes, and took a long weekend every week.

This informality was my undoing. The last weekend in November Mum and Dad were staying with the Cheltenham Manns, my grandmother and Dad's three brothers and their families. I was to join them for a grand family reunion. The journey involved changing trains at Birmingham New Street, a station I hardly knew. As I staggered from my Nottingham train a couple of RAF police pounced on the hapless airman who presumed to go about with his greatcoat buttons undone. 'AIRMAN!! GET THOSE BUTTONS DONE UP.' 'Yes, corporal.' 'WHERE'S YOUR PASS, AIRMAN?' 'I'm sorry, corporal, I don't have a pass.' 'NO PASS!! WHY NOT, AIRMAN?' 'It's not the custom in my station, corporal.'

I spent the next hour or two in a police cell, and was allowed a quick call to Cheltenham to explain that the exigencies of the service meant I would not be coming after all. Dad could not figure it out. His brother Harold was in no doubt. When my police corporals came off duty they drove me to their station, and I was solemnly installed in another cell. Thirty-six hours later, and a nervous, bespectacled visitor arrived, Corporal 252 Smith from Watnall. Corporal Smith was on the admin side, nicknamed 252 for his addiction to handing out charges on Form 252, and supposedly rich beyond an airman's dreams with an inheritance of twenty or even thirty thousand pounds. He came apprehensively, armed with handcuffs, thinking he knew the huge desperado he'd been sent to fetch. His relief when we met was palpable. We were to return to Watnall by train and he thought it would be less embarrassing for both of us if we could dispense with the handcuffs provided I promised not to run away. In my situation it seemed as well to stop digging so I gave my word and we travelled companionably back to Watnall. There the solitary cell behind the guardroom was warm and ready. Senior NCOs, the orderly officer and even the station adjutant called to ask whether I was comfortable. I ate NCOs' rather than airmen's meals. My friends called with books and magazines. Another day passed without any charges being brought. On Tuesday I polished my boots and buttons and was marched off to see the Squadron Leader, a wartime pilot. 'It is,' he said, 'people like you' going about with my greatcoat buttons undone 'who are spoiling the service for people like me who are giving our lives to the RAF.' I did my best to look suitably abashed. 'Case dismissed.' Perhaps he thought a lost weekend and four nights in the cells was enough. Perhaps even in the RAF habeas corpus requires some sort of charge to be brought within forty-eight hours of an arrest.

The RAF was a kindly employer. The station hockey team played almost every Wednesday, and there was always transport for away matches. I acquired some useful life skills; since all organizations abhor the appearance of idleness even in the armed forces you're rarely challenged if you march about briskly with printed papers in your hand. My good friend George spent several weeks re-cataloguing the station library while the rest of us were on fatigues. For some reason he dropped out just before finishing so I took over, had of course to begin again, and spent several weeks on the task before handing over to yet another bookish volunteer. My winter reading included G.K. Chesterton's *Life of St Francis*, Maurice Ashley's *Life of John Wildman*, De Tocqueville's *Ancien Régime et La Révolution*, and plenty of Stephen Leacock, Dorothy Sayers, Ngaio Marsh and Simenon. I went often to the cinema and saw several classics, including Alec Guinness in *Kind Hearts and Coronets*, Danny Kaye in *The Secret Life of Walter Mitty*, Lawrence Olivier as *Hamlet*, James Stewart in *Harvey*, A.E. Matthews and David Tomlinson in *The Chiltern Hundreds*, Orson Welles in *The Third Man*. Michael Denison in *The Glass Mountain*, Sylvana Mangano in *Bitter Rice*, Douglas Houston, Alec Guinness and Joyce Grenfell in *Run for Your Money*, and many others like *Kidnapped*, *Joan of Arc*, *Rebecca*, *Revenant*, and *La Femme Perdue*.

In January my persistence in applying for almost any kind of course whether in moral leadership or the arts was at last rewarded. I became a guinea pig at Porton Down, the Chemical Warfare Research Centre. We were told we were testing the protective capacity of various kinds of material. Patches about three inches square were attached to our arms, and the patches were then painted with some kind of chemical. If our arms fell off, turned red or blistered the material was clearly inadequate. In my case nothing happened so presumably my patches were satisfactory. Or so I thought at the time. Half a century later I've been referred to a dermatologist and wonder whether it's too late to sue.

Every now and again management flexed its muscles. On parade one week we were roundly chastised, 'Ninety per cent of you need a haircut, and the other ninety per cent have dirty boots.' They asked for volunteers to help in the docks; but none of us volunteered. In the billet we became concerned about some petty pilfering. I lost £2. John Dan and I planted one or two items and found irrefutable evidence which we passed on. Our erstwhile friend Frank went down for 112 days, a stiff sentence by RAF standards. When I met him by chance in Reading many years later we talked affably enough about old times.

As spring turned to summer I began to buy civilian clothes, a jacket, trousers and shirts, and was measured for a suit. We spent a glorious day at Trent Bridge, watching the three WWWs, Clive Walcott, Everton Weekes and

Frank Worrall, amass 479 for 3 in reply to England's 223. One demob party followed another. We all celebrated 252 Smith's departure. Ben went, John Dan on 18 August, George Edmundson on 25 August, John Mann on 1 September, and Sean McGrath a few days later. I had a month to collect my thoughts before heading for Oxford.

CHAPTER 5

Trinity, Oxford

We were brothers all
In honour, as in one community,
Scholars and gentlemen.

WHY OXFORD? Why Trinity College? Dad spoke rarely about his own feelings or ambitions. But for him Oxford was the ideal, a community of gentlemen and scholars. A place at Oxford was the supreme accolade for achievement at school, an Oxford degree the open sesame to a life of opportunity. His ambitions for his sons were happily consistent with those of Whitfield and Anderson for their school. Whereas my termly reports had been the only line of communication between Poole Grammar School and home, at Tavistock the Parents' Association and the Parents Evenings inaugurated by Whitfield allowed parents and teachers to share their hopes and fears. By the time I was half-way through my sixth-form career I too had grasped that Oxford was the target at which I was to fire my arrows.

The *cognoscenti* were well aware of course that at Oxford and Cambridge candidates had to apply not to the university or a subject faculty but to a specific college. In those days all the colleges were single sex and most admitted only men. Each college reckoned to have its own strengths, its own specialisms, and sometimes its own long-standing connections with particular schools or districts: Trinity Cambridge and Eton, New College Oxford and Winchester, The Queen's College and the North of England, Exeter and the West of England, Jesus and Wales, Hertford and Essex. Pretty well every college offered valuable entrance scholarships, some open to any candidate, others restricted in various ways. Small groups of colleges ran competitive scholarship examinations at different times of the year, in December, January and March or April. They also offered ordinary places known as 'commoner-ships' to some who failed to win scholarships and others who applied only for places.

The mysteries of this arcane world, well enough known to many famous schools, were not widely understood in West Devon. I fired my first arrow at Merton College, chosen mainly because my cousin George had read medicine there, and then one at St John's and another at St Edmund Hall, better known as Teddy Hall. On each occasion the written papers were spread over three or four days. This left time also for interviews with college tutors, and at Teddy Hall time to become acquainted with their friendly shove ha'penny table. Most of my rivals looked formidably scholarly but few of those with the highest brows were to be found in Oxford when I got there. We history candidates translated passages from Latin and a modern foreign language, took English and European History papers and a General Paper, and wrote one long essay. At Teddy Hall the Vice-Principal, the Reverend J.N.D. Kelly, announced that the subject for essay was Illiteracy. 'Judging by the papers you have already written, this subject should suit you well,' he said. It suited me well enough for them to offer me a place. With this offer in reserve I fired one last arrow at Trinity, chosen I fancy because its social kudos was a little less than that of, say, Christ Church, its academic kudos a little less than that of Balliol or Magdalen. One of those who interviewed me was Tony Crosland, not long back from war service with the Parachute Regiment, an intimidating presence with his Presidency of the Oxford Union and his First in PPE. His only question was whether we in West Devon had much trouble with the CP. I'd been to odd meetings of the Young Conservatives and whatever Young Labour was called, but despite my election success in 1945 the Communist Party was something of which I knew little. However feeble, my answer did not stop the College offering me a Minor Scholarship worth £80 a year to read History or PPE. I had found at last a target I could hit. The scholarship entitled me to a supplementary State Scholarship whose value depended on parental income. In practice I received almost the maximum grant and was able to live in moderate comfort in term time, relying on free board and lodging at home to keep me going in the vacations. That apart I was financially independent from the moment I left school.

Twenty-one months sped by between my first and second visits to Trinity. Was it, I wonder, what Wordsworth had in mind by 'a community of gentlemen and scholars?' The college was small, with some two dozen Fellows, a small number of postgraduates and about 200 undergraduates. Eton and Winchester were strongly represented among the undergraduates, as well as many other well-known independent schools like Rugby, Westminster, Charterhouse, Marlborough, Cheltenham, Tonbridge, and Roman Catholic Schools like Ampleforth and Beaumont. A sizeable contingent of Rhodesians and South Africans came mainly from comparable schools in their own countries. Another contingent came from somewhat less famous independent schools. Just a handful, barely a dozen in all, were from maintained grammar schools.

Three or four of these groups were large enough to be almost self-sufficient, displaying a bland and almost Devonian disregard for those from a different milieu. They lived their own inward-looking lives, civil enough for the most part, but doing little to make the college an inclusive community of gentlemen or scholars. On the contrary, some quirky droit de seigneur ensured that our Junior Common Room Presidents and Secretaries were always Etonians, the annual elections a formality. In 1952 however a mild American

Rhodes Scholar, Buzz Baldwin, went around quietly stirring up disaffection. At the traditionally ill-publicized and ill-attended hustings his group of dissidents seized power and my good friend Tony Fathers from Charterhouse was elected President. Red Revolution it was not. Tony was no sansculottes. But the victims were furious. They demanded a re-run at a better publicized meeting, when as I observed they would have had a few days respite to organize themselves. The controversy filled pages of our JCR suggestions book. No other event in my three years at Trinity excited such emotion, such bitter recrimination.

A social seismograph would have recorded other tremors. Perhaps in deference to the supposed feelings of the contingent from southern Africa, Trinity was an all-white college. This was no great surprise. I had been to all-white schools, and served in what was in effect an all-white air force. But it was, or so we understood, in marked contrast to our neighbours in Balliol whom we challenged from time to time to 'Bring out your white man'. At Trinity, the first harbinger of change arrived in 1951 when T.R. Anantharaman, a brilliant Indian engineer, came to take a postgraduate degree. 'My admission,' he wrote later, 'was not welcome to many in the College, particularly the large group of Etonians there. Some of the Grammar School boys assured me that I had nothing to worry about since they also felt equally unwelcome.' When he invited as a dinner guest a Ghanaian chief who later became a university vice-chancellor, all the English students 'marched off suddenly from our table'. In much the same way when my chess-playing friend John Black invited an African guest one of the backwoodsmen wrote an open note in the JCR suggestions book asking whether JB could not be restrained.

At that time the idea of legislating to promote equal opportunities and root out racial discrimination lay some way ahead. Even when these laws came they were designed as much to change the climate of opinion as to reflect current thinking. In the 1950s colleges could hardly be expected to have formal policies or rules on such matters as equality or discrimination. In other respects however Trinity had elaborate codes defining what was and what was not acceptable behaviour. The authorities were much concerned to update these codes in line with changing fashions. At least re-writing the rules gave crabbed age an opportunity for ponderous wit. 'Games may be played in the Quad on payment of £1 for each throw, catch, drop, kick, dribble, shove, pass, run, hack, bowl, hurl, toss, hit or miss, cut, drive, slog putt or push with any stick, wicket, club, bat or bat-like thing...' 'It is permissible to...walk or run over grass in the Lodge Quad...on payment of 5/- a time.' 'Gentlemen coming from homes where bread throwing at the dinner table is habitual...will be permitted to continue their domestic pastime, on a payment of 5/- a throw...' Horn-blowing and whip-cracking in the quadrangles had caused some concern before the 1914–18 war but were rare occurrences afterwards. In 1927 the authorities of another college asked whether the practice of undergraduates treating one another to beer in hall had spread to Trinity. It was thought to be a new custom which had come in with the Colonials. And by 1938, since 'wireless has now become commoner…some definite ruling should be made'. This had been done by the time I arrived in 1950. You needed the Dean's permission to have a musical instrument, gramophone or wireless set, and these could be played only in the afternoons between 1 and 5 p.m. or in the evenings between 7 and 10 p.m., with the windows closed.

The process of initiation to this esoteric world was grander, it's true, than that of joining the RAF, but hardly less convoluted, and almost as frenetic. We freshmen attended a formal ceremony to be admitted as matriculated members of the university. We swore solemnly to observe the College Statutes and learned that we scholars shared the daily lesson reading in Chapel and were expected to attend the Sunday evening service. We acquired the scholars' long black gowns, far more serviceable especially in winter than the commoners' short bum-freezers. Like my RAF best blues, the gown had to be worn for every formal occasion: from matriculation, chapel, lectures and tutorials, to meetings with the President or any other Fellow, and dinner in college. We tried to memorize the lengthy Latin grace and I at least lived in fear thereafter that by some malign misfortune I might be the Senior Scholar at dinner one night and have to say grace. As a Minor Scholar in a low-ranking subject I was much safer than I knew, and was never called on. It was not the thing, we learned, to talk shop at dinner, to mention any woman by name or to use more than five consecutive words of any foreign language. Bread-throwing, bad language, singing, *outré* clothing and being more than five minutes late were all forbidden. The penalty for any of these social gaffes was sconcing, which involved buying a five-pint flagon of beer and trying to down it in one long gulp. We visited the President, J.R.H. Weaver, an otherworldly spirit absorbed in his superb photographs of Moorish Spain. We assembled for a group photograph. We met our own tutors Bruce Wernham and Michael Maclagan, were told when we would meet again for tutorials, and were advised which of the university lectures to attend, and which to miss.

For Oxford as a whole the immediate post-war years were a time of restrained turbulence. 'So much here has been changed by the war,' wrote Michael Maclagan in 1948. Before the war the colleges had seen themselves *in loco parentis* and their undergraduates *in statu pupillari*. Regulations which the colleges thought appropriate for that kind of relationship seemed unduly restrictive to the seasoned warriors who entered the university after the war. Many of these regulations had apparently been jettisoned by the time my generation went up in 1950. But some remained, and any infringement of these rules or any other unruly behaviour was severely punished. Walking on the orchard grass cost 2/6, throwing part of a chair through a window £2, and using the Fellows' Guest Room, when his own bed had been removed, cost another unfortunate £4/4/-, the same price as someone else paid for being drunk and shouting obscenities. Among the most expensive japes at £5/12/6, even though the miscreant 'admitted his misdeed and behaved comparatively well both in Balliol and on his return' was entering Balliol and damaging a window and some trellis work. You had to have the President's permission to stay in Oxford during the vacation and both his and your Tutor's permission to spend a night away from Oxford. Those who returned after term had begun were usually fined a pound or two, but someone absent for two nights was fined £6, and my friend Richard Honey was fined £4 for arriving three days late and failing to offer any kind of explanation. Not even having trouble with his fiancée saved another from a £2 fine for returning late. Someone else whose landlady reported a second unauthorized overnight absence was sent down. You needed the Dean's permission to be absent from Oxford during the day. No stranger was allowed to come in to the college after 10 p.m. and no one was allowed to enter or leave the college after midnight. The buildings were relatively secure but there were one or two illicit entrances, and one or two rooms looking on to the Broad had easily accessible windows which were much in demand. My friend Peter Mooney complained once that his sleep had been interrupted on fourteen successive nights at times ranging from five minutes past midnight to 5.30 and announced that in future his windows would be locked unless a prior booking was made.

After six hundred years as an exclusively male institution the university came slowly to terms with women. The rule which prohibited a woman undergraduate from the rooms of a man undergraduate without the consent of her college principal and the company of another woman was rescinded in 1935. In the following year the Vice-Chancellor and the Proctors decided to withdraw experimentally the general prohibition of 'mixed' acting, and by 1950 women were allowed to become members of OUDS, the university dramatic society. But it was still the Trinity rule in 1950 that 'No ladies are allowed in College before 1 p.m. or after 7 p.m. except that, in the Summer Term, ladies, accompanied by a member of the College, may remain in the Garden until 9 p.m.' I don't remember ever taking advantage of this concession or of the implied licence we had to entertain young ladies in our rooms all the afternoon from 1 to 7 p.m. Exceptionally, ladies were also allowed to be present at parties which went on after 7 until as late as 8 provided of course that the Dean had authorized the party if alcohol was to be served and more than ten people were to be there.

No doubt these rules were the outcome of centuries' experience of the young males' innate and infinite capacity for boisterous behaviour. The senior members of the university were concerned to create civilized communities in each college, and harmonious relations between Town and Gown. In all this the college authorities worked closely with the university's Proctors and their 'bulldogs' who were responsible for undergraduate behaviour in the city at large and were doubtless responsible for there being no such thing as a Rag

Day at Oxford. When they stopped one young undergraduate in the company of a well-known lady of the town he explained that the lady was his sister. This effrontery so astounded the Proctor that he forgot that a gentleman's word is not to be questioned. 'But sir, the creature's a notorious strumpet!' 'Yes indeed,' said the young man, 'mother and I worry about it continually.'

When I went up to Oxford in October 1950 I was directed to my rooms on Staircase 4 of the New Building. Behind a double door I had, like all the other young gentlemen, a small suite consisting of bedroom and sitting room. If I wished for total privacy I had just to 'sport my oak', a process which involved only closing the outer door. I'd hardly stepped inside and was just examining a pile of invitations from university and college societies when there was a thunderous knock. In the gloom of my second floor landing were two enormous men who demanded, 'Are you going to row?' I took one look at their barn door shoulders and delayed not one second. If giants like these went round canvassing support for the college boats, rowing was certainly not for me. I learned only later that my visitors were Christopher Davidge and David Callendar who were to row as a pair for Britain in the Olympics. Trinity was, I found, the pre-eminent rowing college, Head of the River for more than a decade. There was nothing as crude as a rowing scholarship, but the College Bursar and Law Tutor Pip Landon was said to double as governor of several independent schools and talent scout. If the best oarsmen had any difficulty passing Oxford's low-level admission hurdle, Landon took them under his own wing to read law. No wonder there was a fracas the following year when the Trinity boat was overtaken and 'bumped' by our neighbours Balliol on the last night of Eights Week. It was the end of an epoch. As the dean observed sorrowfully after fining the culprits, 'hostilities were thereby rendered almost inevitable'.

My next encounter had more lasting consequences. My next-door neighbour was another West Countryman, Ronald Moore, a Devonian who had also been educated in Tavistock but at Kelly College. He too was one of Trinity's Minor Scholars, in his case in Modern Languages. We met for the first time in 1948 as fellow members of the Post War Society Committee. Now we became the closest of friends. He was my best man in 1966, and we are still frequently in touch more than fifty years after graduating.

The New Building was not so new as to have running water in each suite. Amenities such as a laundry and a surgery lay in the distant future. The devoted 'scout' who looked after our rooms and kept a general eye on our comings and goings and goings-on was Spanner, a venerable college servant, one of Alexander Pope's 'abbots, purple as their wines'. Each morning he delivered a steaming jug of hot water for washing and shaving. Taking a bath was a much greater adventure. 'Damn it, they're only up for eight weeks,' was what Jowett the legendary Master of Balliol is reputed to have said when the question of installing baths was raised there. At Trinity all we had to do was to walk a hundred yards or so across three quadrangles and into a fourth courtyard to find a suite of bathrooms of which the RAF would have been proud. The bath house was open before breakfast, and from 4 p.m. to 7 p.m. for those who had been playing games. On a good day I could wallow happily in my tub there listening to majestic operatic arias emanating from Jeremy Thorpe's neighbouring tub.

He was on his way of course to becoming Leader of the Liberal Party, and was already one of the leading lights of the Oxford Union, the university's debating society. Among its giants were broadcaster Robin Day, philosopher Bryan Magee, journalists Keith Kyle and William Rees-Mogg, journalist and political commentator Anthony Howard, columnist Godfrey Smith, journalist and man of affairs Jeremy Isaacs, politicians Tony Benn, Norman St John Stevas and Gerald Kaufman. To have known them, even at a distance, provided a lifelong interest, though the Union's debating style was too contrived for me to wish to speak. Its library and billiards table were more to my taste.

I had the good fortune to enjoy some very minor sports. Untutored, I had played a fair amount of chess and happily assumed the undemanding task of arranging inter-college matches. As our weakest link, I usually played board three but when we played Balliol to give John Black and Bruno Ryves a better chance of winning I played board one against the international Leonard Barden. He won of course, and we lost the match in spite of my stratagem. I was too an enthusiastic hockey player and without knowing it had become a pretty low watt bulb in perhaps the brightest galaxy ever seen in a single college. Landon's successor as Bursar, Robin Fletcher, played for England in the 1952 Olympics and five of my Trinity contemporaries played against Cambridge in 1953. Ian Burnett and Pat Walker, a future Director General of the Security Service, played for Scotland against an England team which included Richard Norris and John Strover, a future Olympic Captain. It was a delight to play with these people, if not often in the needle matches.

For the summer I found one or two tennis players of about my own standard, and found my level in the college's second cricket XI. Once at the end of term when they were really strapped for players I was conscripted to the first XI for a match against Brasenose, one of the most famous sporting colleges. In the hot sun I toiled in the deep all day while they amassed a ridiculous score like 350 for 2. At a lower level, my diary records one series of five matches towards the end of term when my cunningly flighted lobs deceived no less than thirteen of our opponents, whose wickets fell for 81 runs in 25 overs. Most enjoyable was the kind of social cricket of which Oxford had an abundance. We of the Trinity Haymakers played a few village teams in term time and then took off for Kent. An agreeable pub served as a splendid base for a week of daytime cricket and night-time roistering. My easy relations with the landlord's nubile daughter led Christopher Martin to predict that I would be first among the Haymakers to marry. An ominous prospect.

I also had some sort of association with another cricket team, the Harvesters. Most of the Harvesters were at Pot Hall, aka St Peter's Hall, a college with a fair number of northerners, among them my air force friend George Edmundson and several of his Blackburn friends. I don't remember playing for them more than once or twice but was a loyal supporter of their annual dinners, slap up do's at Long John's, where we caroused and sang into the small hours. One year the peerless commentator John Arlott enthralled us with an endless fund of salacious stories. Another year George struck gold when his friend Brian Statham came as our guest, Brian Statham, the Lancashire and England fast bowler, already a Test cricketer and an icon. He was just a couple of weeks younger than me.

I joined one or two agreeable outings to delightful villages like Bibury with a team led by Arthur Norrington, a direct and friendly man who was Secretary of the Oxford University Press and destined soon to succeed J.R.H. Weaver as the College President. Norrington was to achieve lasting fame for devising league tables showing the relative academic performance of the various Oxford colleges, a truly magnanimous act on his part since in their early days Trinity held only a modest position in these tables. Despite that about half a dozen of my year achieved some sort of fame, as senior partner in a leading city law firm, queen's counsel, company chairmen, ambassador John Shakespeare, and High Commissioner Sir David Goodall. It was one of these grandees, a Wykehamist (motto, 'Manners maketh man'), hotfoot from National Service in the army, who was so taken by my first contribution to the common room suggestions book that he exploded: 'A joke's a joke, but fuck a pantomime.'

We historians had two terms in which to work for 'prelims'. We were to be examined in Historical Geography, on which the dry and bloodless lecturer was C.F.C. Hawkes, whose wife Jacquetta later left him in favour of bluff Jack Priestley, Political Science, De Tocqueville's brilliant analysis of the causes of the French Revolution *L'Ancien Régime et La Révolution*, and the Venerable Bede's *Historia Ecclesiastica*, an account in medieval Latin of the conversion of Britain to Christianity. Our own tutor, Michael Maclagan, delivered the twice-weekly university lectures on Bede, compulsory reading for all first-year historians, of whom there were 350 or more in those days. The hall in the Examination Schools was crowded for the first lecture, a little less so for the second. By the fifth, the hall was only half full. What happened after that I can only surmise. There was little in the lectures that was not clearly set out in Maclagan's annotated edition of Bede. His *'Clemency' Canning* was to win a prize for its index.

It came as a great surprise to me some years later to learn that there were teaching universities which required their undergraduates to attend twenty or thirty hours of lectures each week. I averaged about five a week in my first year and never went above eight including two special French classes. I learned a great deal from listening to people like Asa Briggs and John Habbakuk, more like a successful lawyer than a don, whose university lectures included material and interpretations which were not yet available in print. But I missed out shamefully on other famous Oxford historians like A.J.P. Taylor, Hugh Trevor-Roper and Robert Blake. For the most part we historians usually worked at any time with two or three tutors. The normal practice was for pairs of undergraduates to meet each of their tutors for an hour each week. Each tutor would suggest a theme, some books which dealt with that theme, and a topic on which to write an essay. We would go away, read, and write, and the next week one of us would read his essay aloud and our tutor would comment.

It's been well said that historians learn more by writing than by reading because it's only when he writes that a historian has to express precisely what he understands about the past. I'd kept up an unfocused programme of reading while I'd been in the RAF, but had written nothing except a few letters. Writing was to remain a painful chore for my first two terms at Oxford. It became bearable only towards the end of my first year. Perhaps that's why I managed to satisfy the examiners in only three of our four subjects and had to resit the paper in Political Science. This was a puzzling blow, since I'd enjoyed the set text for this paper, Sir Henry Maine's *Ancient Law*... Maine's attempt to describe primitive societies as they were was a useful corrective to the entirely imaginary societies invented by theorists like John Locke and Thomas Hobbes whom we had to read later on. And his argument that primitive communities tend to move steadily from relationships based on status to relationships based on contract is a useful starting point for considering such current issues as the place of students in a university, or the place of hereditary peers in our legislature. For the time being however the need to tackle Maine again meant I was obliged to take the summer term a little more seriously than I might have done.

Oxford terms last exactly eight weeks. In my three years as an under-graduate I spent just seventy-two weeks in Oxford, a fraction less than my seventy-eight weeks in the RAF. The vacations were opportunities for recreation or reading. My reading was usually pressed into the last two or three weeks of each vacation. Just as the prospect of hanging is said to concentrate a man's mind, the prospect of 'collections' at the beginning of each term had a salutory effect on me. These collections were college examinations, not unduly serious but holding the possibility of a summons to explain one's performance to the President. For prelims our tutors used a comical three-point scale, S, VS, and NS. These letters stood for the Latin Satis, Vix Satis, and Non Satis. Satis (satisfactory) and Non Satis (not satisfactory) were clear enough, but Vix Satis (scarcely satisfactory) for a passable piece of work seemed rather grudging. After prelims they tended to use a more refined grading system which ranged I fancy from alpha double plus (A++) to gamma double minus (C--) through such subtle gradations as beta double plus query alpha double minus (B++ ? A--), a good solid performance with just a hint of real class. We all knew the difference between that and alpha double minus query beta double plus (A – – ? B++), a moderately classy performance with just a hint of stolidity.

Apart from my routine commitment to ten or twelve hours' reading a day for the last two or three weeks of each vacation the rest of the vacations were my own, opportunities to be out of doors, to do something quite different from reading and writing. Each Christmas I spent ten days or so helping the Post Office as a temporary postman, up early and off duty well before lunch time. In my first summer vacation I became a guinea pig again, joining my school friend Dennis Penny at the Common Cold Research Centre near Salisbury. We were isolated from other people, and lived in a comfortable old nissen hut to which container meals were delivered three times a day and left in a large 'post box'. We were given a daily pint of beer and a few shillings as an honorarium. We had to do our own washing up which we tended to pile in the bath and tackle in one fell swoop every three or four days. We could play tennis and a game new to us called padder tennis, a game like tennis played with solid bats on a smaller court, and were free to walk on Salisbury Plain provided we didn't approach anyone else. In between times we sat on the grass between the huts and chatted, across a twenty-yard cordon sanitaire, with two lissom girls and two fellows from neighbouring huts. Not quite Club Méditerranée, but an agreeably inexpensive and relaxing ten days. And we didn't catch anything worse than a lifelong interest in news about the common cold.

A day or two later I joined my Trinity friend Richard McWatters at Copford, a few miles north of Salisbury in the Wylye Valley. Richard was a year my senior, also reading History, a personable and multi-talented Etonian who sang in the Bach Choir, played a powerful game of tennis and a keen game of bridge, and obtained a good degree with no sign of having sweated over his studies. Richard had invited me to join him and two or three others in a woodland clearance project on an estate near Copford. We laboured in the July sun under the watchful eye of a forester and enjoyed lardy-cake teas at the local cricket club. After about a week, the middle finger on my right hand began to swell with what proved to be an ever more painful whitlow. A few days later I went off to Salisbury to have the whitlow excised. By this time the throbbing finger filled my little world. But the last words I heard as I succumbed to anaesthetic were 'this is not a very interesting case'. I was mortified. When I returned to Copford a couple of weeks later, finger much restored, I found Richard in some distress. He and I shared a room in the house of Captain and Mrs Smith. More than once while I'd been away, he'd woken in the night to hear the sound of beatings, sobs and screams and Mrs Smith saying, 'I shall call Richard, I shall call Richard.' We spent some time wondering what we would do if she did call for help.

The following year Tony Fathers and I spent a few days tramping over Dartmoor. We happened to be there on 15 August, one of the wettest days ever recorded in those parts when a few miles further north nine inches of rain fell in twenty-four hours, and the resulting floods cascaded over Lynmouth. We were soaked, but unbowed.

I'd just spent several happy weeks in Newcastle. The University Appointments Board had publicized Thomas Hedley's offer of vacation traineeships. Hedley's were in the habit of offering these traineeships to a few science and engineering students each summer, but I was the first arts student ever to be selected. I entered a new world, a factory where everyone donned overalls, a factory where even the manager Bob Chester was known by his first name, a factory and a city where everyone seemed very friendly, a city where many of the men were not much over five feet tall in marked contrast to my immediate circle at Oxford, most of whom were well over six feet, a world where I had great difficulty understanding the local Geordie accent and they had some trouble with mine. My induction was thorough, a quick survey of Hedley's and its place within the Procter and Gamble empire, and a whirlwind tour of the Tyneside factory where Oxydol, Fairy Soap and Drene were the main products. The factory buildings had grown piecemeal over many years, never purpose-designed for their current use. The delivery and storage of the various chemicals used to make Oxydol, Fairy and Drene, and the bottles and boxes used to pack and despatch them, had never been thought out systematically. Bearing in mind that some of the old floors could support only limited loads my task was to examine the flow of goods and materials in and out and make recommendations for improving Hedley's use of storage space. This kind of assignment was very similar to the kind of problems and puzzles to which I was much addicted at that time. One which engrossed me and various friends and relatives was how to determine in just three weighings with a balance which of twelve similar balls was the odd one and whether it was lighter or heavier than its fellows.*

My assignment also gave me every reason to wander freely through the factory, and to talk to all and sundry. Len took me on a tour of various depots and warehouses across the city, and introduced me to Flo as 'John who's come all the way from Devon to see you'. Merry laughter, and later on he kindly handed me a sheet of paper with her address and phone number. He was very disappointed next day that I'd been too busy to call. I watched women slapping labels on Drene bottles hundreds of times a day, an undemanding occupation which left them free to gossip all day about their lives and loves. There was one whose right arm had grown with this constant exercise to enormous proportions, twice or three times the circumference of her left arm.

At weekends I and another trainee, an engineer named Donald, visited

*The number of weighings with a balance required to determine which of a number of balls is the odd one and whether it is heavier or lighter than the others is determined by the formula: $(3n - 3) \div 2 = X$ (n is the number of weighings and X the number of balls; i.e. three weighings, 12 balls; four weighings, 39 balls; five weighings, 120 balls, etc.)

Durham, went to Whitley Bay for an hour or two of group tennis coaching by Fred Perry and Dan Maskell, walked in the Upper Tyne valley, and on the August Bank Holiday followed the Roman Wall almost all the way to Carlisle. When we crossed the divide into Cumberland and dropped into a rural pub the locals might as well have been speaking Mongolian, their intonation and pronunciation were so unlike anything I'd ever heard previously.

Six or eight weeks at Hedley's was I'm sure no less educative and no less stimulating than the European tours which some of my fellow undergraduates undertook in their vacations. When we returned to Oxford in the autumn my tutorial partner described such a tour to Michael Maclagan's great interest and evident approval. When Maclagan asked what I'd been doing I undersold my summer by saying I'd been working in a factory. Maclagan, grandson of an archbishop, son of the Director of the Victoria and Albert, Wykehamist and future Richmond Herald at Arms, managed to look patrician, disdainful and dismissive. Though he often emphasized the importance of historical imagination, of empathizing with the people of history, he never heard how much a summer on Tyneside could extend a southerner's horizons.

One university myth was that you would get the class of degree corresponding to your natural talent if you worked for four hours a day. The formula lacked specificity. It wasn't clear for example whether four hours a day was for seven days each week or just weekdays, nor whether you were supposed to work for the whole year or only in term time. Suffice it to say that I recognized the need to compensate in my third year for some shortfallings in the second if I was to avoid a third or fourth class degree. From the end of August I would work at least a forty-hour week. This proved increasingly difficult as the year progressed because my eyes became steadily more troublesome. By early in the New Year the eyes needed half an hour's rest after an hour and a half's reading or writing. The rest periods gradually became longer and more frequent. I spent an hour in one library and then took a short break by walking to another, from the New Bodleian to Rhodes House, to the Union, to the college, and then to my own room. In the end of course I had to wear glasses. But by the time I waited for tests and waited again for glasses to be made many weeks had passed. For much of the third year achieving my forty-hour target was quite a burden.

It represented a sharp increase in my work rate. For much of the second year I'd been exercising my mental powers at the bridge table. Dad had introduced me to whist and I'd picked up the rudiments of bridge in the RAF. At Trinity there were a good many enthusiasts, some of them experts in both theory and practice. One of the most entertaining was Richard Honey, apparently in training as a dandy and dilettante, master of the King's Arms bar billiards table and the Oxford Union billiards table, tennis player, table tennis player, film buff and good friend. I never thanked him properly for taking me home and putting me to bed one night when I fell asleep at the bridge table after imbibing deeply of an apparently innocuous fruit cup at one of Ronald's excellent parties. Nor for recounting his boarding school housemaster's memorable homily after an unfortunate liaison between one of the boys and a housemaid, 'better little boys than babies'. After a good many years Richard went down without completing his degree in medicine. He loved to tell the story of how he was sitting at his downstairs window one afternoon when a party of American visitors walked past, saw him there, and observed, 'Gee, a stoident woikin.' He knew better than any what an implausible example they'd chosen.

I listened carefully to the bridge experts, read S.J. Simon and Iain Macleod and other pundits, spoke confidently of Culbertson and Acol, and sometimes played from lunchtime till 2 or 3 a.m. with only a minimal break for dinner. We played for the most modest stakes, a penny a hundred points, just enough to curb the most imaginative bidding and play. Even at this level I spent enough time at the bridge table over one twelve-month period for my winnings to pay for one supper a week. Without having any ambition to play in more formal settings, I found it a most stimulating and satisfying pastime, requiring a unique blend of analysis, psychology and quick response. Bridge engaged me to a degree that nothing else did. What I learned through playing bridge was in its way at least as important as anything else I learned at Oxford.

I also played another card game with my friend Paddy Passmore. Paddy was a modern linguist whom I first met through my friend and staircase neighbour Ronald Moore. Paddy was a friendly giant from Bristol where he'd been Captain of Bristol Grammar School, a straightforward man who hated spin in any form. 'Play it straight up and down, as God meant it to be played,' he would say if an opponent sliced or cut a table tennis ball. Paddy and I decided to live more economically out of college and found pleasant digs in Bickerton Road, Headington. We each had our own bedroom and shared a sitting room in which Mrs Stone served our breakfast and a Sunday lunch. Occasionally on Sunday afternoon when we had exhausted the Sunday papers and our books we would play cribbage, the only game we knew for two people. Every Sunday was the same. We played. We played again, double or quits. We played a third time, double or quits. It did not matter how many games we played or how often we played. Good linguist though he was Paddy had a blind spot when it came to seeing the scoring combinations at cribbage. On Sunday mornings we would read the papers, perhaps take a gentle stroll, and be in for lunch. Then Mrs Stone really went to town with enormous helpings of meat, potatoes, brussels sprouts and other vegetables. As soon as she had brought our meals and left the room, I would shovel my sprouts and sometimes more on to Paddy's plate. He could easily put away his own lunch and half mine. This went on for several months, until one unfortunate Sunday when Paddy was away. Mrs Stone served the usual plateful of brussels sprouts. It was much too late to explain my lifelong aversion. I hastily wrapped them in half the *Sunday*

Times and hid the parcel behind a chair. Mrs Stone removed my gratifyingly empty plate as she served my pudding. Sometime during the afternoon I managed to smuggle my parcel across the hall and up the stairs and hid it in my wardrobe. Getting my parcel out of the house was not so easy. When I left in the morning there were usually members of the Stone family milling about downstairs. I began to suspect they were waiting in the kitchen to jump out on me as I passed. Several days went by, until even I was aware that the damp sprouts in my wardrobe were becoming malodorous. I began to think I could smell them downstairs when I entered the house. The time had come for desperate measures. One evening I seized my parcel, crept downstairs, and let myself and my companion out as quickly as I could. I did not anticipate any difficulty in finding a quiet moment when I could tip my parcel over a nearby fence. But there are more people about in the evening in Headington than you might think and the streets were well lit even then. People are watching me and my swag, they can see from my shifty demeanour that I am up to no good. What would it be like trying to dispose of a dead body? I traipse from street to street. At last, a quick heave and the stinking remains go flying over a hedge. I creep away from the scene and sneak quietly into Number 33. Nothing is ever said but the next time Paddy is away on a Sunday I make sure I am out for lunch.

Cricket in the Parks to watch Cowdrey, Hutton and other stars, help paint the scenery for St Peter's play, to Woodstock and Blenheim, Trinity JCR debate, tea with George, read the Lesson in Chapel. Peace Association, see Christopher Fry's *Venus Observed*, tutorial with shrewd and kindly Bruce Wernham, tramp Port Meadow on a frosty morning, tea with John Black future Professor of Economics, to the Dragon School with Richard to see *The Gondoliers*, walk up Cherwell, tutorial with Father T.M. Parker, walk along the Broad with the stunning Normandy blonde Marie-Claire and every head turns, Psychical Society, bridge in the Judges' Lodgings where Richard and his father live, to the cinema with future QC Peter Horsfield to see *Jour de Fête*, observe King George's funeral by playing bridge and squash, tea with Anne, lose my twenty-first birthday watch, World University Service committee meetings, tutorials with C.T. Atkinson: life at Oxford was indeed a delightfully diverse sequence of events and sights, an ever-changing kaleidoscope.

At that time all Oxford historians took three papers in English History and one in Political Science. Beyond that we had a wide choice of special subjects, original legal documents and cases relating to some aspect of constitutional history, and periods of foreign history, which in that eurocentric world meant European History. College tutors usually taught only two or at most three papers each so the more exotic our choice of subject the more likely it was that we would be farmed out to some other college or some unattached lecturer waiting and hoping for a college fellowship. C.T. Atkinson was one to whom I was farmed out, a retired Fellow of Exeter College who taught the History of

War. This was my special subject. We read Clausewitz's *On War*. War is, he said 'an act of violence intended to compel our opponent to fulfil our will'. It is 'the continuation of policy by other means'. We noted his useful distinction between the absolute wars of a nation at arms like Revolutionary France and a limited war. I knew of no one since Machiavelli who had written so clear-headedly about the conduct of state affairs. We studied Nelson's tactics and read the American Admiral Mahan on *The Influence of Sea Power on the French Revolution and Empire*. We learned about the strength of a defensive position based on short interior lines of communication, like commanding the middle of the chess board, and the risk of overstretching oneself quite literally with overlong lines of communication, like Napoleon or Hitler in Russia. We thought we understood the merits of avoiding battle so that your forces were not overwhelmed and were still there to embarrass the enemy; it was not so novel a doctrine: 'He who fights and runs away, lives to fight another day,' my mother would have said. We understood that Admiral Byng was executed not for cowardice nor as Voltaire put it ironically 'pour encourager les autres' but because supine politicians had failed to equip the navy adequately and poor Byng had no alternative but to try to keep his 'fleet in being'.

All this proved of some lasting value in trying to follow the wars which punctuated my adult life, in Korea, Suez, Vietnam, Falkland, the Gulf and elsewhere. But it was as nothing to the delightful memory of being tutored by C.T. Atkinson. We had to go to his own house in Chedington Road, North Oxford and ring the bell. When the door opened we faced a diminutive Scots terrier, more animated mop then dog, with whom we had to shake an extended paw and greet formally, 'good evening, Lucy,' before we were allowed in. Our 'private hour', for CT would not allow a vulgar modernism like 'tutorial' to be used in his house, ended with a similar ritual. Throughout our private hour Lucy dashed hither and thither, jumping on the chairs, dancing on our papers, and giving us a splendid practical demonstration of the difficulty of sticking to a plan while under hostile fire.

Choosing freely from the university's range of optional subjects and its extensive *à la carte* menu of lectures, and then reading and writing alone for our two-to-one and sometimes one-to-one tutorials meant that we historians each worked in his own way on his own programme. It's hard to imagine a better way of fostering independence and self-sufficiency, precisely the qualities needed by colonial administrators for whom by that time there was a falling market. By chance I'd found just the place for doing it 'mine own self'. No thoughts of community or team work diverted us from single-minded concentration on the days of judgment awaiting us in the Examination Schools.

CHAPTER 6

North Essex

And he would gladly learn, and gladly teach

QUEEN ELIZABETH'S Coronation Day was a disaster: 2 June 1953, the day before my final exams began. I'd planned a day off, a relaxing day in the sun, a stroll, some gentle tennis, and watching cricket in the Parks. Instead it drizzled all day and nearly everyone was glued to a radio or just possibly a television. I did not know anywhere I could watch television. So I moped in the rain all day.

The next day was much better. I enjoy competing against examiners however badly I'm doing, and on that occasion the examiners were kind. My viva three weeks later lasted only a few seconds and I emerged with second class honours. I would have had to work twice as hard to have had the slightest hope of a first, so honour was satisfied. Most employers regarded both second and first class as 'good honours' so I'd reached the qualifying level for most large companies and organizations. But I had already failed to clear the hurdle for entry to the administrative grades of the Foreign and Home Civil Services. Only candidates who achieved a total of 260 or more in their written examination went forward for interview. Even a creditable mark for precis brought my total to only 258 so I was spared the later rounds. It was a lucky escape. Dad would have liked nothing better than for one of his sons to enter the highest civil service grades, but I realized later on that the Civil Service was like Ray Kroc in believing 'We cannot trust people who are nonconformists.' I had the good fortune to find more flexible employment.

Some bump of caution made me wary of the Newcastle soap people Hedley's. None of the managers I'd met was much over thirty, and I wondered what happened when they crossed that threshold. Did they live to draw a pension, or were they all put out to grass? I was not eager enough to phone Hedley's, and they did not phone me.

I closed two other doors during the summer. Following a short visit to the University Appointments Board I approached the Legal and General Insurance Company. Perhaps on the strength of my interest in puzzles and problems they and another insurance company offered starting posts where I could study to become an actuary. I went home, found a tutor, and enjoyed working hard through the summer at A-level pure mathematics. But the starting salary was only £350 a year and I doubted whether I could live in London on that sort of money. More seriously, I had growing doubts about committing myself to a minimum of five years' hard work with very little play. Could I stick at it 'unto the end until it be thoroughly completed'? I was much too easily diverted from the task in hand. So at the eleventh hour I wrote to say I wasn't coming after all.

That left me in limbo. Dad and Mum were very good. They put up with me for a few months while I studied the job ads, went to see Dexion who make the grown-up Meccano for shelves and storage units, applied for a tutor's post in Kenya, and tried to learn to touch type. My closest school friend Dennis Penny was also at home, so we relieved the tedium with badminton and table tennis, and resumed our old places in the local hockey team. Early in November I spotted an advertisement for a graduate to teach English and History at a boys' grammar school and undertake some residential duties in the school's boarding house. The post was temporary for two terms, which would provide a few months' space in which I could look around for a permanent post. Accommodation and board were free, and the starting salary was £508 a year. Within a couple of weeks I had been to Colchester for an interview and was preparing to join the staff of the Royal Grammar School in January 1954. I had signed on fairly casually for a six-month cruise, but as things turned out the voyage went on for half a century.

What a stroke of fortune! No historian could ask to live and work in a more memorable town. The legendary home of Old King Cole, with its Roman walls and Norman keep, its priory and abbey and medieval churches, an extensive Dutch Quarter, many handsome properties of the sixteenth, seventeenth and eighteenth centuries, and Jumbo, the magnificent nineteenth-century water tower, no town epitomizes British history better. Modern Colchester was too, as I soon found, a civilized town with a decent repertory theatre shortly to be graced for a season by the young Harold Pinter, a respectable public library, a nascent museum and gallery at the Minories, a lively Literary Society where a young writer named Ronald Blythe played a leading role, Tony Doncaster's superb Castle Bookshop, and an outstanding local newspaper edited by Harvey Benham.

Colchester had too an ancient grammar school. Colchester Royal Grammar School traces its origins to charters granted by Henry VIII and Elizabeth I. After many vicissitudes the school fell on hard times in the late nineteenth century, and by 1898 it had just 29 boys and one master. The four headmasters who spanned more than half the next century transformed it into one of England's foremost maintained grammar schools.

In those days grammar school heads were omnipotent. They hired and fired. Within traditional boundaries policed lightly by external examining bodies they decided their school's curriculum. In Minister George Tomlinson's immortal words the Minister of Education knew 'now't about t'curriculum'. The Ministry, someone wrote more formally in his name, was 'zealous for the freedom of schools and teachers', so its Annual Report for

1950 had nothing to say about educational methods or the school curriculum. Bliss was it in that post-war dawn to be a head, but to be a young teacher was very heaven. Few doubted then that the professionals had the ability to assess and the capacity to meet the country's educational needs.

J.F. Elam was already the experienced head of the Sir George Monoux School in Walthamstow when he came to CRGS in 1948. By 1954 he had ten years' headship behind him. A shy, gruff, unyielding Yorkshireman, Jack was almost good enough a cricketer to win a place in Yorkshire's First XI when Yorkshire were pre-eminent, but he was first and foremost a scholar, a historian by training, with a passion for art and church architecture, and a great interest in gardens. He took morning assembly for the whole school and usually dropped into the staffroom at morning break to exchange a few words with some of his senior colleagues. Otherwise he was rarely seen and we imagined him spending his days on his scholarly pursuits. For a man not much given to declaratory statements Jack was remarkably successful in communicating his values. His ideal school was a civilized community, committed to the pursuit of excellence in the classroom, on the playing field, and on the stage. There were few school rules but Jack expected the boys to behave in an orderly responsible way. He devoted much of his own time and energies to trying to enhance the appearance of the school buildings and grounds, and boys who failed to respect their environment might well be asked to perform some sort of community service like removing litter.

Jack was not one to walk about, nor one for meetings or mission statements. His style was unique. The school year began with a short staff meeting and there were no others. He fostered a sense of collegiality in the staffroom by fighting to secure equal allowances for all the academic departmental heads at a time when the authorities were trying to impose a divisively hierarchical structure. No time was set aside for internal school examinations, because Jack thought they took a slice out of the working term and encouraged staff and pupils to rest on their oars after the exams were over. Jack expected us all, staff and boys, to go on working up to the final assembly each term but he was happy enough for staff to use their 'free' periods to go to the bank or get their hair cut. Benignly liberal and progressive, Jack Elam was an amazingly effective conductor of his chorus of prima donnas.

'People don't change, they just grow more so,' is one of the abiding truths my friend Tony Fathers propagates. Of no group is this more true than it is of schoolmasters.* Every master plays a larger-than-life, star role on the classroom stage half a dozen times a day.

Almost all my new colleagues were in their forties or fifties, gnarled veterans of many a campaign at home and abroad. Many had served in one of the World Wars or had worked overseas. 'Sam' Hughes, il s'amuse, lived at the

*'Schoolmaster' – in 1954, the invariable name for the male teachers in grammar schools, just as the female teachers were all mistresses.

Scheregate Hotel, and was thought to own it. A mathematician, he was said to play the stock market and to be rich beyond the dreams of any avaricious assistant master. There were several cricketers and rugby footballers of almost county standard, and several distinguished scholars: Dr Purkis edited an Italian dictionary and A.F. Hall had worked with the famous archaeologist Christopher Hawkes on Roman Colchester, while Ralph Currey was establishing an international reputation as poet and broadcaster, and classicist Arthur Brown was even better known as the outstanding local historian of Essex.

Their wide-ranging interests and achievements enriched the staffroom. Fred Seymour invited me home to meet his daughter Anne, a pretty girl of about my own age, but I couldn't find much to say to a bedridden girl dying of multiple sclerosis. A mere twenty-three year old, I was the only one under thirty. Indeed, four years later I was still the youngest master though there were by then three or four more under thirty and a few not much older. What the common room lacked in youth was more than made up by a glorious range of originality verging sometimes on eccentricity.

Algy Batt was a harum-scarum figure on his old upright bike. He lived near the school with his aged parents who had pioneered their own system of student loans. On the day Algy took his degree, his father is reputed to have said that since they had kept him up till then, he could now keep them. Unhappily his career as a science teacher was abruptly curtailed when the head of science expelled him from the labs following a minor explosion. Despite a contorted cockney accent which did daily violence to the English language he was relegated to teaching French to the younger boys. We marvelled. Through all these misfortunes Algy always had a cheerful friendly smile, and invincible self-confidence. Armed with nothing more than some time-expired experience as a motor cyclist, at about fifty years of age he went off to Ipswich one day to buy his first motor car, asked a few questions about the controls, and drove it home. Each summer he travelled, and each summer he learned and murdered a new foreign language. By the mid 1950s he had got to Welsh.

Another of the junior form teachers was Packo to the boys and Packy to his colleagues. Michael Pakenham was a wrinkled humorous Irishman, humpbacked because of the wracking asthma for which he always carried an enormous nebulizer. When the boys' cheerful disrespect irked him beyond measure he would detain some after school. To stop them escaping early he resorted to taking their shoes, returning them only when he thought the culprits had expiated their crime. One day Packy forgot to return a couple of pairs, and after an hour or two their owners set off shoeless for home. Packy's informal approach to keeping order ended abruptly.

Hairy, Weary and the Baron were the core members of what Hairy Daniels liked to call the nucleus. In eight years at CRGS I never heard their first names, nor those of several other senior men. The nucleus stood for traditional values, of which the most important by far was faith in the character-building properties of Rugby football. Fortunately J.C. Vickery had fostered a little Rugby at Tavistock Grammar School and as a boy I'd played a few games against teams from Kelly College and elsewhere. I'd even watched a few high-class games when Oxford University was still stiff with ex-servicemen and could hold its own with any club in the country. Now I was pushed willingly enough into the second or third game on Saturday mornings to get some hands-on experience, and took my lowly place in the staff team which ran the fifth- and sixth-form games afternoon on Wednesdays. Perhaps the lads benefited from this homely illustration of the abiding rule that the worst players get the least competent referee. I supported the First XV's home matches loyally on Saturday afternoons. I did my bit to support the true faith.

Hairy Daniels must have survived the closure of the old preparatory department. A talented man, church organist, violin-maker, and much else, he taught games and general subjects and came to specialize in History. Unfortunately he hated what he called the 'snarling periods' of social change, industrial development, trade unions and trade disputes. As he grew older, his snarling periods grew longer. For his own health we had to ask Hairy to stick with early and medieval history with junior forms.

Casey, 'the Baron', was said to owe his soubriquet to his prowess at Colchester's Rugby club. We could never discover whether a 'Baron' was an obscure liquid measure denoting the quantity of beer he could consume, or a sincere tribute to the way in which he outperformed his team mates at the bar. A stocky gargantuan Orson Welles prototype, Casey ruled the Rugby field like a medieval fiefdom, and taught a little Latin. One day as I conducted my cheerful class on one side of the folding windowed partition separating two adjacent rooms the boys next door hoisted a small placard saying 'HUSH!! THE BARON'S ASLEEP'. And so indeed he was, head resting on the master's desk on the dais at the far end of the room. I gestured hastily to my own lads to read the notice, and they subsided into total silence.

Both these forms were more tolerant than those who used to wipe a young colleague's board clean as fast as he could write on it. He did not stay as long as Doughy who often had a day or two off when the rest of us would cover his maths classes. They never seemed to know what they'd been doing in the previous lesson. A cruel satire in the school magazine had a master saying 'Turn to page 232,' and a boy observing 'That's more than he said last time'. Doughy and my very good friend John Morris left at the same time in July 1958. Jack was unaccustomedly eloquent in his farewell to John, whose contributions to the school were described and lauded for fifteen or twenty minutes. 'As for Mr Baker,' said Jack, 'we thank him for what he has done.' What he had done became apparent during the summer holiday, when the courts heard that Doughy's love of photography extended to using the school as an illicit accommodation address for trading stimulating self-portraits.

On an altogether more innocent occasion I watched through the folding partition while fifth-form boarder Nick Hodges climbed out of the window beside the master's desk where my colleague Robert Hey was dealing with another boy. Moments later to my amusement a smiling Nick came through the door and went straight to the master's desk with his own query. Unsurprisingly, Robert believes I invented this whole incident to tease him. Not so: although we teachers claim to have eyes in the back of our head, we also have a remarkable ability to focus on the matter in hand. A couple of sixth formers told me once how, like a pair of con men, one of them would approach Bodger Currey's desk and engage him in conversation while the other stood a little to one side shuffling his teaching notes. By this device they claimed to have enjoyed substantially the same lesson four times over. The same pair, Ian Beckwith and Bill Dodd, took to heart my own injunction to read widely for their history essays and quote their sources. They ransacked the library and found one or two authorities unknown to me. Their quotations grew increasingly bizarre until in exasperation I was reduced to writing 'Balls! Even if X was daft enough to write this you should have enough sense not to quote him.' All was then revealed: X did not exist, and I'd been led up the garden path for several weeks.

Bright boys have this knack of exploiting a situation. One winter Wednesday the frost made Rugby football impossible and we set the lads to run eight times round the field instead. The tuck shop supplied a stock of bottle tops and our idea was to sit in the pavilion and issue one bottle top each time a runner passed the pavilion. The runners could knock off once they had collected eight bottle tops. We hadn't appreciated how soon runners would start lapping each other, nor the scope for trading in bottle tops. The runners found other bottle top suppliers. The first to collect their eight tops reported almost immediately. The scheme collapsed in ignominious disarray.

Having arrived in mid year I inherited a teaching timetable: a Games afternoon, a couple of periods of Religious Instruction with my own form, some History with various forms at different levels, and quite a lot of English with fourth, fifth and sixth forms. Given the preponderance of English, my mentor was R.N. Currey, Head of English, and Housemaster of Harsnett's, the house to which I'd been assigned. I had of course no training as a teacher and no previous experience so Ralph arranged for me to sit in on some of his lessons to see how to do it. He had been a wartime army officer in India, and had still a somewhat military bearing and manner. His relations with the boys resembled those of a Guards officer with other ranks. He did me a great disservice. In my second observation lesson some wretched youth committed a minor misdemeanour, was hauled out, and dressed down sharply. Instead of seeing this as Currey intended, an example of how to control a class, I saw it as a totally disproportionate response to a fairly trivial infringement, and resolved never to go over the top in the same way.

It might have saved me a good deal of trouble if I had received then one piece of inestimable advice for a beginning teacher: 'Don't smile for the first two terms.' I went instead for the natural style, smiled often, admitted when I did not know things, and fraternized with the boys in Saturday games, school societies like chess, debating and railways, and the boarding house. Since I was only five or six years older than the sixth form, and much nearer their age than I was to my colleagues' ages, all this went down very well. As a resident master living and breathing school twenty-four hours a day seven days a week, I learned a great deal about the school very quickly. Only a few weeks into my first term I was sharing this expertise with an old fellow I met on the way to a school match. After a while he observed in a puzzled way, 'You look rather old to be at the school.' I drew myself up to my full five feet eight inches, 'Actually, I'm a member of staff.' 'Oh,' he said apologetically, 'You look very young.' This lack of gravitas was a bit of a problem, and I had my share of boisterous lessons in the first few terms. The Head called me in to see what we could do about this distressing state of affairs. In the end I was greatly helped by one untoward incident. In those days there was no bar on corporal punishment. It wasn't common at CRGS, but slippering, tweaking and clipping were endemic, and I sometimes clipped an obstreperous youth or two 'pour encourager les autres'. On one unfortunate occasion, a cheerful cheeky fourteen year old turned his head as my hand fell. My knuckle caught him just below the eye, and he soon had a wonderfully multi-coloured bruise. There were no complaints and no repercussions but within a few days the school grapevine credited me with having boxed for the university. I had no more serious problems.

'The boys like you,' Jack Elam had said. That and various other unspecified credits on my balance sheet led him to offer me a permanent post and one of the first special allowances. I enjoyed being a teacher, so the immediate future was settled. From September 1954 I was however to teach mainly History. The Head of History was A.F. Hall, known to his colleagues as AF to distinguish him from the senior chemist, R.L. Hall. The boys called him Hiram, perhaps a long-forgotten but no less scholarly reference to the King of Tyre who supplied Solomon with cedar wood for his temple. AF was a tall, benign and somewhat ponderous figure. No one else would have presumed ever to sit in his grand armchair by the staffroom fireplace. Silent and inscrutable, AF rarely spoke except occasionally to recall some half-forgotten soldier's witticism about World War One trench food, "'orses 'ooves and ruddy great lumps of fat'. He evidently thought it unnecessary to offer any guidance to his fledgling colleague. We never had anything like a departmental meeting, though after a year or two we exchanged a few words when he asked if I had any thoughts about new books for the library or new texts for my own classes. The unwritten syllabus was much as it had been in my own school days. We began in Form I with the ancient world, plunged into Roman Britain, and worked our way more or less chronologically through English History quickly enough to reach the nineteenth century in the fifth form. A few years later when we faced the imminent threat of inspection by Her Majesty's Inspectors I had to compile a written history syllabus, perhaps the first the school had ever had. One of the reasons for learning history was, I wrote, to develop a degree of scepticism. For a different audience I might have been more forthright. As Premier Macmillan observed 'the main purpose of education is to know when someone is talking rot' or as Hemingway put it, to equip young people with 'a built in crap detector'. Jack raised a sceptical eyebrow, but did not demur.

AF had little faith in text books. With the third form he used an ancient history of Tudor England by Meiklejohn. His pupils had to search Meiklejohn to compile a list of everyone the Tudor monarchs had put to death, for what supposed offences, and how they'd been executed. This gruesome task enthused thirteen year old boys, who began to learn how to search a text to extract information. The next step was to send whole forms to the library to find what they could on some topic or other and write a short essay. AF would tell them which shelves to use, but not much more. Some responded well to this approach, and these AF designated 'gentlemen scholars'. The rest were 'cads'. It was just about possible to win promotion, or be relegated, from one group to the other. By the time they reached the sixth form the 'gentlemen scholars' knew how to use a library and how to write a scholarly essay. Though many specialized then in Classics or Modern Languages rather than History or English, AF's training helped many generations to win university places and scholarships. By the mid-twentieth century CRGS was often at or near the top of the Premier League, the annual list of schools whose pupils had obtained open scholarships to Oxford or Cambridge universities. When AF retired three years later and 'wafted by a favouring wind' I took his place, the school's standing was such that the Cambridge Examinations Syndicate invited me, sight unseen, to become an A-level examiner.

In the meantime I went on working closely with Ralph Currey because I was still teaching a fair amount of upper school English, and was also a member of his house, Harsnett's, whose name commemorated a seventeenth-century Head who rose effortlessly to become Archbishop of York. Ralph had a particular affection for the house system which CRGS had borrowed like so many day schools from the great independent boarding schools. It's a concept without very much meaning in a day school except for organizing competitive sports internally, and fostering loyalty to a middling-sized group, somewhere between the class of about thirty and the school of several hundred pupils. We had six houses and the boys and masters attached to each house used to have lunch together every day. The masters sat together and kept an eye on the proceedings. This modest responsibility earned us a free lunch. Having lunch with the same small group every day for almost eight years might seem tedious, but half an hour or so each day was just enough to savour their idiosyncrasies. There was John Rodgers, a warm friendly craftsman from Rotherham, missing one eye because of some industrial mishap, and in charge of wood and metal work, which were a bit below the salt at a school like CRGS. We came to enjoy the way in which he always top-sliced a pudding to give himself the fruit or treacle-coated top and leave us the pudding. 'Eh, ah've gout a naice coup o' teay waaitin foer me at quaairter tu vour,' 'Flash' Rodgers would say as he dashed off at the end of afternoon school to pursue his interests in property and market gardening. Perhaps I missed a trick when he invited me home and I failed to date his only daughter. Eric Richards was another sociable, party-giving man, who opened a new world for many of his colleagues when he and Thelma divorced. In those days few of us actually knew anyone else who had divorced, and certainly not a teacher. As Head of Physics Eric was always complaining about a few enquiring spirits who badgered him with questions instead of writing down what he told them. Eric also opened the batting for Colchester and East Essex, the leading local cricket team, and was in charge of school cricket. He coached by example. He would don his pads, say 'toss me up a few, old boy,' and spend half an hour or more at the nets, giving the First XI a demonstration of how to bat and himself some midweek practice. Eric and I enjoyed encouraging Ralph Currey to talk about his wartime experiences with the army in India. We scored one point each time we led Ralph to say 'when I was in India', three points for each 'when I was on the Times of India' where he ended his military service, and six for a very rare reference to 'Poona'.

These little games add a little spice to every day life in a closed community. George Young used to challenge his forms to find the unusual word he would introduce in his English lessons, and later on my History colleague Phillip Crittenden and I played the same game together, picking a way-out word we would each use and challenge our forms to identify. Gerry Fancourt was the subject of a somewhat wider conspiracy than Ralph Currey. A friendly energetic geographer, voluble, dark, short and a bit podgy, Gerry was a replica of his Portuguese ancestor who had settled in Bradford a century earlier. With him 'az ma faayther uzed to saay' was worth one point, 'az ma grandfaayther uzed to saay' three points, and the very rare 'az ma greaat grandfaayther uzed to saay' at least six we thought. Gerry was in charge of Geography and form master of Five G. Colchester Royal Grammar School had three and sometimes four forms in each year, known not as A, B, C and D as in most schools, but somewhat misleadingly as C, R, G and S. In theory 'we all shall equal be' but in practice everyone knew that C stood for Classics and top, S for Science and second best, R for Remove and next best, and G for General and worst. 'I was a G man' was Gerry's mournful reference to his many years as Five G's form master. Though CRGS did outstandingly well by its cleverest boys, like almost every other selective school CRGS was generally disposed to write off its lower streams. They often did badly in external exams. The boys in G and R would stop in their tracks when I reminded them from time to time that they were the cream of the country, among the ablest 15 per cent of the population. It was up to schools like ours, as Councillor Lovelock put it so memorably at one of our annual Speech Days, to take clever boys like them and add 'the final blemish'. We did our best.

As one of the three resident masters I lived at first in Gilbert House, a mid-Victorian villa named after William Gilbert whose pioneering book on magnetism appeared in 1600, which gives him some claim to be one of Colchester's most distinguished sons. The house had a small turret room which was said to have served as an observatory or to have accommodated a former Mormon owner's spare wife. It was a fine white brick mansion which housed the Housemaster Jim Donson, a fellow travelling member of the character-building nucleus, and his wife Dorothy and their two daughters. After lights out at 9.30, leaving Dorothy in charge since she was the matron, Jim and I would slip out to the Hospital Arms, unsubtly known as Ward Nine since it was virtually an extension to the Essex County Hospital across the road. There we were joined by Ralph Currey and sometimes one or two others for a convivial half hour. The short walk home sometimes gave Ralph the opportunity for more housemasterly homilies. Later on after a few staff changes, I moved out and my good friend and gifted colleague Godfrey Sullivan moved into the boarding house. When my own modest researches into local history revealed that the number of licensed premises in Colchester had fallen dramatically from a peak some fifty years earlier to just over a hundred in the mid 1950s Godfrey and I thought it might be fun, over a few months, to survey them all. We gave up despairingly after the first three samples and went back to Ward Nine. There Godfrey was a man of such regular habits that the landlord had his first pint ready at precisely 9.32 p.m., with others to follow at 9.45, 10.00, and 10.15. Unhappily his regular habits did not save Godfrey from a fatal stroke only five or ten years later.

By this time I was already a car driver and owner. We had no family car after 1939, and very few of my own friends had one in the early 1950s. Driving a car looked as if it needed awesome powers of concentration and co-ordination. But I looked about me, saw the people who were already driving, and was much heartened by Sylvanus P. Thompson's maxim 'What one fool can do, another can' (Introduction to Calculus Made Easy). I would buy a car, and my new colleague Bob Falkner who was an enthusiastic driver but had no car would be pleased to go out with me and his wife Peggy in return for driving some of the time. Another colleague, H.H. Billett, was happy to sell his 1935 soft-topped Austin 10 for £55. I took some lessons and failed the test. Some weekends or evenings Bob and Peggy held their breath while I careered rapidly round the Essex coast and countryside. With their help I passed the test second time round, just in time to set out for the West Country and home. Through London, and out on to the Great West Road where I stopped to pick up three hitch hikers, huge young South Africans with enormous rucksacks. My little Austin groaned. We decided to look at Wookey Hole en route for Weston-

Super-Mare. Too late, or too early: either way, the Hole was closed. I opted for the direct route up and over the Mendips and we began the long haul from the valley floor. I dropped from fourth to third gear, and then from third to second. I slipped out of second and made as if to hold the car on the handbrake while I tried too slowly to double de-clutch and engage first gear. The cable brakes would not hold and we began to roll slowly backwards. I contemplated the prospect of rolling several hundred yards down a twisty lane, and decided in favour of turning into the steep bank at the side of the road. It wasn't quite steep enough. We rolled obliquely up the bank, and half-way up turned over. 'Dowse your lights,' came the cry from one of my smoking passengers. He managed to open the nearside door, and we all climbed out. They picked the car up, turned it over, and turned it round to face downhill. It seemed intact so we all climbed in and as I was shaking one of them kindly offered to drive round, not over, the Mendips. I took over when they left me at Weston-Super-Mare.

Another colleague with whom I developed close links was Arthur Brown, an Oxford classicist whose pupils won open scholarships year after year. Arthur had taken two or three years from school teaching to be a full-time tutor for the Workers' Educational Association. One of his core beliefs was that adult education should be a voluntary movement and when he went back to school teaching he took on almost single-handed the task of orchestrating WEA activities right across Essex. He soon enrolled me as a member of the Colchester branch and part-time tutor. I enjoyed Professor John Morris's course on Roman Britain, Doris Wheatley on Psychology, Dr W.H. Swinburne on Appreciating Music, and a scholarly Congregational Minister on Theology. Fellow members Doug Baker, Tony Duke, Winifred Duke and Mary Walsh became close friends. As branch chairman I brought in visiting speakers like barrister V.G. Hines, local MP 'Cub' Alport and his successor Antony Buck, and only realized many years later how humiliating it was that the inveterate cottager Tom Driberg never made a pass when we adjourned to the pub after his talk on Beaverbrook. We joined other branches at day conferences in lovely Suffolk towns like Lavenham and Thaxted and Long Melford, and went on in the evening to their superb wool churches for London Philharmonic Orchestra concerts. How oddly disappointing it was to find the musicians in the bar before us. During all their sublime music making they'd obviously been thinking mainly of how to get to the bar first.

Each autumn and spring I would drive one night a week through the Essex fogs to WEA branches in places like Tollesbury, and Frinton, and Bocking, and Great Bentley, to instruct and perhaps to entertain from my pot pourri of English social and local history. By far the most successful class was at Great Bentley where the branch secretary used to invite a select group to her home to take a glass, or two, or three, of sherry before the class. By the time we settled down both class and speaker were strangely warmed, and I was unnaturally fluent. My Frinton class was even more rewarding. Two class members from Thorpe-le-Soken took pity on their exhausted lecturer and invited me to drop in for coffee on my way home. Margot Simpson and her dentist husband David became very good and most hospitable friends. Their monthly evenings at home were not to be missed. Margot's cooking, David's fiendish games and carefully chosen records, and an interesting mix of guests all made for great evenings. I was always delighted to drive the ten or fifteen miles from Colchester to see the Simpsons. On the way home one night a dark shape materialized too late for me to miss it. 'It's a cow,' came a gentle feminine voice from a car facing me some twenty yards away. But no, it was a prize bull which filled the road, and we only escaped when it decided eventually to graze on the grass verge. I threatened to sue the farmer for damage to the car. He threatened a counter-claim for damage to his bull. We agreed to call it a draw.

On another of these evenings I armed myself with a bottle of wine for my hosts and went to collect my car from the small service station just across the road where it lived. I opened the passenger door to put my bottle on the seat, and stepped back into an open inspection pit. There was time as I fell to review most of my life, and to wonder how many sharp objects might be lying on the floor. I hit the floor with a thud. The bottle broke. I whimpered. The proprietor came rushing from his house. He sat me down. No bones were broken. I went on my way. I bought another bottle. I arrived late. By way of explanation I added simply, 'I fell into a pit.' 'An elephant pit, I presume?' asked my unkindly host.

Encouraged and ably supported by their wives, David and a dentist friend of his named Kit Hughes and I were the core members of a short-lived Pudding Club. The Club used to meet from time to time to dine richly from a menu consisting of such delicacies as Black Pudding, Pease Pudding, Yorkshire Pudding, Steak and Kidney Pudding, Chicken and Bacon Pudding, Rice Pudding, Sponge Pudding, Christmas Pudding, Fruit Suet Pudding, Baked Custard Pudding, Lemon Pudding, Spotted Dick Pudding, Bread and Butter Pudding, and Treacle Pudding. After only a few meetings the gourmet cooks and the gourmands agreed regretfully to abandon the challenge.

As well as engaging me in adult education Arthur Brown also introduced me to W.R. Powell, the local editor of the Victoria County History, who commissioned me to write the histories of Colchester's many Nonconformist churches. The influx of Dutch Protestants in the sixteenth and French Huguenots in the seventeenth century had reinforced a natural East Anglian tendency to religious dissent and there had been a strong Nonconformist tradition in Colchester from that time on. Even in mid-twentieth century Colchester I heard it suggested that the Congregational Church was still the real seat of power in the town. My task required background reading as well as work on original sources, made me a bit more of a historian, brought me many more acquaintances in Colchester, and added depth to my evening and my daytime classes. In some ways it was rather like taking a postgraduate course, and it had the added advantage of providing a conversational topic of common interest when I visited my Methodist parents. All this meant I had no feeling of regret or disappointment when editorial policy changed a few years later and my thirty or forty precious little pebbles were cast aside.

There was more time for these extramural activities when I succeeded A.F. Hall as Head of History, gave up my residential duties, and took a first-floor front room in a tall semi-detached Victorian boarding house in Victoria Road, about half-way between the school and its playing field. I was to live there with Mrs Amand and Miss Steele and three or four other lodgers for the next four years. A few days after moving in and well before I'd established myself with Mrs A or my fellow guests I arrived home in the small hours after an evening's bridge at the Morrises to find I had no house keys. To avoid waking the whole household I tapped as gently as the enormous front door knocker allowed. No one stirred. I considered climbing in at my first-floor window, but there was no way I could cross the open area round the basement window. It might be possible with a ladder. I went off to one or two building sites in neighbouring streets to see whether the builders had left a ladder lying about. There was only one, too heavy to carry several hundred yards. Who else might help at that hour? In the golden age of Dixon of Dock Green you could always 'ask a policeman'. So I trudged off to the police station to ask an amused duty officer whether by chance they had a spare ladder, and was disillusioned when he didn't offer me a cell mattress for the night instead. But in those golden days there was still one refuge for the temporarily homeless. I legged it to the railway station, settled down by a roaring fire in the waiting room, and was home in time for breakfast.

One of my fellow guests, a young man named Brand, was a veteran car buff. He took a great interest in the gleaming two and a half litre MG saloon which had taken the Austin's place in my affections. It was a car to cherish, the only one I've owned which could attract small crowds of admiring peasants in remote French villages. Only two or three hundred were ever made, and its spare parts fully confirmed my father's dismal prophecy that as a car owner I'd always be poor. Engines were an impenetrable mystery, but the school of experience is a tough one, and I learned to bandy terms like big end and cylinder head gasket with the most expert mechanics. It was however a more difficult proposition when John and Ros Morris and I went off to France together. John and I had forged a close friendship during our years together as resident assistants in the school boarding house and had similar interests in books and theatre. I had been John's best man, and now I offered him and Ros a lift to Provence and back. I was to continue to Cavalaire to stay with the Renards, whose two children I would coach in English for a couple of hours each day. All went well until we were approaching Vichy. The engine showed distinct signs of distress. We found a smart city garage who soon had us running again. We set off into the hills. Half an hour later more ominous sounds of distress, and a distinct lack of power. We limped into Thiers, a tiny town with an enormous reputation for its cutlery. We found a small garage whose owner had no English. John Morris had fluent French but knew nothing of engines. I had little French and less motor mechanics. It took a couple of conferences to establish that the garage needed two or three weeks to get a new gasket from England. The onward rail journey from neighbouring Clermont Ferrand south across the Cevennes really is one of Western Europe's most scenic routes. John and Ros had a splendid holiday in Provence, I found my way to Cavalaire, and we are still close friends.

The following year I left the car at home and went by train for a week of High Renaissance culture in Florence and a scenic week on Lake Garda. The train from Florence was packed, but I was lucky enough to find the last seat. Delighted by this success I settled down, pleased to find myself surrounded by smiling faces. Even without any Italian I eventually grasped that I was sitting under a sign indicating that my seat was reserved for the war wounded and pregnant women. I couldn't claim war service but I had worn the King's Uniform and was still liable for immediate recall in any dire emergency so I sat tight and happily no more deserving candidate appeared.

Neat, flat Holland was more of a shock to the system. The bicycles had white tyres, some men were pissing in the streets while others ate raw fish fillets, and in Marken rough little boys wore skirts. As if this was not enough you could see the painted ladies of Amsterdam town taking their ease behind vast plate-glass ground-floor windows, behind them beds ready for use. How different, how very different, from the home life of the English as portrayed at one of Amsterdam's secondhand bookstalls. 'I swear by all sacred things I will never purchase love,' said *The Etonian* by A. and C. Askew. 'Cyrus old man we're not going to quarrel and part over this thing just because you love a woman and I don't,' wrote A.W. Marchmont with a stiff upper lip in *By Snare of Love*. Some of the CRGS nucleus, I knew, would still go all the way with Hugh Walpole's *Jeremy at Crale*: 'To play in the School First Fifteen is the greatest honour a schoolboy can have.' But the nucleus did not convince everyone. Even in the 1950s there were one or two rebels at CRGS who played soccer for their village teams in preference to Rugby for a school team. There was an eerie silence in the staffroom when Old Colcestrian apostate Philip Palmer won the school's first Cambridge Blue, for *Association* Football. And, perhaps even more surprising, at least a couple of boys refused the Headmaster's Commission and declined to be prefects on the grounds that power corrupts. I sometimes wished I had enough self-confidence to reject such an offer. As it was I was still wrestling with these novelists' concepts of honour when I saw an American soldier resisting eviction from a bar. An enormous landlady blocked the doorway, two armed policemen were standing nearby, and his pal was trying to persuade him to leave peaceably. His pal's words came straight from Hollywood. 'Look, Joe, you walk into the washroom with me, or else…I waalk right out o' youur life.'

In Spain, driving south from San Sebastian, the roadside lined with civil guards in cocked hats and Sherwood Green, we're suddenly directed imperiously on to the grass verge. The guards are armed so we don't delay. Outriders on motorbikes, and then a motor cavalcade ferrying Franco and his government to their summer retreat on the Bay of Biscay. Towns dense with priests and the maimed survivors of the Civil War. In the countryside oxen and donkeys, rarely horses, pulling flat wooden boards or metal plates across the wheat to separate chaff from grain. To my Etonian companion's enormous satisfaction I have to search for tracksuit bottoms to cover my knees before the state possada will let me in for lunch. Tim Card won fame later for his revelatory history of Eton College and was honest enough to confess that he had been obliged to find a tie before a posh London hotel would let him in. We reach Lisbon, a city of shoecleaners, Mercedes taxis, and women walking in from the countryside with enormous loads on their heads. To Nazare, then an attractive little village whose fishermen had light complexions and grey eyes and whose boats had high painted prows like those of the Phoenicians who were said to have settled there. Thought I'd come home on a banana boat, but you travel first class with the captain and it's much more expensive than a cruise ship.

The 1950s were my first opportunity to travel abroad, and after my first hesitant trip to Auxerre to tutor the young Renards, I began to savour the delights of foreign travel. I explored the Ponte Vecchio, Vermeer's Delft and the Left Bank, gazed at Notre Dame, Cologne Cathedral, Chenonceaux, Salamanca and the Jeronimos, and savoured the Uffizi, the Louvre and the Rijkmuseum. It wasn't just a new world, but glimpses of new galaxies of art, architecture, history and customs. L'appétit vient en mangeant. I've been a devoted traveller ever since.

In Britain, at least once a year Ronald Moore and Tony Fathers and I refurbished our Oxford friendship, taking advantage of my half-term breaks for short walking holidays in areas like Radnor Forest, the Surrey Downs, the Cheviots and the Cairngorms. Despite our preference for hilly areas Tony usually insisted on routes based on the 'Fathers' Principle', following the contour lines wherever possible. That and the need to find lunch time sustenance did much to improve our map reading.

One year Phillip Crittenden, Godfrey Sullivan's successor as my main colleague in teaching History, suggested a Whitsun break of another kind. We and half a dozen sixth formers drove north in two cars to spend ten days or so in the Iona Community. Perhaps Phillip saw to such things as insurance and parental letters of consent. We left after school one Friday and drove overnight, snacking en route. It was, I hope, the experience of a lifetime. Twelve or fourteen hours of sitting and snacking generates several days of painfully explosive wind. We did odd jobs like tidying the graveyard and cleaning memorial plaques in the church and enjoyed mingling with the mixed assortment of people who were staying in the Community. The most exciting for us were a falcon and his owner. There was ample time for four-a-side football, evening rambles, and enjoying the serene Atlantic sunsets. We were amused to see that most of Iona's cinema audience came by tractor. On one memorably rough day we were offered a boat trip to bleak basaltic Staffa and peered into Fingal's Cave.

Our expedition to Iona was a one-off. At that time CRGS was not much into school journeys or educational visits, but I was soon drawn into a good many out-of-school activities. Youth was my only qualification for helping with Saturday morning Rugby football, long experience of second-team cricket at school and college the best of reasons for asking me to run the Second XI cricket. There were net practices after school on Thursdays and matches on Saturday afternoons, home or away, every Saturday in season. I even joined a car load of colleagues on a course for cricket coaches. Later on when some of the lads expressed an interest in mixed hockey with girls from the High School, my friend Oliver Atkinson and I were hijacked into acting as coaches because we were the only men still playing club hockey. Similarly when new music master Peter Isherwood established a school choir I was drafted into the basses on the grounds that I'd sung along with choirs before. The chess club needed a mentor for its weekly meetings and occasional matches and I enjoyed the opportunity of playing some of the school's cleverest and most senior boys. Perhaps they picked up the useful lesson that although some games end with a sudden *coup*, most proceed, as world champion Steinitz observed, by the accumulation of small advantages. I used also to meet a somewhat larger group of sixth formers in the debating society, which Ralph Currey thought needed rather more support from young masters like John Morris, John Kirkman and myself. My continuing responsibility for General Studies with the Science Sixth and my own interests both pointed the same way, so I went to many of the meetings, and perhaps once a year was invited to make a set speech. The railway club also needed a figurehead, and I've always found it hard to resist a direct request for help. I knew little about railways, but the club had several enthusiasts who were eager to organize meetings and expeditions as long as I was nominally in charge. Before long I was traipsing round engine sheds and railway sidings at remote places like Stratford-atte-Bow and Willesden Junction, trying vainly to ascertain whether I still had twenty-two or was it really twenty-three small boys in tow. In those days no one thought of questioning the sense or safety of one master leading two dozen lads across a dozen railway tracks sixty miles from home. And no one ever questioned my proficiency before leaving me in charge of a swimming pool full of boys. Luckily, their instinct for self-preservation saved me from ever going home with fewer boys than had set out.

One of Jack Elam's most admirable decisions was to entrust his own son's education to CRGS. Nick still relishes his memory of our first meeting, a January evening, cold, dark and dank, when he answered the ring of their front door bell and a dim mist-shrouded figure dolefully announced, 'I'm Mann.' Three years later Nick was in one of my sixth form history groups, a somewhat testing experience for both of us because his own father had also taught history and took a professional as well as a paternal interest in Nick's progress. From time to time when I suggested a particular approach, Nick would observe 'I have been advised' to tackle the question in a somewhat different way. His father's name was never mentioned. Trying to strike a judicious balance between his two mentors may have been the most valuable training Nick had for his future role as diplomat and UK ambassador. Never underestimate the importance of a school's hidden curriculum. And teaching your boss's children is a salutary experience for teachers too. One of the things I learned in Colchester was the need to be on guard. Every now and again when I was out and about in Colchester or the surrounding countryside one of my pupils would leap from an alley or a hedge and greet me. Sometimes the boot was on the other foot. Discretion seemed the best policy for example when I and a few colleagues dropped into the Golden Fleece and found a group of cheerful under-age sixth formers including the Headmaster's son already enjoying themselves. Experiences like these confirmed what Tavistock should have made plain, that teachers in a small town's leading school cannot live entirely private lives, and that grammar school heads are among the most public figures in their own local communities, as well of course as being both the supreme appeal judges and the chief executioners in their own schools. Twenty four/seven propriety and dealing with naughty boys who'd defeated one's colleagues were not very appealing prospects.

Despite these reservations I knew there had been a fashion for appointing very youthful heads to small country schools and this seemed a possibility. So too did teaching history to somewhat older students training to be teachers. Encouraged by HMI Cresswell's kindly comments I began to read the job ads at the back of a still slim *Times Educational Supplement* and occasionally shot an arrow or two into the air. I still enjoyed CRGS enormously, but I didn't want to reach the stage in ten or fifteen or twenty years when I was repeating one year's experience again and again. My good friend John Morris seemed to lead a challenging life as Jack Tillett's assistant in the West Essex Education Office. Perhaps that was a route to explore.

CHAPTER 7

Leeds

The industrious apprentice

Little matter well or ill
Sentiment is more than skill
Sing together with a will
Floreat sodalitas – tas Colcestriensis

DECEMBER 1961, and for the last time I join in a rousing end-of-term rendition of Cuthbert Cronk's *School Carmen*, wondering all the time whether a grammar school ought to rate sentiment above skill. My sixth form greet me as *The Lost Leader*. Can it possibly be 'never glad confident morning again' for them, or do they really think it's 'just for a handful of silver he left us'?

In truth although I read *New Society* and *New Scientist* and my colleague John Kirkman did his best to keep me *au fait* with 1950s jazz, the cultural gap between me and my pupils was bound to grow, and once the boys no longer knew which war I was talking about when I casually mentioned 'the war' it seemed time to give up teaching.

I had travelled on Thursday 19 October to Leeds, my first visit except for rare forays from Harrogate where I'd stayed occasionally with my friend Ronald Moore. On Friday I breakfasted at the modest hotel recommended by my hosts, strolled back to the railway station and City Square to orientate myself, found Park Row and began to walk northwards past the Bank of England towards Victoria Square. Facing me on the left is Cuthbert Brodrick's monumental Town Hall, on the right the City Art Gallery and the City Library, and a few yards up Calverley Street, only just visible from Victoria Square, the City of Leeds Education Department.

When the Leeds School Board came into being in the early 1870s they soon covered the city with elementary schools built of tough Pennine grit. For their own use they commissioned a handsome Italianate pavilion with solid walls to ward off industrial smog and northern weather. Up its steps and through its portico I went for a preliminary interview with the Chief Education Officer Mr George Taylor, his Deputy Mr John Taylor, and his two Assistants, Mr Wood and Miss Ayres. Some sharp questions, and then Mr George Taylor made it clear that it was the Committee who would make that afternoon's decision. They were shrewd, experienced, and well-informed, and were on no account to be underestimated. And so indeed it proved. Alderman Walsh and his Conservative shadow Councillor Crotty were both solicitors, omnivorous speed readers who knew their onions. They led their regiments of party veterans seasoned by many a caucus campaign.

I was dismissed for lunch and instructed to return to the waiting room at 1.45. My rivals and I exchange a few words, but our minds are focused on the interviews to come. Interviews are always held in the same room, the Small Committee Room on the right just inside the entrance. Lofty, but quite small as committee rooms go, it is furnished with an enormous horseshoe table. There are about twelve or fifteen places round the outer rim, fewer on the inside. The Chairman sits at the head of the table flanked by his officers and Committee Members. The hapless candidates sit in the middle of the horseshoe facing the Chairman. The nearer they are to the Chairman the more likely they are to have Committee members on either side and even behind them. They have somehow to hold these invisible members' interest without losing the Chairman's ear. They have no chance of hiding their least attractive profile, they sweat, they flounder, they gabble, they hardly hear the questions. Only later do the survivors realize exactly what has happened. For almost a century the bond which unites every head teacher, every college principal, every education officer and many others in Leeds is the knowledge that they have shared and survived the same initiation ceremony, not perhaps as rich in symbolism as Aztec or masonic rites, but hardly less significant in its own world. Two years later when I had graduated to the outer rim of the shoe one of the sacrificial victims was a raven-haired young physicist.

The formal written offer of appointment arrives on Monday 23 October. I give two months' notice in accordance with my contract. Jack Elam is furious. 'How can a so-called Education Department do this, taking a key teacher when it's too late to find an immediate replacement?' My Essex friends are amazed. What could possibly induce a person of apparently sound mind to leave the delights of East Anglia for a northern industrial city?

Perhaps it was their concern which led me to look for lodgings outside the city. I advertised and enjoyed a day inspecting the respondents. I resisted the blandishments of a comely young single parent who seemed to need a companion, and settled on Mrs Hirst at Bardsey, a pleasant village a few miles north of Leeds. John Morris offered his shooting brake to carry some of my books and furniture north, and we set out to drive in convoy from Colchester to Yorkshire without thinking about the Cambridgeshire fogs we were likely to meet en route. After fifteen or twenty miles we lost sight of each other, drove separately, and arrived in Yorkshire without John knowing precisely where to go since I had not given him an address. It was not perhaps the best advertisement for our administrative competence. Fortunately we each had the wit to telephone John's wife Ros, and reached Mrs Hirst at about the same time. A proto-typical West Yorkshirewoman, bandy and bluff, she relishes the old Halifax story about a couple of locals spotting a stranger: 'Dust a' know 'en?' 'Naay, durst a' know 'en?' 'Nay.' 'Well, sod 'im!!' For a West Countryman it's a most helpful introduction to the inner world of West Yorkshire.

It's 2 January 1962: a word of welcome from the Deputy, and another from the Chief, and then to Miss Ayres, the Assistant Education Officer (Schools) who is to be my immediate boss. Tiny, birdlike, lively, quick, intuitive, she's the sharpest person I've ever worked with; in her case Maths, History, French and Latin for Higher School Certificate led on to a degree in Maths. Luckily I'm fairly comfortable with such modest calculations as my post requires. She doubles as AEO and the Chief's personal assistant. The head of the typing pool does his typing, but Miss Ayres spends an hour with him every morning and comes away with mountains of paper to add to her own formidable in-tray. She introduces me to Douglas Smith, the grey Glaswegian with whom I'm to share a large office. She suggests some preliminary reading and mentions people I'm to meet and places to visit as part of my induction. I finish the reading and at about 11 o'clock potter back to her office to ask if there's anything else I can do. Four years later I'm allowed to take another breath, but only when I'm leaving Leeds.

I'm the Administrative Assistant for Secondary Education. There are sixty-one secondary schools in Leeds and, to use terminology fashionable forty years later, they all outsource some of their personnel work. I help to draft and then place all their advertisements for teachers, arrange interviews and obtain written references, ensure that letters of appointment and their conditions of service go to the successful and suitable words of condolence to the unsuccessful candidates, make sure schools stay within budget, and see that all the candidates' expenses are reimbursed. I attend most of the interviews and am soon in a position to tell heads and governors how the candidates they have seen compare with the current market in a particular subject. If councillors are involved I often double as mini-cab driver: I enjoy every second when Mesdames Fish, Hammond, Happold and Henson, a mixed bag of Labour and Conservative *tricoteuses*, unite in slagging the Liberals for spoiling the neat symmetry of two-party politics.

None of the schools has much in the way of clerical or administrative support, and most of the secondary modern schools are quite small, so it makes good sense for them to use my specialist personnel services. Each spring we interview scores, hundreds, of young students in their last year and offer posts for the next September. I spend two or three days with Miss Keeling, our prim little housecraft adviser, interviewing a bevy of capable young women from the Yorkshire Ladies College of Housecraft. 'Perhaps it would be easiest,' I say, since at that time no young lady would think of coming for interview uncovered, 'to pick the ones with the nicest hats.'

From time to time I broker the transfer of a failing teacher or a disruptive pupil from one school to another where he, very rarely she, has the chance of a fresh start. My most satisfying *coup* was easing the chairman's brother into a new post as teacher librarian which we funded from our float. Since about a quarter of the city's 800 secondary school teachers leave the city or change schools each year I lead an active life. I dash from one school to another and teachers file in and out of my office all day long; and sometimes parents or pupils or councillors drop in too. It's an exhilarating and rewarding life. George Taylor obviously feels I'm not sufficiently '*serieux*' when I say I've no need to play bridge any more because the job gives me much the same sort of mental and psychological satisfactions.

I'm encouraged also to win heads' confidence and widen my knowledge and understanding by showing an interest in what the schools are doing. Along with a good many of my departmental colleagues I attend music and drama festivals, school plays and gala sports days. I enjoy Anouilh, Ibsen, Obey, Molière and Miller, as well as Britten, Coward, Fry, Shaw, Shakespeare and W.S. Gilbert. I become one of the grey men whose presence on speech day platforms is the cause of such puzzled wonderment to the assembled parents, teachers and pupils. I'm buoyed up by memories of Fred Geary, the local education officer who sat, year after year, right through the two or three hours of our CRGS speech days without moving a muscle or showing a flicker of emotion. I'd welcome a fraction of his fortitude.

But in the course of a couple of years I hear and meet a canon and a chief constable, local MPs Alice Bacon and Keith Joseph, college principals, city librarians, bishops, professors, judges and vice-chancellors. The readiness of so many eminent people to give their time and talents to the city's schools is marvellously impressive. My own constitution survives innumerable School Meals Service sausage rolls, and countless renderings of Brother James's *Air* and *My Bonnie Lass She Smileth*.

Less exciting are the termly meetings of the Area Advisory Boards the City Council has established to govern their secondary schools. These Boards consist of councillors and other known supporters of the prevailing party in each area. Each Board is responsible for six or eight schools and meets once a term to hear their heads' reports. The heads file in one by one, and are dismissed after fifteen or twenty minutes. My task is to write the minutes of these meetings.

This fairly undemanding rite is useful training for the more exposed task of writing the minutes of the Education Committee itself. The Committee's monthly meetings begin at 2 p.m. and usually end well before 2.30. This is one of the great advantages of the caucus system. Every major political decision is made in party meetings. The Labour Party caucus includes key party, trade union and trades council members as well as councillors. The Education Committee's role is in effect to ratify the decisions taken in caucus, and decide a few relatively minor issues. George Taylor liked one or two of these to be mildly contentious so that members felt their meeting had been purposeful. My target is to get the minutes to Jowett and Sowry the printers within fifteen

or twenty minutes so that they can be printed immediately and posted in time
for the next week's City Council meeting. I write the minutes before the
meeting, phrasing my draft so that the removal of a few words would cover
any possible decision. I bear in mind the young East India Company clerk who
asked his Director, 'What style, sir, is most to be preferred in the composition
of official despatches?' 'My good fellow,' responded the ruler of Hindoostan,
'the style as we like is the Humdrum.'

My draft began with a complete list of all those who might attend so that I
only had to delete the names of those who were absent. Then for each item I
would write something like 'The Committee considered an application and
resolved that the application be approved/rejected.' I had to stay awake and
make the appropriate deletions as the meeting proceeded, clear my amended
text with the Deputy as soon as the meeting ended, and rush pell mell to the
printers half a mile away. I was usually there by 2.45 or 2.50.

My training in these day-to-day duties proceeded alongside my halting
induction to this new world. At Roundhay Boys' I introduce myself,
improbably, 'I'm from the office and I've come to help.' Mr Howarth greets
me politely and chats pleasantly enough; but after half an hour the penny
drops, I'm supposed to be next door at Roundhay Girls' with Miss Lee. At
Allerton High School I trip over the rug in the unlit passage linking the
secretary's to the head's office. The rug yelps. I've trampled Miss Morton's
peke. She never forgives or forgets. I get a more cheerful welcome at Leeds
Modern whose head is Frank Holland, to be immortalized anonymously in
Alan Bennett's *Forty Years On*. Have I heard about the guy who was asked why
he was carrying an enormous clinical thermometer round the streets of Cairo?
'No.' 'It's to take the rectal temperature of a camel.' 'Why on earth would
anyone want to do that?' 'Because it's there.' George Taylor encourages me to
inspect a few lessons. The boys at South Leeds seem to be painting a storm at
sea but there's such a deafening row I can hardly see what's going on.
Mendelssohn's *Fingal's Cave* at full blast is the young art teacher's idea of mood
music.

My mail bag is another source of innocent merriment. 'I have been asked',
writes one correspondent, 'to give a talk on "education for women" with
particular reference to the Leeds area…including future developments.' 'To
complete my master's degree', writes another, 'I am required to prepare a
10,000 word dissertation on the work of the Leeds Education Committee.
Please send me all the relevant information. Please could you reply by return
of post.' That at least I can do.

As Administrative Assistant (Secondary) I was the most junior of the senior
officers, an elite cadre who lunched together at 12.45 p.m. every day round the
horseshoe table. The Chief sat at the head of the table flanked by the Chief
Inspector on his right and the Deputy on his left with the Assistant Education
Officer (Schools) on the deputy's left. Beyond that there was no strict order of

precedence, but the five or six young men in their thirties tended to sit at the far ends of the horseshoe, a little apprehensive that the Chief Inspector's occasional absences might prompt a summons to sit next to George Taylor. Though a slightly daunting experience for the young assistant, this was probably a welcome change for him. George was a man of many talents, purposefully crisp, a linguist and a barrister with a research degree in history, a teaching certificate and an LRAM in piano. He had been a grammar school head and chief inspector in Leeds before, having bypassed the more humdrum jobs which fall to administrative assistants, he became Deputy and then Chief Education Officer. Like George the Chief Inspector William Taylor had also been a grammar school head but William, garrulously near retirement, was a plonker before the word came into general use, and George once uncharacteristically let fall that he felt William's referees had misled him. By 1962 they'd long since stopped speaking meaningfully with each other. At lunch George would sit slightly aslant, presenting a cold right shoulder to William while he chatted with Deputy John Taylor and Miss Ayres on his left and toyed with the ascetic milk pudding made specially for him every day. John on the other hand was an eminently clubbable man, something of a bon viveur, member of the Leeds Club, the Yorkshire County Cricket Club and the Territorial Army, always bowler-hatted, always sporting a home-grown rose in his button hole, an oddly incongruous picture on the Leeds Corporation bus he took daily to and from the office. Every now and again, usually when George was away in London, he would lead half a dozen of us younger men across the road for a quick pre-lunch snifter and when we came tumbling cheerfully into lunch a few minutes late Miss Ayres would look down her beak and sniff disapprovingly. She could never understand why every few weeks I felt a need to escape the claustrophobic club for a quiet lunch alone.

Among ourselves we clearly had to distinguish the three Taylors by job title or first name, particularly as another Taylor, David, the Chief School Dental Officer, was also a member of our luncheon club, and Eric Taylor and Iris Taylor were college principals. Nothing irked any of them more than the slightest hint of some mafia-like relationship between them. But within the Department George Taylor and Miss Ayres maintained a formal style of address. To them I was always 'Mr Mann' as long as I worked there. She clearly disliked her given name, and although we might talk of Nellie Ayres in private she was always Miss Ayres in public and Sally privately to one or two personal friends. None of her assistants would ever have dared to say they were learning their trade by 'sitting next to Nellie'. Outwardly formal, our relations were no less friendly and mutually appreciative. Years later I warmed to see the young N. Ayres named on the honours board at London's Central Foundation School.

It was doubtless John Taylor's clubbability which forbade 'shop' at lunchtime. John Taylor was also the chief guardian of what might be called the traditions of the regiment. He would regale us with gently spiced recollections of our talented predecessors and of by-gone councillors and principals and heads. Like George and Nellie, John Taylor was a great reader. Holding your own with them and the two politicos, Josh Walsh and Paddy Crotty, was a full-time task. Every six weeks or so I was overwhelmed by black despair, wondering how I could ever survive among so many clever well-read people. Perhaps that's why I took the Mensa tests, though I soon found like Groucho Marx that a club which would have me was one I didn't want to belong to. And in case I needed a quick re-entry to teaching I continued my A-level examining. 'Please be merciful,' wrote one young Malaysian at the end of an unusually lightweight script, 'I too am a Christian.'

Not all my new colleagues were quite as formidable as my chiefs. Of about my own age there were the glum grey Scot Douglas Smith, the jovial West Yorkshireman Jack Mayman, the Liverpuddlian Leavisite Peter Williams, and, from Fleetwood, published author Brian Yeo whose declared aim was to travel through life with no more impedimenta than he could put into one suitcase. His *Place of Stones* caught to perfection what I could remember of the misery of the Lancashire marshes from a few days at a bleak midwinter teachers' conference. John Tunnadine seemed rather posh for Leeds but there was no doubting his expertise and keenness as a Youth Employment Officer. The Further Education Assistant was John Wood, a dry sardonic man who'd narrowly missed going on Mallory's Everest expedition and had had like many others a rough time in the North Riding at the hands of Frank Barraclough. He espoused the eccentric view that British weather ran in nineteen-year cycles, and that the cold spell of 1963 was bound to persist for a long time. I bet him a penny a day that the lake in Roundhay Park would not stay frozen over. The ice lasted until Easter and I paid my debt in wine.

Lunching every day with fifteen or twenty colleagues sitting at one large if oddly shaped table meant I was soon well acquainted with most of the senior officers and inspectors. Some of my early assignments obliged me to work closely with many of them. George and John Taylor were good at devising challenging jobs for their young assistants. I prepared the brochures for the Official Openings of new schools like Matthew Murrary, arranged Common-wealth Institute Lectures for schools, and interviewed young applicants for Outward Bound courses. These young fifteen year olds from secondary modern schools were the biggest fish in their ponds, mature and personable young men. After meeting them it was no surprise to learn that two or three hundred boys and girls from Leeds secondary modern schools were achieving much better GCE results than two or three hundred grammar school boys and girls who failed to fulfil the promise they showed at eleven.

George took his role as mentor most seriously, and when the Robbins Report on Higher Education appeared he asked his young apprentice for a considered commentary. When it was time for a new edition of Taylor and

Saunders, the definitive guide in those days to the Law of Education, George Taylor had his apprentice do some of the devilling for him. From time to time he would also ask for notes for some speech he was about to make. He always received my contributions courteously though what use he made of them remained a mystery.

John Taylor, being the clubbable man he was, seemed more concerned about helping his young assistants to feel part of the community of education officers. With my letter of appointment came the suggestion that I should spend a few days at Grantley Hall near Ripon where there was a course for young officers. Two of the country's best-known education officers, Alec Clegg of the West Riding and his brother-in-law Frank Barraclough of the North Riding would be speaking and so too would Alderman Hyman, the opinionated bruiser who chaired the West Riding County Council. John Taylor told us the ability to write with force and clarity would be our greatest asset, and Jim Hogan implied a possible conflict between being a good administrator and having sympathy. Among my fellow students were two of the rising stars of my own generation, Donald Fisher and Dudley Fiske, and another able young man whose claim to have 'rumbled' his own eminent director in three months compared with the three years it had taken his predecessors brought a twinkle to George Taylor's eye. It was John Taylor too who encouraged us all to play an active part locally and nationally in our own Association of Education Officers where I met colleagues from scores of other localities.

After only a few months John Taylor asked me to draft our Leeds Education Committee's annual report, a printed booklet of some seventy or eighty pages covering every aspect of the city's education service. Others would supply the raw material but I was to ensure that the various parts cohered and the same editorial style ran through the whole report. It was a splendid opportunity to get a bird's-eye view of the whole service.

The last forty years have seen such enormous changes in British public services like health, welfare, employment and education that it's hard to discern how they began. First the government created a national system of elementary schools in the nineteenth century and then in due course it made local councils responsible for running the schools. When it became apparent that disability, poverty, malnutrition and ill-health prevented many children from benefiting fully from their schooling government gave these local councils power to tackle these problems. They could set up special schools for handicapped children, relieve children's poverty, provide meals and milk and offer medical inspections and simple treatment. As late as the 1960s there were still huge local variations in poverty between different areas as George Taylor and Nellie Ayres were to show in their book *Born and Bred Unequal*. In the meantime these same councils had been charged with providing secondary schools and technical colleges, providing an employment service to put school leavers and employers in touch with each other, and giving grants to enable young people to stay at school and to take technical and university courses. Miss Ayres assured me that somewhere or other there was an enabling law which allowed us education officers to do virtually whatever we wanted to do.

For three or four decades in the mid-twentieth century a council's Education Department was in effect a one-stop shop for most of the public services intended for children and young people. This edifice, built laboriously in the century's first three decades, was largely dismantled in its last three decades. For a few months in 1962 however my task was to prepare a report on this intriguing conglomerate. This meant soliciting material from colleagues like the Chief Education Welfare Officer, the Principal School Medical Officer, the Chief Dental Officer, the School Meals Organiser, the Principal Youth Employment Officer and officers responsible for further and higher education. What they had to say was a revelation. We were giving five or six thousand clothing grants each year and free meals to about four thousand children. We were spending more than a million pounds a year on milk and meals, an eighth of our annual budget. The School Meals Service produced nearly eight million meals a year, making it surely the largest caterer in the city. We were issuing National Insurance cards to almost three thousand school leavers, placing about two thousand in jobs, and paying unemployment insurance or national assistance to several hundred young people. We were spending almost five times as much on medical inspection and treatment as we were on school inspections. At that time the department was running enormous and far-ranging health and welfare services. and our higher-level colleges had as many students as Leeds University. But the idea of an Education Department carrying such diverse responsibilities would become deeply unfashionable when a new generation of gurus told us later that one of the secrets of excellence was to stick to the knitting, to focus on your key task.

Another of the pundits' mantras a generation later was 'stay lean', avoid organizational flab. The Leeds City Council had anticipated this teaching a generation before it became fashionable. The council's spending on admini-stration and inspection was the lowest in England and Wales, only three-fifths of the average for county boroughs and less than 2 per cent of the budget for education. George Taylor had perforce to run a tight ship.

Surprisingly enough the tight-fisted party caucus who ruled Leeds did not take the view that one size fits all. Not for them the uniformity parodied by Eugene Richter in *Pictures of the Socialistic Future*: 'it is an inspiring thought to reflect that in every cookshop in Berlin on one and the same day exactly the same dishes are served.' Several decades before government discovered the beauty of specialist schools, Leeds encouraged diversity by providing the rooms and equipment its schools needed to specialize. Foxwood had an organ and an auditorium as part of its provision for music and drama, and another comprehensive school had the staff and equipment to teach about one-third of the curriculum, including science, in French. The boys at Belle Isle built a swimming pool as part of their building trades course. Another school had special facilities for athletics and sport, and a third had gardens and greenhouses for horticulture. Several Leeds primary schools were teaching French, and one Italian, forty years before the government discovered the virtue of an early start to learning foreign languages.

Diversity and specialization were the council's guiding principles in its provision for older students too. Writing two successive annual reports had acquainted me with the names and functions of the city's many colleges, the four Branch Colleges of Building, Commerce, Engineering and Science, and Institutional and Domestic Economy, the three major Colleges of Art, Commerce and Technology, and the four colleges for training teachers. Many of the city's teachers had trained at City of Leeds, Carnegie, or James Graham Colleges, or the Yorkshire Training College of Housecraft, and I'd interviewed scores of their students. George Taylor had prompted me to take a deeper interest in Higher Education by asking for some sort of appreciation of the Robbins Report. Then to my surprise he suggested that I might be interested in an impending vacancy which involved working with the colleges. The Committee usually followed George's lead when it came to appointments in the Department, and in due course I became the Organizer of Further Education. This grand and misleading title meant only that I was paid rather more for attending meetings about colleges than I had been for attending meetings about schools. But for the first time I enjoyed a modest perquisite. I was eligible to join the exclusive but inexpensive luncheon clubs at two of our colleges which trained students of catering and hotel management. Otherwise I was soon immersed in an arcane world peopled by experts in everything from painting, decorating and plumbing, to accountancy, banking and insurance, librarianship and social work, civil, mechanical and electrical engineering, architecture and town planning, and graphic and three-dimensional design. There might have been some debate about whether the most civilized and thoughtful people were to be found at the College of Art but there was no doubt that mastic asphalters were at the bottom of the vocational training heap. I attended advisory committees, governors' meetings, speech days and job interviews. Immediately after a preliminary lunch-time chat about Leeds United I heard Councillor Underwood baffle a would-be Senior Lecturer in Estate Management with his opening question, 'Are you one of life's natural centre forwards, or are you like me, one of the goalkeepers who take everything that's coming?'

Councillor John Underwood represented the Methodist and Non-conformist wing of the Labour Party. He was Deputy Leader of the Labour Group in the Education Committee, and one of the Three Wise Men along with Alderman Walsh, Labour and Jewish, and Councillor Crotty, Conservative and Roman Catholic. The Three Wise Men exercised some delegated powers for the Committee. One of their most important duties was to make discretionary grants to students who were not eligible for major awards for ranking degree courses. Many theological courses had somewhat lower entry qualifications than other degrees so they qualified only for discretionary grants, but in truly ecumenical mood the Three Wise Men always approved applications from Nonconformists, Jews and Roman Catholics.

It was at about this time that George Taylor asked me to tackle the most demanding of all the tasks he set. He had made a very public display of his own dissatisfaction with Allerton High School and its Head, Miss Morton, by moving his daughter Elizabeth from the sixth form at Allerton to Miss Lee's care at Roundhay High School. Now he, another historian, asked me to help Elizabeth to make up lost ground by visiting his house on my way home to coach her in A-level History. For several months Elizabeth and I met in their front room for an hour each week to discuss topics vaguely related to her A-level syllabus. Mrs Taylor would offer cups of tea, and from time to time I stayed on after the tutorial for a quarter of hour to chat with Mr and Mrs Taylor, an unprecedented honour for any of his young assistants. On one occasion George offered me a can of beer he'd found buried at the back of his garage, gave it a good shake and seemed surprised when the beer frothed up and hit the drawing room ceiling. My dexterity in opening the next can without causing another catastrophe was much admired.

All this occurred at much the same time as my move from schools to colleges in May 1964. By September I'd relinquished any remaining responsibility for schools and was conscious of no impropriety in inviting the slim, long-legged, blue-eyed and raven-haired young woman who was now Head of Physics at Roundhay High School to continue the conversation we'd had across the horseshoe table some months earlier. We found we had enough in common, books, theatre, food and being strangers in Leeds, to enjoy meeting once every week or two. She suspected me of some deep ploy when we ran out of petrol one evening only to realize much later that an engrained insouciance was more to blame. Even when I left my Bardsey digs and moved into a Leeds flat near hers we found there were too few weekday evenings and we needed to meet at weekends too.

This was something of a problem because my move to Leeds had proved more of a landmark than I expected. After eight years I'd many friends and acquaintances in Colchester literary and educational circles. These links ended abruptly when I moved to Leeds. I was no longer young enough or good enough to play hockey, and there was little scope for social tennis or cricket among my new colleagues. But by great good fortune my old Trinity friend Ronald Moore was working for ICI Fibres at Harrogate and had few weekend entanglements. Before long we were meeting most Sundays for walking and talking endlessly about books and the organizations in which we worked. A great conglomerate like ICI could not be represented by a simple organization chart; it had at least a three-dimensional structure, with separate divisions for each of its major products like paint, or fibres, or chemicals, other divisions offering a particular service such as personnel or finance, and in many parts of the world a local manager to pull together all the company's activities in that area. We admired Sir Arthur Wellesley's bold claim from his command head-quarters in Portugal, 'I make it my business always to complete the business of the day on the day.' Most of the functionaries we knew massaged their egos daily by going to bed with a full not an empty pending tray. We identified a new sub-species, distantly related to Neanderthal Man and *Homo Sapiens*, whom we christened Otley Man. Otley Man's distinguishing characteristics were turning right across on-coming traffic without signalling, steering a meandering course and in every other respect exhibiting a bland disregard for other road users. Forty years later Otley Man seems to have disappeared, unable to cope with the pace and stress of life today. The Ordnance Survey maps enabled us to plot our routes with care, walking just as far in the morning as would deliver us to a convenient hostelry shortly after opening time at 12, with perhaps another halt at about 1.45 just before closing time at 2. We completed our twelve or fifteen mile circuit in the afternoon and retired to his flat or my digs for an evening of dining, wining and dissecting the Sunday papers. After a hard day's walking and two or three bottles of plonk it was usually Wednesday or Thursday before I felt fully restored and ready for the next weekend.

Greatly daring I now persuaded Ronald that Margaret should join some of our long weekend treks across the Pennines or the Yorkshire Wolds. She passed this test with flying colours and our Sunday duumvirate became a triumvirate. Margaret and I also went together to a convivial Oxford Society meeting where we met and chatted with another Oxford man, John Taylor. 'You're on to a rich seam,' he observed slyly the next morning. With such an endorsement from my new Chief I had to press ahead.

CHAPTER 8

Essex Revisited

Nor rural sights alone, but rural sounds
Exhilarate the spirit

L EEDS WAS EASY to get out of. That was the kindest thing its young people had
to say about their native city. Or so at least I was told by former colleague
John Kirkman who happened to mark a bundle of their A-level scripts while I
was working there. I was working *in* the city, immersed in a sea of schools and
colleges, but not really *of* the city. It was no great wrench to leave the city itself
after less than four years and return to the sights and sounds of rural Essex. No
county has lovelier villages than Essex, and for two years I was to revel in
places like Abbess Roding, Sible Hedingham, Good Easter, Helions
Bumpstead and Tolleshunt D'Arcy.

Following public advertisement and a few nail-biting weeks for him John
Taylor succeeded George in the summer of 1965. His new deputy was Dudley
Fiske, a year or two older than me, more experienced, and a remarkably
professional outside candidate. If Spenser was 'the poets' poet', the education
officers' administrator was Dudley Fiske who had prudently ascertained
Alderman Walsh's and Councillor Crotty's particular interests before coming
for interview. I was less thorough, but John Taylor thought I'd done well
enough to look for further promotion elsewhere. By November I had moved
to my fourth job and my fourth house in a little less than four years.

The Tower of the Old Vicarage at Roxwell provided daily lessons in
organization and planning. My accommodation was on five floors, two
bedrooms at the top, then on each succeeding floor: bathroom, living room,
kitchen and front door. I soon learned to pick up toiletries, briefcase, breakfast,
topcoat and post as I tumbled headlong down the stairs each morning.

My job was equally novel, to me at least. Large parts of Essex are among the
most urbanely civilized parts of rural England, carefully cultivated for more
than two thousand years. The county once reached as far west as the River Lea,
itself now engulfed by London sprawl. But for centuries London and its people
have looked to Essex for the living space they could not find within the city or,
later, within the wider boundaries of the London County Council. The
expansion of London was acknowledged again in 1963 when Essex lost a large
swathe of land and people to the new Greater London Council, but the exodus
continued and when I went there in 1965 many Londoners were still settling
in what remained of Essex. Harlow and Basildon were New Towns and

Witham and Braintree among the Expanded Towns designated for London 'overspill', an unlovely name for uneasy people moving to unfamiliar surroundings. Many of those moving to the New and Expanded Towns were parents with young children and others on the way. These children needed schools, primary schools from the moment they arrived and secondary schools a few years later. It was the County Council's duty to ensure that schools were available both in the New and Expanded Towns and in the many other towns and villages which were growing rapidly at that time. I was one of the cogs in the machine the council had built to perform this duty.

Schools do not materialize overnight. You need land, buildings, furniture, equipment and materials, and for all these you need funds, and the expertise of land agents, surveyors, lawyers, architects, designers, educators, builders and suppliers. Above all, the most invaluable aids are well-burnished crystal balls to help you forecast exactly when new buildings will be needed. But, I was warned, administrators with crystal balls are very vulnerable.

It was not too hard to obtain details of the live births in each part of the county, rather more difficult to get details of how many new houses would be built in each of the next five years, and an act of faith to estimate how many children of school age and below might move into these new houses or be born later to the families which had moved in. My mentor was Jack Springett, a high-flying Cambridge mathematician, sharp, kind, insightful and amazingly enthusiastic. 'It was', he would say of some pedestrian occasion, 'the kind of party that made you want to leap on to the table and shout "fuck".' Fortunately for my peace of mind by the time I inherited the crystal balls Jack had evolved elaborate and well-tried formulae for estimating the relation between the numbers of births and new houses and the demand for school places in three or five or ten years time. There was of course a special formula for the lively young philo-progenitive army couples living in the new houses at Colchester barracks. Only if there was a demonstrable gap between the demand and the existing provision would the government, speaking via the Department of Education and Science, allow the County Council to borrow money to finance more 'roofs over heads'. My task was to assemble the data, and construct the best possible case. Doing this appealed enormously to the chess-playing, bridge-playing problem-solver.

If extending an existing school met the need for new places this could usually be done on land the council already owned. But the council was building and opening a new school every two or three weeks and had a constant need for new sites. One of my most agreeable tasks was to go out, usually with my long-serving Sites and Buildings colleague Cecil Dowsett, to meet surveyors and architects to examine plots to assess their suitability for whatever scheme we had in mind. Someone would have to get planning permission, make sure there were no restrictive covenants to stop us using a site, and sometimes take steps to buy land compulsorily. Cecil was a splendid companion on these jaunts, a cheerful episcopalian figure with a curiously high-pitched and somewhat parsonic voice who liked nothing better than a country picnic. We would go into some village store, buy bread and cheese and a raw onion or two, and find a field where we could sit in the sun, enjoy the Essex countryside, muse over what Cecil termed the kalliber of our colleagues and prepare to breathe our sulphurous fumes over the afternoon's adversaries.

But most of my day-to-day contacts were with architects in the County Architect's Department, Derek Senior, Bill Smith, Maurice Cramond, Tinker Bell, Alan Jeffery and Arthur Jennings, as humane and civilized a group of colleagues as one could wish for. In consultation with the county's school inspectors and advisers I used to prepare the first briefs for the architects and then collate the Education Department's comments on their drawings. As far as primary schools were concerned preparing the brief usually meant searching a file for the standard brief for an infant or a junior school or a combined infant and junior school. Sometimes however the task was more complex. Particularly when we were extending a village school we liked to explore the possibility of using the school hall as a village hall or using the classrooms for adult classes. Even these relatively simple concepts raised intriguing problems. Do adults using the hall need separate cloakrooms in schools where every classroom has its own pegs? Will outside users leave the kitchens immaculate for the school meals staff? Is there a risk of damage to any children's work that is on display? Will adults be at ease with child-sized water closets and infant chairs? The County Architect, Ralph Crowe, arranges his six feet four inches and 220 pounds on an infant chair to illustrate his claim that it is far easier and far healthier for someone of his bulk to sit on a small chair than for a small child to balance on a full-sized chair. But others argue that children cope somehow with one-size-fits-all water closets at home so there's no real need for child-sized loos in schools.

Similar questions arise when we are planning secondary schools. The possibilities included the shared use of a swimming pool, a sports hall, a stage and green rooms, or even a library or a clinic. What all these schemes had in common was the need for the Education Department to find a partner who could put up some of the funds. We could fund the school, but we needed a parish or borough or district council or in some cases a church or some other County Council department to meet the cost of any extra facilities. We had no doubt about the potential benefits of dual use, the economies, and the synergy when different users interacted with each other. I trekked to Clacton, Corringham and Chigwell, to Braintree, Basildon and Benfleet and many other places to discuss the issues and explore the possibilities with one potential partner after another. From time to time to our delight the different government departments which controlled our partners' spending each gave the requisite approvals at the right time for an agreed joint scheme to go ahead.

Our school designs had to meet all sorts of regulations. Central government specified the maximum permissible cost of each new building and laid down the size of playgrounds and playing fields, the minimum size of classrooms, laboratories and gymnasia, the recommended number of workshops and laboratories, and the maximum amount of space to be allowed for corridors, cloakrooms and storage. These limits led many councils to system building, using factory-made components of standard shapes and sizes. These building systems saved time in the drawing office and on site and we firmly believed that counties like Essex and Hertfordshire depended on them to complete the dozens of schools each had to build in the mid 1960s. Whitehall's Architects and Building Branch also sponsored a number of projects and published many helpful Building Bulletins which described and illustrated interesting and well-conceived solutions to many of the problems involved in school design. But the government's preoccupation with controlling costs meant that we could not afford the durable materials and finishes or the climate control systems which might have saved money over the whole life of a school building. Perhaps it's a bit much to hope that Ministers will ever look far beyond the date of the next election.

Despite the amount of new building, we were adding only a small fraction to the county's stock of school buildings, many of which went back to the previous century. Since for many years the traditional styles would predominate we felt we ought to be making some provision for teachers who favoured team teaching and group activities in more open spaces. Many of our new primary schools therefore had open areas for groups of about sixty children, with specially equipped corners in each area for activities like pottery and crafts, for science, for library and sometimes for story-telling and drama.

When it came to designing new schools the most intractable requirements were the need to provide suitable areas for assemblies and school meals. The regulations said the whole school should begin each day with an act of corporate worship. This was not so great a problem in primary schools, where a hall accommodating the whole school could also be used for physical education and perhaps for drama and music if it was a little removed from the classrooms. But the new secondary schools of a thousand or twelve hundred pupils had few other uses for a room which was large enough for the whole school and they soon concluded that assembling so large a number of teenage pupils in one space got the day off to a bad start. They preferred smaller groups of pupils, sometimes houses of two or three hundred, and sometimes year groups or upper, middle and lower schools. Right from the start of a new school, and well before head or governors were appointed, planners and architects had to make assumptions about the size and number of these groups and design schools with six or eight rooms in which groups could assemble for worship. In almost every case these rooms doubled as dining rooms. That meant they needed serveries, and kitchens to supply the serveries. The kitchens needed vehicular access for their daily deliveries of provisions, and it was an article of faith that the kitchen staff needed windows and an outside view. With those constraints it was almost impossible to design a kitchen to supply more than two dining rooms. In school after school we provided six or eight rooms for assembly and dining and three or four kitchens each with its own vehicular access. If Napoleon's armies marched on their stomachs, so too do schools. The School Meals Organizer, Joan Halsall, was perforce one of my most constant associates.

The rest of the site was left for classrooms, laboratories and workshops. The architects wanted to know exactly what happens in schools so that their designs matched the users' requirements. The science advisers asked for suites of laboratories so that one prep room and one technician could serve more than one laboratory, the linguists and the geographers and the historians asked for their own suites of specially equipped rooms, the drama teachers asked for studios, the PE people preferred to have a gymnasium, a pool and a sports hall, and everyone else asked that the music and practice rooms be some distance away from their classrooms. The specialist advisers subjected me to intensive lobbying on every aspect of a school's curriculum and organization, though when I needed their comments the part-time fruit farmers and chicken breeders among them were strangely hard to find.

And since we knew the schools we were building would probably be in use for sixty or eighty years we began to prepare for modern technology by installing the ducts for closed circuit television and I went off to seminars about the school of the future. As part of my on-the-job training I was also despatched to meetings of building and furniture consortia like the South East Architects Consortium and the Counties' Furniture Group. These were impressive examples of how local councils could pool their expertise and buying power to secure good design and good value for themselves well before Terence Conran and IKEA brought similar concepts to their High Street stores.

These new tasks were challenging, and required a brisk response. But the County Council offices were remote, and curiously impersonal. I missed the constant human buzz of life in a city office. No teacher ever crossed the council's portals. If Essex teachers or parents had a problem they contacted one of the eight divisional or borough offices, though even they were further from the action than a city office. Now and then a county officer was deputed to keep an eye on some potentially explosive matter like the sacking of a head. I may have earned a place in the education officers' hall of fame for sitting through one disciplinary hearing which began at 6 p.m. and ended at about 4 a.m. the next morning. As far as I know the sacked head did not complain about the unsocial hours or the possibility that someone's attention might have wandered at a critical moment.

The council itself had among its members a good complement of deputy lieutenants, magistrates and retired brigadiers and colonial officers who treated the council officers very civilly, as one would a promising subaltern. But even the recently promoted Chief Officer seemed rather insecure, pacing up and down with his head jerking and his limbs flying off at odd angles as he spoke without looking at you. David Bungey seemed particularly nervous of the Divisional Officers, accepting them almost at their own valuation as local satraps or Norman barons. In mid Essex Bill Primmer introduced an unusual kind of feudal levy, appropriating bits of timber from every school site he visited for the boat he was building. Two or three of his colleagues were old colonial officers who were probably used to running half a country and for whom one division was small beer. Overseeing the whole service was Elizabeth Coker, Chair of the Education Committee, tall, crisp and brisk, a stainless steel battle axe who drove round the county in a long low-slung sports car. Being driven in it, some said wistfully, must be rather like being in bed with her.

One of the pleasures of returning to Essex was the opportunity it gave to revive old friendships made during my previous stint in Colchester. The Simpsons, the Walmsleys, the Morrises, the Crittendens and others welcomed the prodigal back from the north, and readily extended their friendship to the raven-haired young physicist who was soon driving south from Leeds every second or third weekend. Margaret was not deterred by what she saw of the south and its people, and Jane Austen insisted that a single man in my position must be in want of a wife. Before long we were looking for a house and planning a summer wedding, a relatively modest affair because in 1966 we did not think of challenging the convention that the bride's parents provided the reception, and we did not want them to be unduly burdened. We endured the bells of Lincoln Cathedral on our wedding night, and drove off swiftly to observe the storks' nests in Alsace, and to admire with Byron the cascades at Pissevache and the shores of Lake Neuchâtel. Margaret soon found some exciting part-time physics teaching at King Edward's, Chelmsford, and we began together to explore Essex and Suffolk.

CHAPTER 9

Sheffield

The biggest village in England

Fᴙᴏᴍ ᴛɪᴍᴇ ᴛᴏ ᴛɪᴍᴇ we ventured further, visiting some of the many friends and relatives who came to see us in Chelmsford. Margaret was an enthusiastic Girl Guide leader so we bought a frame tent, something I thought I'd left behind with the RAF on Pevensey Marshes. We set out for France, stopped briefly in the Black Forest, and in a trice were camping in Vienna with only a clapped-out cylinder block to detain us for a day or two. We explored the Hofburg and the Schönbrunn Palace, peered into the Kunsthistorisches Museum, and resolved to spend a lovely Sunday afternoon admiring the Danube from the Belvedere terraces. There, sour black-gowned matrons taking their Sunday constitutionals tightened their corsets, pursed their lips and glanced sideways when Margaret's shapely young thighs crossed their sight lines. We fled.

The next year we settled for France, drove south and tramped across the Cevennes singing a cheerful ditty called *Marching across the Causses*, now lost alas to the world because we recorded neither tune nor words. Through the Gorge du Tarn, clambering briefly over Viollet le Duc's wonderfully restored protective walls at Carcassonne, admiring the great cathedral at Albi, too late by several years to be allowed to see the threatened Lascaux cave paintings but just in time to visit the Bar Pré-historique and the Hotel Cro-Magnon. By now we were expert campers. We applied our limited understanding of critical path analysis to the simple problem of pitching camp and cooking a meal, and on our best days the tent was up and we were sitting down to a hot supper in about thirty minutes. Margaret had too a real Guide's eye for a pitch and when the Dordogne storms lashed us we sat on the crest of a small ridge behind the protective trenches she demanded even on top of a hill and laughed as the flood waters inundated every other tent.

One of our journeys was more momentous. One glorious summer day in 1967 we drove north up the A1, through Sherwood Forest, passing great mansions like Thoresby, Welbeck, Bolsover and Renishaw, all well insulated from the mining villages on which their wealth depended. Past unlovely Mansfield and smoking Staveley one colliery followed another, one foundry another. In spite of the heat we kept the car windows closed fast to exclude the putrid dust and fumes. We wondered what awaited us in steel city Sheffield where we were overnighting on our mystery excursion. On a similar day almost twenty years earlier I'd seen an opaque yellow cloud covering Sheffield while the rest of England enjoyed blue skies and brilliant sunshine. Highly susceptible to dust and smoke, I seemed to have made a great mistake to think of even touching down in Sheffield.

To our surprise, quite near the city centre our hotel overlooked Endcliffe Park, an attractive strip of well-maintained park and woodland along the floor of one of Sheffield's many valleys. To our amazement, when we wandered round the city centre later that evening the air was pure thanks to a programme which soon made Sheffield the cleanest industrial city in Europe, and almost every street offered a distant vista of green or heather-covered hills. We'd seen no city to match it.

My unreserved enthusiasm warmed the Sheffield burghers whom I met the following afternoon. I've no idea what else we talked about, but I did not hesitate when Alderman Dr Albert Ballard asked if I would like to join the city as its Deputy Chief Education Officer. I only realized much later what a critical step this was. For the next twenty years or so my task as a senior education officer would be, in Sir Geofrey Vickers' evocative phrase, less like steering a grand circle course than trying to shoot the rapids. From now on puzzle- and problem-solving would be incidental to the much more serious business of helping to steer the barque.

The immediate question, however, was 'where to live: in Sheffield or in its captivating countryside?' In those days some local authorities insisted that their officers lived on the patch. Sheffield had no such rule, but my new boss Michael Harrison deftly conveyed that it would be most eccentric even to think of living outside the city. My southern friends would have found this odd but in Sheffield his was the almost universal view. Among the great English towns and cities none had fewer commuters, since nearly all those who lived in the city worked there, and those who worked there usually lived there. Uniquely too among English towns and cities the city includes a substantial chunk of National Park. As you approach from the west, the first 'City of Sheffield' boundary signs appear in open moorland with not a house in sight. Vast areas of open country guard Sheffield on the west, and one of Europe's greatest concentrations of rolling mills and forges on the east. The city is in consequence almost an island, and like other islanders its people seem a little less hurried and a little more at ease with themselves than many mainlanders.

They like to think of Sheffield as 'the biggest village' in England. Within a week or two of our moving there Margaret and I constantly met our new acquaintances when we walked through the city centre along Fargate, and when the Crucible Theatre opened a year or two later its coffee bar on a Saturday morning soon resembled a village shop or pub. As 'comers-in' we were surprised and delighted to find after a few months that most of our new friends were native Sheffielders, not other migrants like ourselves.

First the hard rowing…

…and then the favouring breeze.

We bought a neat chalet in a small enclave built by Gleeson and were much reassured to find their regional director Shaun Fahey living two doors away. Two doors the other way David Johnson invited several friends to his house for his stag party and surprised us all by asking for a couple of pounds each to meet his expenses. At the back we looked out on a hilly meadow with a few trees and a school roof just visible on the horizon. Up the lane and two hundred yards away was Lodge Moor golf course and beyond that open country all the way to Manchester. We had almost achieved my ideal, a back door opening on to open country and a front door on a busy street. The city centre was no more than ten minutes by car and not much more by bike. At one stage I bought a folding bike to enjoy freewheeling downhill almost all the way to work. I'd forgotten how hot and dusty it would be going home, and in any case there was no need for so futile a gesture. As one of the perks of my new post I had a reserved parking space for my car, a space clearly signed in Latin 'D.E.O.', 'for GOD': aka Deputy Education Officer. My other perks were a loo to which only I and the cleaners had keys, and an enormous office with an imposing Mussolini desk behind which the craggy Scot William Alexander had once held sway long before he became first Sir William and then Lord Alexander, for twenty years or more the most fearsome broker in English education. The trappings of office were far grander than in Essex, where thanks to County Hall's automatic lighting system I could not even switch my own lights on and off. That was a privilege reserved for the most senior officers.

Soon after my arrival in November it seemed for a moment that my own career in Sheffield might come to an untimely end. Anticipating the Chief Education Officer's Christmas party, the department's senior officers used to entertain him to dinner a few weeks before Christmas. We ate well at the Rutland Hotel, and I stayed right to the end to demonstrate my stamina to my new colleagues. Driving home along the A57 I was alarmed to see a police car just behind me, even more alarmed when I was flagged down. I could see the *Sheffield Telegraph*'s banner headline 'OFFICE PARTY! DEPUTY EDUCA-TION OFFICER ARRESTED'. But the music I heard as I stepped from the car was 'Don't worry if you've been drinking, sir, we'd just like to look inside the boot.' What were they hoping to find?

'Remember Robert the Bruce and the spider. If at first you don't succeed, try, try, and try again' was among my mother's favourite maxims so I suppose she would commend my pertinacity. I'm one those people who average about thirty job applications for every success so I've always been slightly envious of Margaret who hardly knows what it is to be rejected. As soon as we moved to Sheffield she was snapped up by Thornbridge, a small co-educational grammar school on Sheffield's southern boundary which happened to need someone to run its physics department. We settled down happily among friendly people in a most congenial city, a busy double-income-no-kids couple. We enjoyed the

Susan soon takes to hiking, October 1970.

Hallé Orchestra's occasional visits and the Sheffield Repertory Theatre, as well as treasure hunts by car, the Sheffield Teachers' annual opera, and the Lord Mayor's annual dinner. But we never made it to the high point of Sheffield's public life, the annual Cutlers' Feast.

We cancelled France and holidayed instead at Blakeney when a just-expectant Margaret learned that she had a large ovarian cyst. The operation went well and Margaret went on teaching. It was thirty years before the Prime Minister's wife and the Chancellor's wife both had babies while New Labour were in office, and I was surprised that half Sheffield seemed to rejoice with us when Susan was born in the Jessop Hospital on 6 March 1970. I did not realize how very closely our fortunes were scrutinized until David was born exactly twenty-one months later on 6 December 1971 and one of our head teacher acquaintances observed delicately that we must have been celebrating Susan's first birthday. Susan travelled widely, in a carry-cot which was easily hidden under restaurant and hotel tables and then in a back-pack over the Pennines. She enjoyed a long weekend in Appleby without the other hotel guests hearing, seeing, or even smelling her. She explored London from her cot, and visited Syon House and Hampton Court. She partied with our friends. One tiny baby enriched our social life without constraining it and we imagined innocently that life with two small children would be no more complicated than life with one. However, a tent and two infants did not appeal so we bought a caravan and parked it on our small front lawn, obscuring the pleasant view from our front-facing kitchen. This was not at all what we wanted so I asked my colleague Stewart Rodman, now in charge of premises, whether there was by chance a school with spare hard standing. 'Yes indeed,' he said after a day or two, 'have a word with the caretaker at the Mayfield Environmental Studies Centre', once a little school which served a small community of quarrymen. I spent a pleasant hour with her and her husband, the one surviving quarryman, and moored the van in its new berth later that evening. At 10.30 the next morning Stewart phoned, 'The Chief Executive has phoned. Lady Plonk of the Council for the Preservation of Rural England is demanding to know who has had the effrontery to park a caravan in the Mayfield Valley, an area of outstanding natural beauty.' She must have been out at dawn with her spy glass. The van was back on our front lawn within the hour.

Despite this reverse it gave us several years of pleasure. The van took us to Woodhall Spa, Peterborough, Kimmeridge, Lyme Regis and Cricket St Thomas, Billing Aquadrome, Malvern, Cardiff and Dovedale's Ilam Hall. We went via Poole and the Sandbanks chain ferry to Swanage to see my mother and dying father. As we drove off the ferry, the first to leave, our tow bar stuck in the ground and we stood blocking the smooth flow of traffic. A hundred Samaritans materialized to lift the bar and push us out of the way; only to be metamorphosed miraculously as Pharisees who disappeared immediately without pausing to see whether we needed any other help. Twice, greatly daring, the van took us across the Channel to Normandy and Brittany. We swallowed oysters at St Malo and marvelled at the Carnac megaliths. As four year old Susan played with her tall curly red-haired young brother at La Grande Metairie a kindly fellow camper managed to wound them both with one well-meaning query, 'Are your two girls twins?' she asked, assailing both seniority and latent manhood with one well-placed dart.

Margaret and Roy next door rigged up an ingenious and probably illegal two-way intercom between our two houses so that Joan and Roy and Margaret and I could baby sit for each other from the comfort of our own sitting rooms. The sleeping children's breathing was clearly audible and I don't recall any of us ever having to dash next door to help a distressed youngster. The intercom allowed us to lead a fairly active social life. We got to know a young bank manager, young enough to let us know he could easily arrange a loan if only we transferred our account to his branch. We found a lovely cottage at Cropton with what proved a too-demanding garden, but in the short term Cropton was only two hours' drive from Sheffield and we thought we could easily weekend there, dashing off on Friday evening, returning on Sunday. This hardly ever happened but for three years we spent almost all our holidays there, exploring Ryedale, the North York Moors and the Yorkshire coast, especially Flamborough and Bempton where the children's grandparents Pop and Nanny, auntie Liz and cousins Ian, Wendy and Jo, all lived, only a short stroll from Bempton Cliffs and England's largest colony of gannets.

But Margaret was never fullfilled by days at home with young children and occasional exchanges with other housebound mums. Without my pulling rank, though perhaps the name was enough, Susan was offered one of the scarce places at Broomhall Nursery at about the same time as our hyper-active red-head David enrolled at playgroup, making just enough space for Margaret to start another degree course, at Sheffield Polytechnic. It was tough going, biology, chemistry, astronomy and earth sciences to add to the physics and subsidiary maths in which she'd specialized from the age of sixteen. Half-way through her four-year course came a surprise call from Thornbridge School, now somewhat larger and comprehensive. Like Cincinnatus, called from his plough to rescue Rome, Margaret was summoned from housewifery and motherhood to become Director of Studies and Deputy Head at Thornbridge. Councillor Bill Owen, the upright trade unionist Deputy Chair of Education, was one of several councillors who questioned the propriety of my wife holding a senior post in one of the city's schools. Fortunately I had had absolutely nothing to do with filling the post and the cloud soon passed as did another cloud a little later when I was wrongly suspected of having bared my chest and rolled my trousers to join the masonic lodge. Returning to full-time work at a much more senior level was a tough assignment for Margaret, particularly when timetabling exigencies obliged her to add Geography and Latin to her teaching repertoire. Nor was it a great deal financially. Jacqui Kinman, a newly qualified nursery nurse, came full time to look after Susan and David, and we became again a two-car family. When push came to shove I'd been enough of a new-age man to handle nappies from time to time, and now I became the household's chief shopper because I could easily slip out to the shops at lunch time. It was a small step on the way to my becoming the family chef. *Never in the Kitchen when Guests Arrive* became my household bible.

In what I liked to feel was an equal opportunities household and what came to be known as a symmetrical family with both partners working at their spiralist careers, we raised a concerned eyebrow when five year old Susan came home talking about boys' colours and girls' colours as well as boys' and girls' games. That was not quite as disconcerting as the time we suspected David had swallowed one of my pills and took him urgently to the accident and emergency unit at Sheffield Children's Hospital where he was expertly treated by an attractive white-coated black woman doctor. Our three year old could not believe that a woman or a black person could possibly be a doctor. We wondered about the covert values prevalent in Sheffield's under-five sub-culture.

David and two or three of his closest friends were the liveliest elements in his nursery class. What, we felt obliged to wonder idly, were the chances of his being the youngest child ever to be expelled from nursery? He, and we, escaped a more serious hazard when he went on a canal holiday with classmate Richard, Richard's parents and Jacqui. He came home safe and sound and it was some time before we learned that a life-belted David had fallen off the barge to be hauled out of the water with the help of a long pole. But we knew immediately when four year old Susan ran away from home for the first time, fighting her way through grass as tall as herself in the field behind our house. We took a roundabout route and were there to rescue her two hundred yards from home. The next time she ran away we had moved to a big house in Nether Edge and as I ran after her in *déshabillé* early one morning as she sought freedom on the half-mile circuit round our block, Miss Wright drove past, Miss Wright, the esteemed Head of Susan's new school and an active member of the teaching community. What would the village grapevine make of the Deputy Education Officer's inability to cope with just one small child?

CHAPTER 10

The City on the Move

A commonwealth of learning

Iᴛꜱ ʟᴏᴄᴀᴛɪᴏɴ ᴍᴀᴋᴇꜱ Sheffield less one large village, more a cluster of villages separated from each other by narrow, steep-sided valleys down which half a dozen streams tumble from the Pennine block of millstone a thousand feet or more above sea level. 'I've always thought of cities as big and flat,' said an astonished civil servant sent off to explore the 'sticks' by his departmental masters in London during an aberrant moment of *glasnost*, 'but Sheffield's small and hilly.' One of the curious consequences of this unusual topography was that Sheffield had to build libraries and schools for local communities of twelve or fifteen thousand people whereas flat Manchester built for communities of forty or fifty thousand.

To add to its existing townships, in the twentieth century Sheffield absorbed many reluctant villages, some from the West Riding of Yorkshire but most from Derbyshire, once part of the old Kingdom of Mercia and still subconsciously aware that Yorkshire was home to an alien tribe. Forty years after their transfer in the 1920s the people of Woodhouse still claimed the City Council had done nothing for them. When the Education Committee chairman, lithe and dapper Peter Jackson, and I, a more rotund figure whom my warmest admirers never knowingly marketed as either lithe or dapper, went together to persuade the people of Woodhouse of the Committee's wisdom in proposing to close their local school, they smilingly observed that the dragoons had once had to march from Wakefield to restore order in 'Woodus', that 'Woodus' was the last place where the authorities had had to read the Riot Act, and that the village stocks just outside would fit either of us equally well. Their reasoning was irrefutable, and the school stayed.

'Made in Sheffield' has been a byword for at least six hundred years ever since Chaucer's miller carried 'a Sheffield thwitel' or knife on his pilgrimage to Canterbury. For all its antiquity, cutlery remained an industry of 'little meisters' where employees and masters worked together in small units, and where a successful journeyman might move over to set up his own business. There was as a rule no great divide here between masters and men. Much the same was true of the new silver-plating industry developed in the eighteenth century. Even in Sheffield's third great industry, the making of high-quality steels, no caste of wealthy owners or traders emerged. Benjamin Huntsman's crucible process involved handling large buckets of molten metal, an operation requiring great care and total trust in one's fellow workers, re-enacted three or four times a year at the Abbeydale Industrial Hamlet where I watched it being filmed for the television broadcasts of Jacob Bronowski's *Ascent of Man*.

Sheffield's nineteenth-century industries were skilful and dangerous, hot and thirst-making. Beer-houses proliferated and drunkenness was rife. The whole city depended on its industries, but the city had no mass production lines, no great demand for unskilled workers, no lumpenproletariat.

Like London and many other English towns the city's population grew enormously in the eighteenth and nineteenth centuries from about 5,000 in 1701 to 45,000 in 1801 and 400,000 in 1901. Rows of back-to-back houses provided roofs over heads, but until the 1880s Sheffield remained a 'privy-ridden town', insanitary and prone to epidemics.

Such an environment, densely populated and grimly industrialized, was fertile ground for Methodist preachers. Uniquely among England's large towns and cities, in Sheffield the Nonconformists were in a majority of almost two to every member of the Church of England. The Methodist chapels alone had many more sittings than the Anglican churches. As a totally lapsed Methodist I noticed with interest that almost every Sheffielder I got to know in the 1970s seemed to have stemmed from Nonconformist stock and to have the sort of social concerns I recognized in my own family.

A community with such a preponderance of skilled workers and Nonconformists was a splendid nursery for trade unions and radical politics. Alan Cullen caught the knifegrinders' mood of discontent in his splendid play *The Stirrings in Sheffield* about local upheavals in the 1860s. When I went there a century later the Labour party had held the Town Hall for forty years with only the shortest break in the early 1930s. How they ruled was described by Roy Hattersley, former city councillor and future deputy leader of the Parliamentary Labour Party. 'We ran the city with fists of stainless steel, a metal no decent Sheffielder would cover with a velvet glove.' The party caucus ruled as it had in Leeds, but with one great difference. The Sheffield City Council was a remarkably fertile breeding ground for national politics. Hattersley himself and his contemporary Chris Price, a Junior Minister of Education, both achieved high office as did Home Secretary David Blunkett, an astonishingly on-the-ball and open-minded young councillor in those days, and Minister of Sport Roger Caborn; to add to these high fliers, at least half a dozen other Sheffield councillors among my own acquaintance became members of parliament.

Perhaps the most passionate political debates took place inside the Labour party. In 1967 Albert Ballard and his co-eval J.H. Bingham were the last survivors of the Labour Old Guard for whom the Council's grammar schools were the opportunity for able youngsters, however humble their origins, to fly as high as their abilities would take them. It was not so much a question of the Old Guard being converted to another opinion as of their dying and being replaced by a new generation. By 1967 Sheffield new Labour, personified by such people as Chris Price, Roy Hattersley and Peter Horton, had decided, following Tony Crosland's ministerial lead, that comprehensive schools would offer more opportunities to more children.

Price and Hattersley went off to Parliament, and Horton became Chairman of the Education Committee. Following much public debate and thorough discussions with the teachers whose representatives contributed much of the detailed preparatory work, the Committee agreed to replace the city's grammar, technical and modern schools with co-educational comprehensive schools. The Committee published its proposals and invited opponents to send their objections to the Secretary of State. He would decide Sheffield's future after considering any comments the Committee cared to make about these objections.

To its amazement Sheffield woke one day in May 1968 to find the Conservatives in charge at the Town Hall. Would they jettison the Labour proposals? No doubt there was much lobbying and much agonized debate inside the Conservative group. We officers liked to think that we persuaded the open-minded Oxbridge solicitor who now chaired the Education Committee that morale in the schools would be irretrievably damaged if the city changed course at this late stage. At some cost to his own career in local politics Chairman Peter Jackson managed to carry his group, and when I came to draft Sheffield's comments on the handful of objections perhaps the most convincing aspect of our case was that a Conservative administration was seeking to implement a Labour scheme which had the teachers' full support. In the event Labour returned to its inheritance a year later, in time to launch its new schools. Thirty-one co-educational comprehensive schools rose in 1969 from the ashes of fifty-four grammar, technical, secondary modern and comprehensive schools. Posts in the new schools were reserved for people displaced by the reorganization, but those appointed as heads, deputies, senior assistants and heads of department were now leading much larger groups of colleagues and caring for children of all abilities. They rose to the challenge, rethought their aims and methods, and sought further training. Like their colleagues in other parts of South Yorkshire Sheffield teachers were also more committed to developing their own school-based Mode 3 programmes for the Certificate of Secondary Education than teachers anywhere else in England. School staffrooms became animated centres of personal development, learning communities for all their members.

This was the first stage in building an innovatory system of schools. The Committee accepted the Plowden Report's view that on balance it was better for children to stay at their first school until they were eight, when almost all would be capable readers, and to stay at their middle schools until they were twelve when they were more likely to be mature enough to cope with secondary school pressures. As far as possible the city would create first and middle schools, but for some years some old-style infant and junior schools would exist alongside first and middle schools. This duality meant that Sheffield schools had to co-operate to ensure that children enjoyed the same curriculum and reached the same standard at whatever age they changed schools.

This kind of co-operation was facilitated by linking small groups of primary schools with each secondary school. The groups were planned with some care. Many consisted of the schools in one of the river valleys which radiate from the city centre like spokes in a wheel. This grouping ensured that the secondary schools drew pupils from both inner and outer city primary schools. Exceptionally the children from one or two inner city schools bussed past the nearest secondary school to balance the intake at a more distant suburban secondary school.

The Committee assumed that children would normally go on to the named secondary school at which they were all guaranteed places, but parents were free to choose any other secondary school. In practice about 85 or 90 per cent accepted the offered school, and almost all the rest obtained their first or second choice. Parents were well pleased, and in the linked schools primary and secondary teachers could plan their work together and do short job swaps to widen their experience. Since most secondary schools were linked with only two, three or at most four junior or middle schools, far closer relations developed than in areas like Inner London where free-for-all parental choice meant that some secondary schools recruited handfuls of children from each of more than thirty primary schools.

Enabling the primary schools to tackle their new tasks was more difficult. The Committee adopted new standards of accommodation, equipment and facilities for first and middle schools. Their teachers adopted aims appropriate to their new remit and re-examined their curricula and teaching methods. It was another striking example of how structural changes could stimulate new thinking and rejuvenate old hands.

The Committee managed also to tap an entirely new source of energy for their schools. Like their brothers in Leeds, Sheffield old Labour had kept their secondary schools on a tight leash with area boards of carefully chosen loyalists to govern groups of about half a dozen schools. And they managed their 200 primary schools directly without the help of any board of managers. Amazingly, in 1970 Chairman Peter Horton and Chief Education Officer Michael Harrison persuaded the Committee to discard these shackles. Henceforth each school was to have its own board of governors including parents, teachers and ancillary staff, representatives of industry and commerce, representatives of colleges, universities and neighbouring schools, a few council nominees and the head. Each school would have a group of critical friends to act as a sounding board for the head's ideas and represent the school's needs to the Education Committee. Their role was very different from that of the Victorian school managers whose tasks had included the daily inspection, enquiries into absenteeism, the inspection of registers and the enforcement of cleanliness and tidiness. 'Such managers', said retired HMI Blakiston, 'would no more leave everything to teachers than would the colonel of the regiment leave all to the adjutants and subalterns.' Even in Sheffield in the 1970s there were still a few governors who had to be steered away from inspecting lessons and checking registers.

To show the Education Department's commitment to the new governing bodies we arranged for about fifty or sixty officers and inspectors to clerk the meetings, ensured that they were well briefed for their meetings, prepared papers on current issues for the governors to discuss, and guaranteed that there would be replies at their next meeting to any queries a governing body raised. To make sure the system worked I myself became clerk to the governors of three or four schools. The Committee shared this commitment and agreed that a significant part of the funds at their disposal would be spent on improvements requested by governing bodies.

These changes seemed to involve a huge transfer of power from the centre. They certainly empowered governing bodies and their members; but they also empowered the Committee who knew much more now about the schools' needs and wishes, and whose decisions acquired thereby a new kind of validity. Some heads were apprehensive about having to share power with staff and parents but they soon recognized that they were under less pressure and that their school's case had more weight when a body of governors took the strain. Most important of all these changes created a small army of informed lay people with a commitment to the schools.

Many of the new governors joined the National Association of Governors and Managers, whose indefatigably zealous national secretary happened to live in Sheffield. When at the annual Sheffield Show I shared the education desk with Barbara Bullivant her omniscience left me feeling woefully inadequate. She contrived to be both a pillar of support and a spur. The NAGM presence locally was a real help in our new venture, providing information, support and opportunities for governors to meet each other and exchange views. Barbara was too a regular contributor to the governors' training courses which the Education Department ran jointly in the teachers' centre with Bill Hampton and Bill Bacon of Sheffield University's Extra-Mural Department. In each course Peter Horton would take a session, and I would take a session or two to describe the Education Department and what we hoped of the new governing bodies.

The *Sheffield Morning Telegraph* and the *Sheffield Evening Star* also helped to create a well-informed public. Later on when I got to know most of the national education press corps I often wondered why Robert Bennett of the *Telegraph* and Bob Poulton of the *Star* were not among them. Each took an informed and sympathetic interest and ensured that their papers discussed national issues as well as reporting local developments fully. For a short time the *Telegraph* even published a separate weekly education supplement, surely the only local newspaper ever to have done this. Its existence strengthened still further the depth of mutual understanding between press, teachers, governors, students, committee and department.

There was of course no question of there being an Education Party with a written constitution or a list of members. But when the service was threatened everyone knew what to do. Half-way through the 1974–75 financial year the City Treasurer reported that the unexpectedly high level of pay awards and interest rates meant that the city was heading for a deficit of some £3 million. This led the Council's Budget Sub-Committee to impose on 16 October an immediate embargo on all staff appointments and promotions and all advertisements for staff. A Special Sub-Committee was appointed to consider submissions from chief officers outlining the case for filling particular posts and the consequence of leaving a post vacant. By this time the Branch Heads had already let me know that an embargo would lead to our having some 300 vacancies by Christmas in a work force of about 18,600, and the *Sheffield Telegraph* reported that the teachers' associations were prepared to resist an embargo. On 18 October I wrote to every school, college, institution and department outlining the Budget Committee's decision, saying I believed a good case could be made for filling every post already established in the education service, and enclosing a one-side form, most of which provided space for the consequences of leaving the post vacant. I asked the recipients to complete and return these forms immediately so that the best possible case could be submitted to the Special Sub-Committee without delay.

We swamped the Special Sub-Committee with 235 submissions in three weeks. We promised more than 4,000 submissions in a full year, with two or three seasonal peaks. The first batch of submissions showed that some children would not be able to start school after Christmas if seven infant teachers were not replaced and staff would not be paid if two pay clerks were not replaced. If an escort was not replaced children with special needs would not be able to go to school. If a housemother was not replaced incontinent children would go unwashed. If home tutors were not replaced children who could not go to school for medical reasons would not be taught at all. If the head teacher of a large comprehensive school and heads of department at other schools were not replaced external examination courses would be jeopardized. If college lecturers were not replaced vocational classes would be cancelled and when some were cancelled students wrote passionate letters to members of the Education Committee. Members of the Education Committee fought their own corner in the Labour Group. Governors protested, and the teachers undertook their own survey of forthcoming problems in primary schools. The teachers decided not to cover the work of any absent mid-day supervisor and not to cover the work of a hospitalized and a sick colleague, decisions which would almost certainly mean sending children home. The potential effect on working mums was perhaps the last straw for the council's leaders. On 12 November the Special Sub-Committee lifted the embargo on filling posts in schools and other educational institutions. What Professor Harry Armitage liked to call the Sheffield education mafia had demonstrated, rather like the French Resistance in the 1940s or the Shia Imams in post-war Iraq, a remarkable talent for undercover action. By a curious irony, on the day this local campaign ended the government announced that all local authorities were to be asked to cut staff.

CHAPTER 11

Towards Equality

Liberty to the captives, and the opening of the prison to them that are bound

THE PRESS HAD many more encouraging things to report. As the law stood until 1970 the Education Committee had at almost every meeting to make one decision they found wholly repugnant, certifying that a child with severe learning difficulties was 'ineducable'. They were delighted when a change in the law transferred responsibility for these children from health to education authorities.

They were dismayed when they heard that an eleven year old pupil at one of their special schools was to be sterilized. The girl suffered from Soto's syndrome, better known as cerebral gigantism. The symptoms of this rare genetic disorder include unusually large hands, feet and head, clumsiness, and delayed physical and social development. The girl and her family were well known to social workers, teachers and educational psychologists, and councillors were as angry and affronted that their professional staff had not been consulted as they were horrified by the proposal to sterilize so young a girl on the authority of just one paediatrician. 'We dispute the view that the consultant is God,' said their spokesperson. In most respects, however, relationships between education and health services became increasingly close and fruitful.

The Committee were increasingly uneasy with the way in which children with special needs were segregated. As a great metropolitan centre Sheffield had a wide range of schools for children with special needs, including schools for children with impaired sight and hearing and uniquely a school for children with spina bifida. As a result of Bob Zachary's innovatory surgery at the Children's Hospital many more children with spina bifida and hydrocephalus survived in the Sheffield area than anywhere else, a situation to which the Committee responded readily by building a specially designed school. Our appreciation of the social and moral issues was much extended by the passionate debate between surgeon Zachary and physician Dr John Lorber who thought many of the children could expect so poor a quality of life that it was unkind to operate and save their lives. We enthused quietly when Zachary's more optimistic views prevailed.

We were also delighted later to have a supporting part in a cradle-to-grave review of the city's services for people with mental health problems. Funded by Whitehall's Department of Health the review covered health services, social

119

services, housing, recreation and education. Sheffield had been chosen apparently because of the wealth of resources it already had in a compact urban area. We in education were directly involved through our schools for children with severe learning difficulties and children with emotional and behavioural difficulties, our fairly inadequate provision for older college students with similar difficulties, and our limited contribution in old people's homes. We also employed the teachers in hospital schools, and made some contribution to the work of adolescent psychiatric units. I left Sheffield before the project ended and do not know how successful it was. In the short term, however, my involvement as our department's chief representative meant that I became much more aware of mental health and mental health services, got to know many people working in the other services, and explored with them the scope for closer collaboration.

Most of Sheffield's special schools were small and could not easily provide a challenging programme for all their pupils, some of whom were very gifted. In 1972 the Committee asked Ted Mullin, the Head of Mossbrook School for Children with Spina Bifida, Leslie Frost, the Adviser for Special Education, and me to visit Sweden to study both the arrangements for educating children with special needs and their upper secondary schools for students over 16. We found much that was strange. The schools even had street numbers like any ordinary house. The public could get their cars maintained or their hair cut at normal rates by walking into the colleges which taught those skills. I met teenage building trades students who had built their own college premises as part of their practical training and were now building one or two houses for sale. A girl with spina bifida had a personal attendant who accompanied her from when she left home until she returned in the afternoon. I chatted in English with a ten year old with learning difficulties and with an eighteen year old who had no hearing at all. Some things seemed to work better in Sweden.

The ruling Social Democratic Party had recently adopted the Alva Myrdal report *Towards Equality* which argued powerfully that 'integration into ordinary schools is important if we are to break down the isolation of the handicapped and promote their active participation in the community at large'. We found many children with special needs in mainstream schools, sharing the facilities, mixing with other children in their free time, and sometimes being taught in mainstream classes. Integration was also helpful because it increased the other pupils' awareness and understanding of special needs, and because the specialist teachers were members of a larger community concerned with children of all abilities. In writing our report I quoted the Alva Myrdal Report extensively because it seemed to capture the largely unformed sentiments of Sheffield's ruling Labour Group. Either Myrdal's overarching philosophy or the examples we had seen were sufficiently encouraging for the Committee to decide in 1973 to move towards the integration of children with special needs. Like some of the Committee's other major decisions this one prompted city-wide discussion: of educational aims, the limits if any to integration and the action needed to effect integration.

Similarly wide-ranging debates arose from the decision to develop some of the larger comprehensive secondary schools as community campuses, the urban variant of Henry Morris's Cambridgeshire Village Colleges. The intention was to add accommodation and facilities to enable each campus to house a youth club, an adult education centre, and various other community activities such as public use of a swimming pool, sports hall and refreshment facilities. To play a full part in its local community a campus had to be open in the evenings and at weekends almost every day of the year. The campuses were new animals, and we had to start from scratch working out what sort of arrangements to make for security, housekeeping, cleaning, catering, administration and year-round management. Once we saw the need for year-round cover we readily agreed to the head of campus and his senior colleagues working flexibly and taking their holidays at any time which suited them and the campus, but it was the Council's Personnel Committee which dealt with all the ancillary staff and determined their staffing levels, conditions of service and wage rates. Working through Personnel Officers Roy Aitken and John Boothroyd to secure the Personnel Committee's approval was no cakewalk. But we could always hope for piecemeal gains, and we tended to edge inch by inch towards the ideal solution.

Reconciling the conflicting needs and values of the various campus users might have been difficult. In many localities the heads of schools were at loggerheads with the youth clubs and adult classes whom they regarded as lodgers in their school To avoid this kind of conflict, the Education Committee decided that each campus was to have a single governing body responsible for promoting every aspect of the campus's work and a single principal with a management team including senior teachers and the appropriate youth workers, adult leaders and sports centre managers. Underpinning this structure was another consultative system. The Education Committee required each of their schools to say what arrangements they had for consulting staff and identifying the school's priorities before the schools decided how to spend the funds they had for books and materials, furniture, repairs and minor building works.

This insistence on consultation was very much in line with the Education Committee's own practice. In the 1960s and early 1970s the Committee itself consisted of twenty-eight councillors and twelve non-council members including three teachers representing their unions. From time to time the Committee Chairman and other councillors would also meet teacher representatives in their Joint Consultative Committee. These arrangements were not so very different from those in many other towns and cities. What was different was the Joint Committee of Sheffield Teachers, a superbly organized and well-led body which achieved locally what the teacher unions nationally have not achieved thirty years later. On most issues the Joint Committee spoke as one and the Education Committee were happy to deal with a group who could always deliver what they promised. The Joint Committee's effective leader and chairman was Dennis Spooner, a man with many hats. Whenever he spoke in the Education Committee Dennis was always entertainingly meticulous in explaining which Spooner was speaking, the NUT Secretary, the Chairman of the Joint Committee or the Head of Beaver Hill. He and his fellow union secretaries had already undertaken much of the detailed preparatory work for comprehensive reorganization, and they were happy to go on doing this kind of work, not least because it meant they were very well informed about a whole range of matters like staffing, accommodation and catchment areas. Oddly enough the secretaries of all the unions were heads; perhaps they were more easily spared from their schools than assistants would have been. I used to meet them informally for a couple of hours or so every month, and we were able to resolve almost all the minor issues affecting their members as well as airing some of the bigger policy issues which were coming up. I used to enjoy especially my exchanges with big Bill Hill, Joint Four representative and Head of Myers Grove, Sheffield's first purpose-built comprehensive school. 'I'm the captain of the ship,' he declared whenever he felt the divine right of heads to run their schools was threatened. 'Yes, indeed,' I would reply, 'but you are not some freebooter on the Spanish main. Your ship is one of a fleet in convoy. We may not all be sailing at the same speed or even in the same direction at any one time, but we are all heading for the same port.' And then I would add, *sotto voce*, 'You may be captain of the ship, but the admiral commands the fleet.'

Our admiral-navigator was in every sense a big man, a scholar who read Greats at Oxford, a mountaineer and wartime para, determined, loyal and visionary, a man for big challenges whether it was building a huge containing wall in his garden or laying the foundations of a mass education system in Sheffield. A bon viveur and genial conversationalist with family, friends and casual acquaintances, at work Michael Harrison could seem remote, grappling with the major changes in our education service and trying to interpret the social, technological and economic forces shaping our society. He was active in national affairs as adviser to the local authorities' associations, leading member of his own professional association and member of various government enquiries like Dainton on the supply of students of science and technology and Taylor on school government. These wide-ranging contacts ensured that Sheffield was involved in many national initiatives. 'It doesn't matter what educational development you think of,' observed one surprised HMI, 'Sheffield is doing something.' Michael's mission as Sheffield's Education Officer was to create an education system which supported a prosperous, caring and mutually supportive community by developing the personal qualities needed by its citizens and the skills needed by local employers. In this he was at one with Peter Horton and the ruling Labour Party. They wanted an inclusive system in which people of all ages and all kinds of ability had the greatest possible opportunity for personal growth. Michael and Peter shared a faith in teachers; it was our job to create the systems and provide the resources which enabled teachers to do what they alone were able to do, to provide high-quality education for their pupils.

Peter Horton was a most attractive politician: friendly, modest, patient, and entirely without personal ambition. His persistent enthusiasm could be draining and his fertile imagination knew no bounds: like the White Queen he had the ability to believe half a dozen impossible things before breakfast. He would come in early and try these out on any officer who happened to be there, so by the time he reached Michael or me he might have several different off-the-cuff opinions to draw on. He was so boyishly keen one could never be cross for long. And in any case we knew that within the Labour Group he was the most tireless advocate education could possibly have.

Working with these two men was enormous fun and constantly challenging. My role as Michael's deputy was never defined formally by any job description. From time to time he would say that the job of Chief Education Officer was far too big for one person, implying that I was somehow part of the chief officership. His own involvement in national affairs, liaison with Sheffield University, liaison with leading local industrialists and membership of the Sheffield Chief Officers Group, COG, kept him busy enough. The assistant education officers were fully occupied with managing their own domains. I alone was free of other entanglements, as Michael intended, so I had the good fortune to spend much of my time on such major innovations as comprehensive schools, first and middle schools, new-style governing bodies, community campuses, extending the capacity of mainstream schools to provide for children with special needs, and helping to negotiate the mergers whose outcome was Sheffield Polytechnic.

CHAPTER 12

Scalpel or Axe?

Getting things done

IN ALL THIS FERMENT we did not neglect the Education Department itself. Michael had been deputy for long enough before his promotion to conclude there was an urgent need to revitalize the Department. This was to be my key task, and by way of equipping me for this enterprise Michael sent me off to Birmingham University for a senior management course at the Institute of Local Government Studies. We lived, since Birmingham is the home of Quaker chocolate, in a temperance hotel not far from the Institute, and enjoyed watching the students' mass protest meetings in '68, an experience which proved of absolutely no value at all a few months later when students occupied our own offices in Sheffield for ten days or so and posted pickets which most of my colleagues, trade unionists all at the behest of the City Council, were unwilling to cross. That was irritating, but to me the creepiest aspect of the whole affair was the extent to which the police had evidently infiltrated students' organizations across the country.

Since Birmingham might be my last opportunity for intensive reading I immersed myself in Urwick, Taylor, Elton Mayo, Eliot Jacques, Maslow, Stafford Beer, Simon, Likert, McGregor, Vickers and a host of other managerial wizards. After this baptism at least for a while I had some idea what people were talking about when they mentioned such esoteric topics as organization trees, spans of control, the Hawthorne effect, hierarchies of need, systems thinking or Theory X and Theory Y. Perhaps the most illuminating was Alfred Sloane, the prime architect of General Motors. The dilemma he posed was the constant tension between the drive for uniform standards throughout an organization and the need to leave room for creative initiatives.

Time would show whether this was any help in running an Education Department. It was not the City Council's only venture into modern management. Urwick Orr had advised them to bring their departments together under group chief officers, each with a senior administrative officer to overhaul the group's administrative systems. Michael Harrison was to head a group which included Art Galleries, Libraries and Museums as well as Education. Fred Cooper from Esso's Fawley Refinery was to be the Group Administrative Officer. Urwick Orr had laid and the Conservatives hatched this scheme, so when Labour returned to power in 1969 they reversed the process immediately. But they were too late to stop Michael enjoying a Group

Chief Officer's salary, and too late to stop Fred Cooper starting work with no group to overhaul, only a more restricted role in Sheffield's Education Department.

In other respects George Wilson, the stalinist figure who emerged as Labour's Leader, proved to have a decidedly centralist view of Council business. He espoused the newly fashionable doctrine of corporate management if only because it seemed a means of cutting education down to size. The city's education budget far exceeded that of any other council service, and its Education Committee and their Chief Officer had an autonomous life enshrined in law which no other committee enjoyed. The Councillors, who resented this state of affairs, happily replaced their old-style Town Clerk with a more pliant Chief Executive, 'Podders' as Ian Podmore was known outside the Town Hall, a timid young solicitor wafted on a favouring breeze to an uneasy throne. In the name of corporate management George Wilson and 'Podders' tried to extend the remit of the council's Policy Committee, ignoring the terms of reference which allowed the Education Committee to exercise all the council's education functions except levying a rate. Michael Harrison was one of many education officers to challenge this kind of 'creeping illegality' as it became prevalent among local authorities in the 1970s. From time to time I also found myself at odds with 'Podders'. He seemed to expect me to discipline head teachers who publicly questioned the council's policies, and to dismiss detached youth workers who marched with their young people in protest against the council's cuts. We in the education service happily accepted degrees of open debate which he found positively disloyal.

Like all the most successful consultants Urwick Orr understood that their first report was just a toe-hold. They thought further more detailed work in one department would be highly advantageous. We cheerfully volunteered to be the guinea pigs, and with that and further increasingly microscopic studies of particular aspects of our work, over the following years I came to know partner Ralph Bullock and senior consultant Jo Perrigo very well.

Among their early suggestions was the appointment of yet another senior officer, a chief adviser to lead the eight or ten education advisers who had previously worked most closely with the two assistant education officers for primary and secondary education. Adding this new chief adviser as well as the group administrative officer to the existing management group of five, chief, deputy and three assistants, was almost more than we could swallow. This catalyst prompted a radical review of our department's contribution to the education service.

This contribution seemed to have three distinct elements: advising the Education Committee and helping to shape its policy, providing administrative support for Committee and its schools and colleges, and running certain services for young people. The weight of day-to-day business meant that the assistant education officers for primary, secondary and further education had neither time nor energy to think about the future of the education service and advise the Committee about the issues and the options facing them. We freed them by transferring responsibility for day-to-day matters to half a dozen very capable administrative officers, mostly people who had entered local government at sixteen years of age with school certificates as good as mine. They became the heads of new branches for staff, premises, supplies, awards and benefits, finance, and committee services, accountable to Fred Cooper for the quality of their section's work, and for managing its budget. We also ran various services for young people, services like Education Welfare, School Health, Educational Psychology and Careers. The various specialist officers in these services spent much of their time working in schools, as did some of our youth workers, and all our education advisers. We thought all these people might be more effective if they were based in specific schools for some of their time, working in multi-disciplinary teams led by education advisers, each team serving a secondary school and its contributory primary schools. We hoped also to harness their special skills and insights to enrich the schools' programmes of personal and social education and our own in-service training for teachers.

All the Principal Officers heading these services and all the branch heads, now designated Education Officers, became part of a larger management team when it came to matters like preparing development plans and annual estimates or making the cuts which became a regular feature of our lives. We had moved from a narrow pyramidical structure in which Primary, Secondary and Further Education Sections handled most of our work, to a broad matrix in which policy advisers, administrative officers and service principals all had better-defined and greater responsibilities. They seemed to grow visibly. Our matrix liberated and empowered a great many people. I heard only one gentle reproof. As branch head Arthur Hodge dolefully observed, 'It's people like you who make work for people like me to do.'

All this was happening alongside other changes prompted by Urwick Orr and Fred Cooper. Like many consultants our friends from Urwick Orr seemed to earn rather a lot by helping us to be clear about what we wanted to achieve and then endorsing what we believed to be necessary. The process had, however, two great benefits: it taught us to think more clearly about ends and means, and it gave our case for restructuring and strengthening the department sufficient weight to convince the council's Personnel and Policy Committees. We appointed Brian Wilcox as senior researcher to undertake local projects, monitor the work of the many other researchers who were active in our schools and colleges, and keep us and the Committee informed of other relevant research findings. Brian helped us to know our schools, and the schools to know themselves. His secondary school surveys showed the extent to which boys and girls followed different curricula, and the extent to which each school's curriculum depended on what accommodation, like the number and size of its laboratories, it happened to have. Bert Aizlewood's school served a deprived area with high numbers of free school meals, homes without bathrooms, and absent fathers. It was unlikely to appear in any premier league examination table. But the boys' attendance rates were high and teachers' absence rates and turnover were both low. When I had lunch with the Head and saw how warmly Bert mingled with staff and pupils whom he obviously liked and knew well, I thought I understood why morale was high.

We also recruited a management accountant, Cliff Loveday, from a down-sizing Sheffield manufacturer to instil a new rigour into our financial appraisal of any projected scheme. Fred Cooper's influence was even more pervasive. He joined us after thirty years in industry in various private companies, ending with Esso Petroleum where safety and manager-training had been among his special interests. He could be refreshingly down to earth. 'You don't use a scalpel when an axe will do,' was his favourite maxim. He had no time for what was known in Esso-speak as AFD, the interminable 'arse-flattening discussion' to which he found many of us educationists addicted. What he taught was the Systematic Approach. What are you trying to achieve? Why do you want to do this? What information do you need? And then WHTBreaD, not a well-known pale ale but What Has To Be Done? Who will do it? When will it be done? And how will you know it's been done?

Much depended on being able to find the requisite information when you needed it. We scrapped our central filing systems and asked the branches which generated data to store it so that any proper person could get at it easily. We made sure that the information we sent to schools was easy to read, easy to file and easy to use. Each year we published a booklet of statistical information about the education service. Brian Wilcox and his colleague Peter Eustace devised a way of summarizing each secondary school's complex timetable on one side of A4 paper. We distributed the statistical booklets and the timetable summaries widely so that we all, officers, advisers, teachers, governors, committee members and parents shared some basic information when we discussed matters such as staffing, accommodation, equipment and funding.

The Systematic Approach lay at the heart of Ralph Coverdale's approach to developing managers. Fred was so highly esteemed as a trainer that Coverdale asked us to release him two or three times a year to work on their courses for Esso managers. We were happy for Fred to hone his own skills in this way, even happier when we found that in return Esso would allow us to take any late vacancies at no cost to us. It was not always easy at a few hours' notice to find someone who could leave home and desk for a week but we set up an early-warning system to let people know when their number might come up, and when about fifteen senior people had enjoyed a week of Coverdale problem-solving and team-building we took a block booking for another twenty. This shared experience led increasingly to a shared approach to getting things done.

It also helped us to cut a path through a jungle of management theory. The early 1970s were the golden age of Management by Objectives, Planning Programming and Budgeting Systems, Cost Benefit, Critical Path and a host of other analytic systems. Coverdale and Fred Cooper helped to keep our feet on the ground while our heads stayed in the air. 'Never impose objectives,' Fred told us, a common-sense rule which had not reached Whitehall thirty years later. 'Never ask "do you understand?" but "what do you understand?"' We looked constantly for short-term markers by which to measure our progress towards the ultimate personal and social goals to which we hoped an education service might contribute. But the debates were long and sometimes fraught. Week after week Brian Hanson, the Assistant Education Officer for Further and Higher Education, still overworked and overwrought despite our changes, would declare after half an hour or so as he gathered his papers to rush to his next meeting, 'Either we have objectives, or I keep my desk cleared.'

He should have taken a leaf from our colleague Wallace Holland's book. A large man of scholarly tastes and gentlemanly disposition, Wallace would have seemed more at home in a shire county than an industrial city. But he had a wonderfully effective way of seeming to complete the business of the day on the day. When he left for home in the evening his desk was always clear. Not that he had dealt with the growing piles of matters he had to deal with, but his secretary's nightly task was to hide the files in cupboards. Her first task the next morning was to take them out again and build round three sides of his enormous desk a tall rampart behind which Wallace could shelter, secure in the clear evidence they gave to all and sundry that he had an enormous amount of work to do. Wallace sat patiently through our long debates and seemed very happy when the time came for him to retire early.

Objectives, structure and training: we had fashioned the components and began now to assemble them. The department began to feel like a majestic cathedral organ ready to be played, with due regard for a few dodgy pipes and stops, like the adviser who on Friday afternoons always visited the same schools far away on the city's southern border half-way to her home in Lincolnshire, and the Chief Education Social Work Officer who still saw himself as a school bobby and reckoned that as 'kid catchers' all his team needed were height and speed. The hum of debate and the buzz of purposeful activity filled every corner of the building. I was never more pleased than when a young trainee observed that he had learned more in one year with us than he had in three at Oxford.

CHAPTER 13

Playtime

All work and no play?

S OME OF OUR innovations excited a good deal of interest outside Sheffield. We were one of a leading pack when it came to setting up comprehensive schools, changing the age of transfer and developing community campuses. But in reforming school-governing bodies, restructuring the department and setting out to mainstream some children with special needs we were pioneers. Michael was justly proud of what the Sheffield education service had achieved and wanted it to be well publicized. We in the Education Department were key players whenever the city fielded a team to woo new businesses to Sheffield. Imperceptibly I slipped into public relations, encouraged to speak freely to the media, to write for professional journals, and to speak at seminars and conferences. I worked closely with Len Watson, John Davies and David Falcon of the Education Management team at Sheffield Polytechnic and was active in BEMAS, the British Education Management and Administration Society. By the mid 1970s writing reviews and little essays for publication was becoming a fairly serious hobby. The sell-on rate was the best test, and as long as the journal *Education* kept on sending review copies and the Chartered Institute of Public Finance and Accountancy kept on asking me to write the education chapter for *Local Government Trends*, their annual review of local government services, I was happy to go on scribbling. Then Michael put me in the way of a bigger assignment. He himself had neither time nor inclination to write the education volume in a series about managing the public services which Pitman had in mind but he thought I might be interested. Fortunately we had just moved into a rather grand Edwardian house and for the next two or three years I was able to dedicate the floor of one large room to my little piles of papers while I beavered away at this new project. A quarter of a century later there are still a few people out there prepared to pay for the privilege of photocopying odd pages of a book about the management of education which says there really wasn't any.

Like many such books it drew heavily on my past reading and previous articles or talks so there was no great need for further research or new reading. This was just as well as I embarked on various other playtime activities at about the same time. People like John Taylor from Leeds and Michael saw to it that the Yorkshire branch of our professional association was well supported. I was an assiduous and vocal member, and was rewarded by election as branch

A constellation of education officers, Michael Harrison, Bob Aitken, John Mann.

chairman and national executive member. Based in steel city, I must have seemed the right person to represent the association on the Iron and Steel Industry Industrial Training Board, a role which neatly complemented my membership of the British Institute of Management's Sheffield and District Committee who were anxious to promote links between industry and education. A Sheffield Polytechnic team studied school leavers' perceptions and attitudes to school and work. We in the Education Department worked closely with the city's burgeoning industrial museums to develop resources for schools and to devise local syllabuses and examinations which emphasized the geographical and historical factors which accounted for the city's industrial development. With people from industry and our technical colleges we tried to identify the maths, science and technical know-how needed by employees in the city's dominant industries.

In our efforts to foster links I visited a number of local firms and was surprised how small they were, how often those with household names had no more than 200 or 300 workers at each of their factories. When they gave me a pruning saw, a blade, at one factory I remembered just in time to hand over a silver coin in return. Failure to observe this immemorial Sheffield custom can only bring bad luck. In human terms these factories were smaller than most of our primary schools and completely dwarfed by our big secondary schools with up to twelve or fourteen hundred pupils and well over a hundred adults. Schools and companies partnered each other, and some pupils even set up their own school-based businesses. At one school a limited company with 64 ordinary and 54 deferred shares had assets which included rabbits, guinea pigs, hamsters and mice. In eighteen months the company paid a 40 per cent dividend. No wonder the shares sold at a premium. Our active concern about coupling education and employment led to Sheffield's selection along with Inner London as the two English participants in a major European Community study of the transition from school to working life. As a city we applied for Manpower Services Commission grants to match council funding for local projects, and I marvelled at the contrast between our laborious and time-consuming way of securing approval through a hierarchy of committees and the assured decisiveness of two young MSC officials who could deliver £50,000 on the spot.

Michael also suggested that I might become a Governor of Welbeck, the army's sixth form college, housed from its inception some twenty years earlier in part of Welbeck Abbey, the Duke of Portland's family seat. It was still an impressive pile, with an underground railway built, it was said, to transport meals from the kitchens, a hall which doubled as a sports hall though still festooned with battered family portraits, and the great ballroom with its three different kinds of furnishing, one for the annual party for people on the estate, one for county folk, and one for the rare occasions when royalty was present.

Welbeck Abbey is about a couple of miles from Worksop, the Abbey and the college buildings about a mile from the road. The site seems to have been chosen in the same spirit as those of many of the old teacher training colleges, remote from urban distractions and temptations. Arriving there must have been a shock to any city lad. The college recruited boys of sixteen and gave them a tough A-level course in which maths and physics were the core. The aim was to develop young men who would go on to become officers in the army's technical regiments. There was a dearth of good candidates from the North of England and the governors hoped that co-opting a local authority officer from the north would help them to market the college more successfully. Sheffield was near at hand, and Michael Maloney, the Head-master, had been a contemporary of mine at Trinity, a cheerful, gangling and somewhat dishevelled chemist. The governing body consisted of major generals (Dad would have been amused to see his son consorting on equal terms with such grand personages as Henry Wood, another Trinity man and grandson of a former college President, and Pat Cordingley, whose book *In the Eye of the Storm* is the definitive account of the Gulf War), without exception energetic, vigorous, capable men, perplexed by Welbeck's inability to produce enough young men with officer-like qualities. They sometimes wondered aloud in Michael Maloney's presence whether things would improve if Welbeck, like the Duke of York's School at Dover, had a serving officer as head. I had little to offer on that issue and no penetrating insights to help them recruit young men of sixteen from Leeds or Manchester with the X factor they were looking for even though much of my day job consisted of trying to find people with the equally elusive qualities which make a good teacher, a good head or a good education officer. But I had to marvel at Welbeck's success in its secondary objective. Many of the entrants had only moderate O-levels but their A-level results were phenomenal. Like no other school or college I've seen or heard of, Welbeck's staff and pupils had only one career in mind. It was Sandhurst first for all who completed their Welbeck course with reasonable success, and then a degree at the Royal Military College of Science at Shrivenham or even at Cambridge for those who did well. I could not help contrasting Welbeck's success in hitting its limited target with the problems of a comprehensive school trying to accommodate the diffuse and individual aspirations of all its pupils. Comprehensive schools certainly had problems but I was shocked to the core to hear Junior Minister Trefgarne talk openly at a Welbeck Governors' meeting of 'the failure of the country's secondary schools' as if that was received wisdom in government circles.

In another role I was brought face to face with another kind of failure. I became a magistrate, a Justice of the Peace, a beak. I had always had some regrets that there was no one about when I graduated to tell me how to become a lawyer and when the Sheffield Bench advertised I applied and was accepted, perhaps in part because I was a trade union member and this allowed the Bench to claim a wider social mix. The Clerk of the Court, John Richman, was pioneering training for magistrates, and we had an interesting programme of lectures by academics from Sheffield University's Law Department, and visits to different kinds of penal institution such as Strangeways Prison, Lowdham Grange Borstal, and some of the institutions euphemistically and ponderously entitled 'community homes with education on the premises'. Some of these homes were quite small and lacked resources to meet the differing needs of youngsters of widely varying ages and attainments whose individual dates of arrival and departure were determined by the courts. Their few dedicated teachers were sadly out of touch with the new syllabuses and lively teaching to be found in mainstream schools. The least I could do was to offer access to our teachers' centre and its enormous range of in-service courses, occasional help from our team of specialist advisers, and perhaps some links with a nearby comprehensive school. If only my department could have assumed responsibility for educating these troubled young people.

The work of the courts is wholly absorbing but I soon began to have some reservations about their role. In the Juvenile Court I found myself sitting with retired tycoons and the wives of Master Cutlers, and could not help wondering about our ability to empathize with the young defendants above whom we sat in judgement. Coming from a working world in which problems were resolved by consultation and negotiated compromise I was disconcerted to find that victory and defeat were the usual outcome of the courtroom's adversarial procedures. A finding of 'six of one, and half a dozen of the other' was not a verdict we could reach in a domestic dispute. Nor could we arrange for someone to give advice to a small-scale shoplifter with half a dozen overdrawn accounts and a household budget made up partly of alimony in and alimony out. My own financial affairs were simple by comparison, and they were taxing enough. It was no wonder the people who came before us got into difficulties; many seemed more weak than wicked.

There were opportunities too for travel further afield. Early in 1974 Margaret and I joined about a thousand youngsters from Leeds and Sheffield for a Mediterranean cruise on SS *Nevasa*. David Fyfe, the cheerful burly entrepreneur *manqué* who headed Ashleigh School, had briefed the accompanying teachers meticulously. The youngsters were well prepared and well disciplined. For some the highlight was seeing Gracie Fields on Capri, for others it may have been the ruins of Pompeii, a distant view of Mt Etna, the pyjama-clad urchins who swamped the Alexandrian quayside, the Pyramids, Israeli orange groves, the Church of the Nativity, the Parthenon, or St Mark's Square in Venice. The ship's Headmaster, a Richard Dimbleby look-a-like named Richard Harris, enthused us three times a day with presentations which outshone Henry V at Agincourt, Winston Churchill and Richard Dimbleby himself on any state occasion. Robert Bennett's wonderfully perceptive daily bulletins in the *Sheffield Telegraph* kept our own children and the rest of Sheffield informed about our progress. For me perhaps the most immediate benefit was the opportunity of getting to know twenty or thirty of my teacher colleagues a great deal better. Or was it perhaps the moment of truth when I decided against accepting a villainous sheikh's offer of fifty camels in exchange for Margaret?

Despite the financial stringencies of the mid 1970s, in 1975 the council generously agreed to give me £350 to cover the cost of an exchange visit to the USA with other education officers. First a few days' briefing in New York and Washington where we found that a VIP visit to the White House takes place at 7.30 a.m., an unseasonable hour but it does avoid the crowds. After that I was to be hosted by school board officials in two districts and would have opportunities of following up my developing interests in special and vocational education. Earl Grey tea and Scotch shortbread would be highly acceptable gifts, the British Council told us, but we found that both were readily available in every shopping mall.

My hosts could not have been more attentive. From Allegheny County Jim and Vera Jordan took me to the University of Pittsburgh's 42-storey Cathedral of Learning and to Frank Lloyd Wright's Fallingwater, the extraordinary Kaufmann house cantilevered over a waterfall. In Grand Rapids Harvey Ribbens took me to the Dutch Reform Church and said grace before every meal while his wife Netta and grown-up children listened demurely. Harvey had devised a full programme of visits. While I explored resource centres, skills centres and the like, Harvey combined his normal work with training sessions for the marathon he planned to run. Soon after my return to England he ran off with his comely secretary. In Grand Rapids and in Pittsburgh, though not to the same degree as in trend-setting Massachusetts, children with special needs were rather more likely than in England to have the support they needed at mainstream schools. In both areas local employers helped to decide the content of vocational courses and took part in the students' end-of-course assessment. Employability in the local labour market was the main criterion. Both the penal institutions for young people and the special units for drop-outs and disruptives had resources for vocational education to match those in the best-equipped English college. The aim was to equip these young men and women with marketable skills. The worlds of work and education seemed closer in US than in UK.

There was too a sense of purpose in their administrative systems which seemed lacking in ours. The elected school boards were single-purpose authorities with only a handful of members. When a new school was needed the board members and their superintendent campaigned together for electoral support for a tax hike to meet the cost of a loan. There was a refreshing immediacy about all this which contrasted sharply with the complexity of English multi-purpose and corporately managed local authorities. In the areas I visited the school boards certainly had to liaise with similar intermediate boards with responsibilities over a wider geographical area for matters such as in-service training and special and vocational education. Free to decide their own pay scales, they also employed their own negotiators who spent a great deal of time and energy finding our what their neighbours were paying. And every board discussion was overshadowed by the possibility of court action; 'what the judge might say' was a constant preoccupation. But I came away with a strong impression that the Americans had managed to create relatively simple structures in which people of modest ability could perform rather well whereas our structures were too complex for even the most talented people to do well. Since then successive UK governments seem merely to exacerbate the problem. My most abiding memory was however the banner headline about a Chicago school district, 'Gary teachers Pack Guns.'

The council's decision to support my trip to the States caused a minor political storm. Some said it was a gross extravagance, though a hundred years before their predecessors had sent the School Board secretary J.F. Moss to Germany where he had been mightily impressed. He thought the Prussian system 'by its cleanliness might well excite the admiration of the world'. Any guilt I might have felt was assuaged by calculating how soon the cost would be recouped if it helped me to make an almost imperceptible improvement in the city's £50 million a year education service. Luckily my growing taste for foreign travel was also indulged by other sponsors. I was one of a UK party who went to Holland to a conference of Dutch educators to compare our comprehensive schools with the Dutch system, with its Protestant, Catholic and municipal sub-systems, its multiplicity of small specialist trade schools, and its cross-over points between vocational and academic lines. In the United States too people often seemed to have dual qualifications and very often two careers, in for example teaching and social work or law and medicine. At that time this kind of movement from one track to another was almost impossible in England, where increasing specialization made it hard for anyone to change track at any stage. As the old limerick says:

> There was a young man who said 'Damn!
> It's borne in on me I am
> Just a creature that moves
> In predeterminate grooves,
> Not even a bus, but a tram.

Another visit arranged in conjunction with the Nordic Council and the Danish Ministry challenged other preconceptions. With a total population about half that of England, each of the five Nordic countries runs a viable education service, managed at local level by districts of from ten to thirty thousand people. All five countries favour small, unstreamed comprehensive schools for pupils up to sixteen years old. Schools like this are thought to foster personal and social growth. Small is certainly beautiful in Scandinavia.

Norway and Denmark were following Sweden's example in setting up integrated upper secondary schools, each providing a selection of the numerous academic and vocational courses available for young people over sixteen. They seemed to work well. Our visits to Danish vocational schools were specially memorable for the coffee, croissants and schnappes which welcomed us at every school when we arrived at 8.00 or 8.30 a.m. It's a good way to start the working day. Our excursion to Malmo was also memorable, partly because it was my first experience of a hovercraft, but more because the Swedish Director of Education proudly described his active role in the Social Democrat Party. To combine public service and political activism in this way was a novel concept to someone brought up in the English tradition of apolitical public servants. It was one we soon had to grow used to in Sheffield when one of our departmental colleagues, Leslie Frost, was elected to the South Yorkshire County Council. 'You'll know the circles I move in these days,' he foolishly observed while pressing his case for regrading. It did him no more good with his new comrades than it did with us. But he was on stronger ground in complaining when the chief adviser inadvertently referred to him as a 'dogsbody'.

Like many other young couples Margaret and I spent some of our spare time looking at other houses. We thought it was time to put more of our money into property. With neighbours Joan and Roy we inspected one or two dilapidated country houses and wondered how we could turn them into two equally handsome family houses. Margaret and I began to explore Nether

Edge, an area of large Edwardian mansions which seemed to offer a lot of space at a good price. We bought 38 Kingfield Road at an agreeably modest price from a bank after its previous owner, accountant Geoffrey Close, set off hastily for Baghdad leaving debts of over £1M. Number 38 stood on a half-acre site, well back, sheltered from the road by a bank of rhododendron, facing sideways towards its own tennis lawn. There was a fine vine in the conservatory, quinces in the garden and a fertile vegetable garden. I became perforce an untrained gardener. We ate our own tomatoes, ripened slowly in the cellar, till after Christmas, and I made quince jam. An hour a day in the summer, usually at teatime, and a full day every three or four weeks the rest of the year is just about enough to keep the garden at bay but there is no longer time for the Cropton cottage garden too. Susan and David are delighted. At rising six and four they are already demanding plaintively 'why can't we go abroad like other children?' We sell up and go instead for several years to the Tyrol or the Italian Alps. Ski resorts are wonderful places in the summer because there's plenty to do and not too many people. As we balance precariously on a razor's edge with a long drop on either side our waif-like son announces, 'When I grow up I won't bring my children anywhere like this.' After that it had to be beaches at Cap d'Agde, Rhodes, or the Halkidiki peninsula for three or four years.

The house in Kingfield Road matched the garden: there were elegant reception rooms with moulded ceilings, a wide staircase with shallow risers, enormous bedrooms, and all the attics, kitchens and sculleries anyone could wish. But its *pièce de résistance* was its garage. This was Geoffrey Close's Folly, a huge edifice replacing the former coach house. On the ground floor a six- or seven-car garage in which the elderly Mercedes I favoured in those days was lost, and upstairs to the left an exotic bedroom and luxury bathroom fitted with gold taps which Mr Close may have intended for some special friend, and to the right a huge room with bar, dance floor, and low-slung lighting for a full-size snooker table. A couple of young relatives camped there for a while and then a couple of French *assistantes* from local schools, but we never got round to installing a snooker table. Soon after we left Sheffield the Crucible Theatre staged its first great snooker championships. Practice facilities were hard to find and the space above our garage was pressed into service. Nowadays whenever I see televised snooker from the Crucible I wonder whether we might have enjoyed complimentary tickets for life if only we'd stayed in Sheffield and the players had gone on practising there.

CHAPTER 14

The Schools Council

Bliss was it in that dawn to be alive

The Times, the *Guardian* and the *Daily Telegraph* all announced the appointment. The *Yorkshire Post* wrote half a column and the *Sheffield Telegraph* enthused. My mentor George Taylor described it as 'the most exciting and exacting job in education in our time'. *Education* said rather oddly that there had been 'a strong *team* of candidates' for the post of Secretary of the Schools Council for Curriculum and Examinations. Some of the business pages noted with a certain wry pleasure that a key post in education had gone to a Fellow of the British Institute of Management.

For a few months at least I was almost literally at the top of the ladder. My appointment as Secretary in 1978 was reckoned to be a promotion and the civil service rules did not cover any extra costs I had to meet in the period between my starting work at the Council and my family moving to London. Fortunately the Council's premises at Great Portland Street included a tiny rooftop flat, a pimple on top of the five-storey block which housed the Council. This was really intended for the Council's part-time chairman but Don Basey came to my rescue. The most senior of numerous seconded civil servants who provided secretariat and administrative support for the Council, Don relished the freedom he had running the Council's affairs away from his base in the Department of Education and Science and enjoyed the challenge presented by ostensibly inflexible civil service rules. The Council, he thought, might allow me to use the flat free of charge. So for a few months I savoured the curious experience of returning to London late on Sunday nights, letting myself into a huge and empty office block, parking my car in the basement, climbing up to the roof, and negotiating a starlit route among the chimneys to find my own front door high above the surrounding streets of West London.

My day job gave a similarly extended view of the education world. To my amazement, since the job particulars said nothing of this, I soon found that the Secretary of the Schools Council was part of the stage army whose leaders are often described as the education establishment. None of the other actors ever admitted to being as surprised to be on stage as I was. Perhaps they in their dark suits were as iconoclastic as I in mine. My walk-on parts were legion. I attended the Further Education Unit's Board of Management chaired by my Sheffield colleague Polytechnic Director George Tolley, the BBC's School Broadcasting Council chaired admirably by Sheffielder Professor Ted Wragg,

the Council of the National Foundation for Educational Research, the Council
for National Academic Awards' Sub-Committee on Entry Qualifications, the
Department of Industry's Industry Education Advisory Committee, the
National Reference Library of Schoolbooks and Classroom Materials and a
Social Morality Council consultative group. From time to time I was invited to
seminars at St George's House, Windsor, the Policy Studies Institute and the
Royal Institute of Public Administration. Thanks to my chairman, John
Tomlinson, I became a member of the self-effacing All Souls' Group and a
Fellow of the Royal Society of Arts. I was a dim and flickering torch among
two hundred luminaries who signed the RSA's manifesto *Education for
Capability.*

Some of the signatories like Professors Harry Judge, David Donnison, Paul
Black, Peter Kelly, Tyrell Burgess and Dennis Lawton, Commonwealth
Institute Director James Porter and future Vice-Chancellor Bill Taylor were
among the many leading educators who as committee or project team
members occasionally trod the well-worn path to our offices in Great
Portland Street. Another to tread this path was a lively Cypriot teacher who
had taken to politics and was now Cyprus's High Commissioner in London.
When the European Community decided to fund a Mother Tongue Language
Teaching project the UK programme was entrusted to the Schools Council.
The EEC accepted that in Britain the main need was to develop teaching
materials in Asian languages like Urdu, but to legitimize EEC funding
Modern Greek was added to the programme. Oddly enough since most of
England's Greek speakers come from Cyprus we needed to find out how to
engage the Cypriot community in this project. When High Commissioner
Aristo de Mou came to discuss this problem we took him out to lunch in one
of our favourite Mediterranean restaurants only to realize with horror as we
stepped across its threshold that the Babylonia's cuisine and staff were
Turkish, not Greek. We feared a diplomatic incident. But with admirable
aplomb Aristo de Mou switched immediately to speak fluent Turkish with the
staff.

Lunchtime was also a convenient opportunity to meet the chief officers of
other quangos as some publicly funded bodies are quaintly known. Geoffrey
Hubbard of the National Council for Educational Technology, John Sellars of
the Business Education Council, Francis Hanrott of the Technician Education
Council, Harry Knutton and then John Barnes of City and Guilds, Geoff
Melling and then Jack Mansell of the Further Education Unit became good
friends. We shared many interests but none of the others was as much in the
public eye as was the Schools Council.

From time to time I lunched with one or other of the education corres-
pondents, Diana Geddes, George Low, Peter Wilby or even the doyen of their
corps, Stuart Maclure. I never felt my random comments justified a free lunch
but our accessibility in this and other ways may have helped secure the

Council an overwhelmingly friendly education press. Edward de Bono hoped that a couple of lunches at the Athenaeum would be enough to convert me and the Council to lateral thinking, and an aging James Pitman that a meeting at the Carlton Club would enlist the Council in his campaign for reformed spelling.

They were less successful than some of the many other crusaders who sought sponsorship from the Council. We were happy for example to support small-scale trials of Instrumental Enrichment, a highly successful Hungarian system of educating children with severe learning difficulties, and we also supported trials of the elegant Pupils' Records of Achievement devised by Tyrell Burgess and Betty Adams. We partnered various other organizations like the Health Education Council, the Manpower Services Commission, the Law Society and the Association for Science Education where joint efforts seemed likely to be fruitful.

I had to respond also to the enormous interest in the Council and its work. My appointment arose from a constitutional review which also affected the Council's committees. I tried hard to describe the subtle complexity of the new structure in simple terms. There are, I would say, quoting A.N. Whitehead, two kinds of philosopher: those who are clear and those who are muddled. Those who are clear are clearly wrong, and those who are muddled are at best only half right. I hoped my descriptions of our committee structure were at least partly right.

Quite properly there was much greater interest in what the Council was thinking about curriculum and examinations. I spoke about the control of the curriculum, balance in the curriculum, curriculum challenges, supporting curriculum change in schools, the role of advisers in encouraging curriculum development, what schools should teach, curriculum for a changing society, education in the 1980s, the contribution of education to economic recovery, examinations, the alternatives to examinations, planning processes in the Schools Council and curriculum research. I addressed the Association for the Study of the Curriculum, the London Institute of Education, the Institute of Careers Officers, the British Psychological Society, the Manpower Society, the Standing Conference of School Science and Technology, the Council for Environmental Education, the Association of Colleges of Further and Higher Education, the Standing Conference of Regional Examination Boards, the National Union of Teachers, Sheffield Polytechnic M.Ed students, Birmingham University M.Ed students, the Secondary Heads Association, Essex Heads, Hampshire Heads, Hertfordshire Teachers, Jersey Heads, Northern Ireland Heads, Welsh Secondary Heads and Scottish Directors of Education. At the United Kingdom Reading Association I enjoyed sharing a lifetime's interest in reading and writing, 'easy writing makes damned hard reading', and at the North of England Conference I foolishly distributed copies of my paper in advance and listened with increasing horror as 600 people

The Pundit…

…finds an appreciative audience.

synchronized the rustling of their turning pages as they followed my address from the handout.

Some might have said my travels exemplified seagull management: I flew in, squawked loudly, scattered my droppings and flew off into the blue. But I had to tackle a pretty steep learning curve before I could glide with any comfort across this relatively unknown territory. My papers drew heavily on the Schools Council's surprisingly extensive work. From its inception in 1964 the Council had funded about 170 projects covering almost every school subject, every stage of schooling, every external examination and many special needs. Teachers handbooks proliferated along with teaching materials, examination bulletins, research studies and evaluations. I had helped in Sheffield to promote *Health Education 8–13* and *Geography for the Young School Leaver*. Now I became familiar with many other projects from *Art and the Built Environment* to old favourites like Edith Biggs' work on *Primary Mathematics*, as well as *Breakthrough to Literacy*, a best-seller in English-speaking countries, *Cambridge Classics, Modular Technology, Computers in the Curriculum* and many other more recent projects like Peter Mittler's pioneering work for children with severe learning difficulties.

Of outstanding and pressing interest in view of the widespread concern about the poor state of British manufacturing and the supposed failure of our schools to promote a proper appreciation of commerce and manufacturing industry was the Schools Council Industry Project. SCIP was unusual in several respects. It was backed by the Confederation of British Industries and the Trade Union Congress and it was based in the Council itself, whereas most of the earlier projects had been based in universities or colleges. Like the Nuffield Foundation whose projects it inherited, the Schools Council had seen itself as a grant-giving body, considering, modifying and sometimes approving schemes devised by scholarly applicants from all over the country. Successful applicants were usually designated project director, and one of the Council's own Curriculum Officers was nominated to keep in touch with the project and guard the Council's interests. Typically these schemes involved research by a team of scholars, their development of materials for school teachers to use, the trial and further improvement of these materials in a few schools and an attempt to market the finished products in other schools. The aim was to create 'teacher-proof' materials.

To avoid any suspicion of central diktat the Council had never published books or materials itself. Instead leading educational publishers were persuaded to contribute the working capital to produce and market the Council's output. This certainly added greatly to the value of the Council's own investment, but it left the Council at the mercy of the publishing industry's lackadaisical approach to marketing. The publishers stood to gain even more than the Council from successful marketing and might have been expected to be fairly energetic; but it was a world in which there seemed to be no sense of urgency, no critical deadlines to be met, no market to be found and won. No one knew what share of the market spelt success for the Council's teaching materials, though I suppose any manufacturer trying to break into an established market would be happy to win 5 or 10 per cent of the market. There seemed, however, to be a feeling in Westminster and Whitehall that the Council was some kind of educational Pied Piper whose project materials should be promptly adopted in their entirety by almost every teacher in almost every school. By 1978 the Department's carping had made the Council's staff almost paranoiac about trying to measure the impact and take-up of our project materials.

This 'corn flake' model of development and marketing was not at all appropriate for improving teaching and learning. In developing teaching materials the project teams were the innovators and educators, and the teachers in schools were the people to be educated, the learners. In its early years the Schools Council did not appreciate that improving schools was a specialized form of adult education, in which teachers in schools were the learners. The result was that few of the early projects took sufficient account of the increasing evidence that most learning takes place through the activity of the learner not that of the teacher. Even in my Sheffield days I was acquainted with the growing belief, exemplified in the work of people like Per Dalin, Barry Macdonald and Lawrence Stenhouse, that research in which teachers were active participants was more likely than ivory tower research to improve educational practice.

The Industry Project's most revolutionary aspect was the way it involved teachers from several schools in each of five different localities. With support from a local co-ordinator and the active involvement of local employers and trade unionists the schools developed their own links with local businesses, helped teachers and managers in industry and commerce to spend time in each other's workplaces, arranged work experience for young people, and tried to highlight the interdependence of an area's geography, history, economy, commerce and traditional industries. The project's director was Martin Lightfoot, a subtle, brilliant and opinionated man who had run the Penguin *Education Specials* and had been one of the Inner London Education Authority's assistant directors. Although SCIP was in-house and Martin had been recruited to run it the Council maintained its normal practice of nominating a Curriculum Officer to guard the Council's interests. Helen Carter, an experienced Curriculum Officer who had been an Assistant Education Officer in one of the London Boroughs was reduced almost to tears by her dealings with Martin, and Roger Sturge, a tough-minded Quaker, gave up in despair. Determinedly charitable in speech, the worst Roger would say of someone's suitability for any task was 'that is not a name that would have occurred to me'.

Martin Lightfoot seemed to hope that those taking part in the project would learn by doing, and that as a result their attitudes and relationships would change. He believed that to publish aims for the project or to provide interim reports on its progress would affect the sensitive plant he was trying to nurture. I understood that it's not such a good idea to keep on digging a plant up to inspect its roots, but the CBI and the TUC and our paymasters were clamouring to know what their investment in SCIP was achieving. Martin was obdurate. Fortunately he left shortly before the project's main phase ended and there was no cataclysmic explosion. His more emollient successor Susan Holmes readily agreed to satisfy the demand for a visible output by preparing a much-used series of booklets on themes like trade unions, employers, work and the individual, and industry and the environment. What we learned from the participants, however, was that what they valued above all was the opportunity to share their experience with other like-minded people and the support they felt from working in a shared enterprise.

The Industry Project was unique. It differed greatly from the old-style projects, and Martin's commitment to learning as a process rather than a syllabus to be mastered was a neat prelude to the programmes the Council launched after its reconstitution in 1978.

The 1978 reforms were intended to stabilize the Council. Two years after its inception in 1964 the Council had begun a constitutional review which led to a new constitution in 1968. Registration as a charity had followed in 1969 and independence from the Department of Education and Science was won in 1970 when the local education authorities agreed to match the Department's grant. By 1975 the Council was considering further changes to its constitution. The need for change was underlined in 1976 when a Prime Ministerial brief stigmatized the Council's performance as 'mediocre' and asserted that its reputation had 'suffered a considerable decline over the last few years'. Goaded by these remarks by 1978 the Council was ready with another new constitution.

But new constitutions were less common than changes at the top. In eleven of the Council's fourteen years there had been at least one change in the small group of chairman and two or three joint secretaries. In 1973 all three secretaries left in quick succession and in 1975–76 all three secretaries came to the end of their secondment at about the same time and there was a change of chairman as well. The Council's fifth chairman retired in 1978 as the last of its fourteen joint secretaries were preparing to leave.

In 1978 the new Chairman's first task was to preside over the selection of the Council's first permanent Secretary. The most obvious deficiencies of the previous system of three joint secretaries on short-term secondments had been lack of unity and any sense of long-term direction. This new appointment of a permanent head of the Council's paid staff was intended to remedy these weaknesses.

The Chairman's second task was to road test the new constitution. Its most remarkable feature was its ingenious attempt to give appropriate weight to all the various groups who had a stake in the country's schools. Both the providers of schools and their users were represented in the Council: government, local authorities, churches and teachers as providers, lay people, parents, employers, trade unions, further and higher education as users. The interests of the government and the local authorities who funded the Council jointly were safeguarded by their majority on the Finance and Priorities Committee and the interests of teachers by their majority on the Professional Committee. Users were most strongly represented in Convocation, a forum where users and providers could discuss matters of concern to them all. The examining bodies, neither providers nor users of schools but symbionts, were strongly represented in the Examinations Committee. There was no longer a separate Governing Council so any of the major committees might speak as the Council on matters within their remit.

The new Chairman, John Tomlinson, was formidably well-qualified for the difficult task of riding this hydra. He was by nature a scholar, a historian whose published postgraduate researches broke new ground, a man whose wide reading and interests never failed to amaze and stimulate. County Education Officer of Cheshire since 1972, John had already served on the Court Committee on Child Health Services, the Gulbenkian enquiries into Drama, Music and Dance, and the Special Programmes Board of the Manpower Services Commission, as well as being the founding chairman of the Further Education Curriculum Review and Development Unit. His range of interests and sympathies in education was exceptional, and his enthusiasm infectious. But the most remarkable gift he brought to the Schools Council was a singular talent for finding words to express what the disparate and sometimes discordant members of a committee had in common. His talents were deployed to great effect in conducting the Council's three senior committees, Finance and Priorities, Professional, and Convocation. Under his baton they sang in harmony together; their singing in unison would have been an uninspiring alternative.

From its creation in 1964 the Council had seemed to epitomize the English way of running the country's education services. Power in education was distributed among central government, local authorities, individual schools and examining bodies. Yet there was, as Sir Herbert Andrew, a former Permanent Secretary, had observed, 'a general sense of direction' about the service even if there was no single source of authority. For those of a philosophic turn of mind this loosely coupled system seemed to be an effective answer to what Karl Popper believed to be the central question for open or democratic societies: 'How can we so organize political issues that bad or incompetent rulers can be prevented from doing too much damage?' Dr Rhodes Boyson, soon to become a Conservative Minister, was making much the same point when he spoke at the annual prize giving of the Jewish Free School in London on 5 December 1978: 'In education as in society at large it is essential that power and responsibility should be dispersed.'

As a forum where the various parties could meet, the Council was intended to strengthen the general sense of direction. But to prevent the Council doing too much damage should bad or incompetent elements ever take control its authority was limited to advising Ministers on examinations and suggesting how to improve the school curriculum. 'The principle that each school should have the fullest possible measure of responsibility for its own work' was enshrined in the Council's constitution.

So too was the principle that the curriculum should come first and examinations second. This seemed a self-evident truth and I was more than happy to leave our examinations work to the Council's talented examinations team, ably led in my time first by Michael Wylie, an engagingly stimulating HMI, and then by Peter Dines, once one of the Council's Joint Secretaries. Even before their time the Council had produced many excellent research studies on examinations, and the Council was undertaking further studies to ensure that the standards of the various boards were comparable with each other, that the standards in different subjects were comparable, and that standards remained comparable from one year to the next. From time to time the Council also proposed changes in the external examination system. None of these proposals was accepted outright. Successive Secretaries of State and their departmental advisers were reluctant to commit themselves to any change and blamed the Council for failing to deliver advice they could accept.

One of the difficulties was that too much was expected of school examinations. Many employers mistakenly assumed that General Certificates of Education were like swimming or driving certificates and found to their dismay that a certificate did not guarantee any specific level of competence. Many candidates and their parents assumed that General Certificates were like passports and would guarantee entry to employment or university, only to find that the more people take and pass examinations the less value they have. As Fred Hirsch observed in *The Social Limits to Growth*, when one person in a crowd stands on tiptoe he can see better, but when the whole crowd stands on tiptoe no one is better off. 'When everyone is somebodee, Then no one's anybody.'

Now we've reached an odd state of affairs. O and A-levels are at best a rough and ready way of measuring competence and they are too plentiful to be much use for selecting high fliers. But just as Dad went to his grave regretting the day forty years earlier when Britain abandoned the currency Gold Standard, Ministers still cling to A-level as the academic Gold Standard when some more flexible friend is needed.

With wider lay membership, including for example the editor of the *Guardian*, Peter Preston, the distinguished academic Bhikhu Parekh, the consultant anaesthetist and former member of the Taylor Committee Dr A.E.

Edwards, and Mrs Buckley from the National Confederation of Parent Teacher Associations, the 1978 Council seemed even more like a national forum for discussing educational issues. Our Parents Liaison Committee, where my old friend Barbara Bullivant popped up again, was, Dr Edwards thought, 'the only forum in England Wales where all the differing parent bodies and interest groups could meet together, and in conjunction with representatives of the professional organizations, discuss and advise on aspects of the curriculum and examinations in our schools'. Our Industry Liaison and Higher and Further Education Liaison Committees were equally innovatory and equally valuable even if Principal Bill Easton was prone to sleep throughout. It was not too fanciful for the new Council's midwife, Chairman Alex Smith, and his successor John Tomlinson to liken the Council to a parliament, a place where the producers and the consumers could talk about education. Neither was so naive as to imagine it was like the United Kingdom's modern Parliament, a place for agreeing taxes, approving laws and trying to call Ministers to account.

'Had I been present at the Creation,' said Alfonso the Wise, 'I would have given some useful hints for the better ordering of the universe.' Many of the Council's members and staff had a feeling of wonder in 1978 that they were present at the creation of a new order and had the opportunity of giving some useful hints for the better ordering of education. The funds at our disposal were modest. The Council's budget was about the same as the cost of running a very large secondary school and in the early years of the new Council much more than half the budget was committed to completing the old Council's projects. Three years later they were still taking 49 per cent of our funds. How could we make the most of the small sums which were not already bespoke? Just a small meteorite in the education firmament, how could the Council best deploy its tiny resources to implement its terms of reference, 'through co-operative study of common problems, to assist all who have…responsibilities for…the schools' curricula…?'

Archimedes is said to have claimed 'give me a lever and I can move the world', but it was less clear what lever would move 400,000 teachers in 30,000 schools: if indeed that was an appropriate metaphor at all. Perhaps analogies from the garden, or analogies from the kitchen such as adding piquancy with a little zest or a light drizzle, would have offered more helpful insights to the Council's role than the workshop or laboratory metaphor of the lever. What I and some of my colleagues found most helpful was the published version of Donald Schon's Reith Lectures *Beyond the Stable State*. In this he argued that the role of central agencies in a changing world is not to promulgate a central message but to 'help peripheral systems transform themselves and to connect them with each other'. He suggested that 'the design, development and management of networks becomes pivotal to learning systems'. I thought my own role and that of one or two senior colleagues would be to develop networks with other agencies, adding their creative energy to ours. Other

Council staff would be most concerned with building networks within and between schools and groups of schools. Drawing on our experience in the Industry Project we believed we could help schools transform themselves and learn from each other. The value of our limited funds would be multiplied many times if they helped to make every school staffroom a community of adult learners.

The Council had already decided to move from large-scale development projects to programmes of activities. This implied a commitment to action research in schools and incremental progress rather than 'big bang' projects. Although funds were limited we offered to consider any activities Council members and others might recommend for inclusion in these programmes. The lively response was a clear sign of the great hopes people had of the Council. Convocation and the Professional Committee debated the responses and signalled their own preferences. In May 1979 the Finance and Priorities Committee spent twenty-four demanding hours at Bramley Grange agreeing five programme areas and a broad order of priority within each. When two years later John Tomlinson gave the first Schools Council lecture at the British Association's 150th Anniversary Meeting in York he said,

> Programmes as a conceptual framework are, I am sure, sound...*Purpose and Planning in Schools*, the competence of *Individual Teachers*, the *Subjects and Themes of the Curriculum*, the needs of *Individual Pupils*, and the need to evaluate and *Assess Pupils, Teachers and Schools* are enduring and comprehensible imperatives... They have also proved dynamic as tools of management under the leadership of a member group and programme director.

I had already spent many hours trying to synthesize the heaps of suggestions we received. At Bramley Grange John's skills as chairman ably supported by my colleagues' contributions as scribes left the Committee with a cheerful glow of achievement when they went home on Saturday evening. They had decided the Council programmes and, more fatefully, in their final session they had decided to publish a statement about the curriculum. John Tomlinson let me know immediately that he thought the curriculum statement might prove to be a very important aspect of the Council's work. He followed this by writing on 10 July to say that it now seemed even more urgent than the programmes because Lady Young had told the Society of Education Officers that the government intended to prepare and publish a curriculum framework for secondary education. Subsequently the Education Officers had been most enthusiastic when he mentioned the possibility of the Schools Council doing some work on a framework. 'People prefer the Schools Council to do it rather than the Government,' he wrote. 'I'm not suggesting we deliberately try to upstage the Government. But we have published our proposals first and are entitled to press ahead.'

That was not quite how the new Conservative government saw things.

When in August Ministers and the Permanent Secretary received copies of *Principles and Programmes*, the slim leaflet in which we described the new programmes and our intention to work on a curriculum framework, they summoned John Tomlinson to ask what was going on. Fortunately he was able to explain that eight senior officials and inspectors had been involved at every stage of the discussions leading up to this publication. But the incident did little to engender warm Departmental feelings towards the Council.

With old-style projects to oversee and new style programmes to launch, most of the Council's Curriculum Officers were at full stretch. In view of the importance John Tomlinson attached to our curriculum statement I immersed myself in the literature and began to draft an issues paper for Professional Committee. My deputy Keith McWilliams made many penetrating suggestions, and so too did Maurice Plaskow. Maurice had been associated with the Council for eleven years, first as a member of the Humanities Curriculum Project team and then from 1970 as one of the Council's direct recruits. He had seemed so demoralized and so despondent about the Council's future at my first senior staff meetings that I dropped him a line asking whether perhaps he ought to think of looking for employment somewhere else. Within a couple of hours I was assailed by our colleague Helen Carter. Did I not realize how wounding my note was? Was I not aware of the width and depth of Maurice's curricular interests and the enormous contribution he had made to the Council's work? Did I not understand that the Council had no more loyal supporter than Maurice? She was right. I came to have the highest regard for both of them, and certainly never had any further reason to doubt Maurice's total commitment to the Council.

Indeed one of the most extraordinary things about working there was the astonishing enthusiasm members and staff had for the Council. I was constantly surprised at the time and energy innumerable people, advisers like Joan Dean of Surrey, education officers like Eric Briault, Andrew Fairbairn and Michael Ridger, professors of education like Dennis Lawton, vice-chancellors like Clifford Butler, innumerable classroom and head teachers and many others were ready to give to Council committees. Some of my new colleagues were old friends like George Pearson, once a fellow examiner, and Jasmine Denyer, one of the divisional officers with whom I'd jousted in Essex. Other familiar faces in our committees and working parties, from education officers Bob Aitken and Michael Henley to Sheffield heads like Arnold Jennings and Dennis Spooner and former pupils John Percival, now a pro-vice-chancellor, and Laurie South now representing the NUT, made me feel comfortably at home. People like Don Basey, Chris Brookes, Ken Storey and David Noble from the Department of Education and Science worked as hard and loyally for the Council as the researchers and the curriculum and examinations officers who were more directly involved in our crusade for better schools. This loyalty survived even charges of cruelty and victimization brought against me by researchers Lea Orr and Norman Williams when I extended the Council's ban on smoking to our departmental meetings. Two floors above Great Portland Street we had to chose between being asphyxiated by smokers or deafened by traffic if we opened our windows.

One of the strengths of our work on a framework for the curriculum was the range of expertise on which the Council could call. Perhaps the 1978 review should have included a cull of some of the many subordinate committees, notably the primary and secondary curriculum committees and a dozen or more subject committees, none of which had much to do once we had established monitoring and review groups to oversee each of the programmes. As there had been no cull we invited the two curriculum committees to nominate members of a small Framework Working Group chaired by John Tomlinson himself, and the subject committees to comment on an early issues paper. This elaborate process ensured that the Working Group was well briefed. But it was ready to begin putting its own thoughts into shape only in October 1980. The government's *The School Curriculum* was expected later that year and we hoped our own publication would be ready soon after that. Our hopes were dashed when we saw some early drafts of our own booklet. They were verbose, ponderous and convoluted, not at all the straightforward practical material we wanted. Our nominated draftsman was clearly incapable of writing a plain sentence. The need was urgent. I decided to put my own reputation on the line. My hand would hold the pen which wrote *The Practical Curriculum*. It was 'a handbook of working papers to help teachers to test their own ideas…an incitement to critical self-evaluation…a whetsone for teachers to use, not a prescription to take.' 'The heart of the matter', we said, 'is what each child takes away from school. For each of them, what he or she takes away is the effective curriculum.' The four chapters of our handbook were designed to help teachers develop *a rationale for the curriculum, plan the curriculum, monitor the curriculum* and *assess what had been achieved*. Each short chapter ended with checkpoints for action. This was to be a handbook which working teachers could and would want to use.

Then came a last-minute hitch, best described in John Tomlinson's words. The Working Group

> contained both DES officials and HMI. By the Spring of 1981 it was completing its work and final drafts were being circulated. I then became aware of anxiety in the DES. At first it appeared as excessive criticism of the drafting which, when probed, resolved into matters easily accommodated: only to be followed by a repeat performance. Then I was asked to delay the publication of the Council's document until the Government had been able to publish theirs. I knew that if this got into the committee process at the Council it would cause dismay. So I took the responsibility upon myself to accept what was being asked of us.

Two weeks after the Department published *The School Curriculum* in mid March, the Council published *The Practical Curriculum*, sent a free copy to every school and sold many more. At Convocation on 9 April it was widely praised by the local authorities, teachers, parents, CBI and universities. The DES representatives were mute. The press welcomed its realism, and so too did schools. With its initial print run of some 35,000 it was almost a best seller.

As *The Practical Curriculum* took shape the working party began to think it might be the first of a series in which other volumes dealt in greater depth with particular stages or areas of the curriculum. We published a short guide to planning one-year courses for young people of sixteen and seventeen and our Primary Curriculum Committee began to prepare a sequel to *The Practical Curriculum*. The Committee's aim was to help groups of primary school teachers to discuss what objectives and what standards to aim at in Science, Mathematics, Language and Literacy, Studying People Past and Present, Imagination, Feeling and Sensory Expression, and Personal and Social Development. Other chapters provided a similar framework for discussing Topic Work, Pupil Assessment and Record-keeping, Organization and Planning, and Evaluation and Staff Development. Gathering and sifting material and drafting the text for the knowledgeable experts in the Committee kept me happily engaged for several months. When it appeared in 1983 the *Times Educational Supplement* described *Primary Practice* as 'a concise and usable handbook' and thought it struck a neat balance between the considerable benefits of the class teachers' traditional independence and increasing pressure to plan the curriculum in detail and check progress systematically. There was plenty of anecdotal evidence over the next few years to show that it was much used by schools and local advisers.

Very many teachers also took part in activities sponsored or supported by the new programmes. Several local authorities had developed guidelines to help schools evaluate their own strengths and weaknesses and devise strategies for self-improvement. Programme One built on these developments in its own *Guidelines for Internal Review and Development* and helped many schools to use the guidelines. To complement this work I took advantage of a nodding acquaintance with Professor Charles Handy, not yet the famous guru he was to be, to persuade him to bring his business acumen to bear on the problems of managing schools. He welcomed this opportunity to examine a different kind of enterprise and we were delighted to publish his slim essay on *Understanding Schools as Organizations*. Michael Henley, County Education Officer of Northamptonshire, a warm, friendly man with a great understanding of teaching and learning who happily devoted many hours to serving Council committees and working parties, was chairman of Programme Two. His Planning Group took as its guiding principles the beliefs that professional development and curriculum development are in effect different sides of the same coin, that teachers work best on problems they have helped to identify, become more effective when they are encouraged to appraise their own practice and develop professionally by working in partnership with other teachers and other agencies. The programme made ninety-seven small awards of up to £500 to support networks of teachers and others who needed help with problems they had identified, and commissioned a dozen larger activities. The independent evaluator reported that potentially valuable ideas were supported at an early stage, that local groups were enthused by outside recognition, and that in some cases the value of the work done vastly exceeded the grant. In one case a £500 grant had stimulated work worth £15,000.

Our third programme, Developing the Curriculum for a Changing World, adopted a similar strategy, funding activities concerned with neglected aspects of education such as Political and Economic Understanding, Technological Awareness, Environmental Awareness, Logical Skills and Study Skills. Programme Four funded activities to help Individual Children with various kinds of special need, Disruptive and Truanting Children, Ethnic Minorities, and Gifted Children. Like the other programmes it generated many readably slim reports such as Graeme Clarke's *Guidelines for the Recognition of Gifted Pupils*. These were all edited and published in-house by Jean Sturdy and her editorial team.

The most significant critique of these changes was the comment of one long-term observer of the Council. In the days of projects the key words had been target-populations, teacher-proof packages, impact, research, development, dissemination and centre–periphery models. 'With the advent of programmes the key words became negotiation, consultation, networks, social interaction, teacher autonomy, action research, participation, and partnership.' By 1982, through its remaining projects and its programmes the Council was collaborating with three charitable trusts, two professional and two other voluntary bodies, two international agencies, five public bodies and eight government departments, as well as eighty local authorities and a thousand teacher groups. Our two-person press team of Tony French and first Ian Anderson then Nick Tester poured out a stream of succinct informative press releases about all that was going on.

'A new found confidence and optimism began to fill the corridors and committee rooms of Great Portland Street,' wrote Programme Director Don Cooper of the winter and spring of 1979–80. Ministers, from Secretary of State Mark Carlisle to his Minister of State Lady Young and his Parliamentary Under Secretary Neil Macfarlane, spoke quite kindly of the Council. In March 1981 the Department's long-awaited publication *The School Curriculum* referred to the Council's work on records of achievement, curriculum development and links between schools and industry. The Central Office of Information suggested that other government departments should use the School Council's expertise if they wished to develop teaching materials. The Central Policy Review Staff recommended building on the work of the Schools Council and so too did the Manpower Services Commission. Professor Meredydd G. Hughes recommended that the proposed Schools' Management Unit should be established within the Schools Council. Our premises were a-humming with ideas and action. Morale was high, and when a challenge came in 1981 we responded vigorously.

CHAPTER 15

Life in the Great Wen

Earth has not anything to show more fair

WHEN I JOINED THE Schools Council in 1978 our six year old son David thought I could easily commute from Sheffield since I often went to London for meetings and came home the same day. But he soon became a confirmed Londoner, reluctant later on to contemplate a university or a job more than an hour or two from Hyde Park Corner. Knowing little of London, Margaret and I thought we ought to live as near the centre as we could afford. That way the whole family would be able to get to know the capital before we moved on to somewhere prettier. Still tourists at heart we thought of 'London' as the patch roughly bounded by the Circle Line, with a few Monopoly board tentacles like the Old Kent Road and Pentonville Road. London was the City's 'square mile' plus Westminster and the Thames, with a few more distant highlights like Hampton Court and Greenwich, Lord's Cricket Ground and Hampstead. These were the gems to seek out in what had been, since we knew a little history, the 'great smoak'. This was the Great Wen, a vast workers' dormitory filled still with little Pooters, all scriveners, bank clerks and civil servants pouring into the centre every day. It all came to life twenty years later when I suddenly realized that my roots lay in nineteenth-century London. All four grandparents' families had been sucked into the Great Wen. On Dad's side Euston, Marylebone and Hammersmith, on Mum's, Bermondsey, Brixton and Clapham, were all part of my family history even though my forebears quit the metropolis by 1900.

The gentrified houses in Islington and Camden were already pricey for people from the north, and I didn't fancy taking on an unimproved house at the same time as a new job. So we ended up in Willesden Green, in Saxon times a green on a hill with a stream, and just a couple of hamlets surrounded by manor farms until the late nineteenth century. By then railways criss-crossed the area and fertilized the growth of handsome villas. In the end even the Ecclesiastical Commissioners succumbed to Mammon and sold their remaining land to builders who drove long straight roads across the fields and filled them with comfortable family houses. By 1978 the area was well served by bus and tube for work and pleasure in the West End, and motorways for friends and relatives to the north, east and west. The house we liked had a lawn for family cricket and football and was only a short safe walk from a well-regarded primary school.

153

House and area met our criteria well. It took us a while to grasp that London was not just ten or twelve times larger than Leeds or Sheffield. In England's largest village we had all lived, worked, shopped and played together in the same place. In London we all lived and worked and played in different places. I bumped into colleagues by chance in Gloucestershire, Scotland and even Mexico more often than I met any colleague by chance in London. We have never met any of our London neighbours when we've been exploring other parts of London.

Our borough, Brent, was already among the most culturally diverse in Britain. There were more temples, mosques and synagogues in our patch than there were churches, and I was staggered to find more than two dozen Irish local papers at the local newsagents. After a year or so of the usual round of children's games and parties we realized that of the children who had crossed our front doorstep our own two were the only ones whose grandparents had all been born in Britain. Some like Snow, whose mother was one of a wealthy chieftain's several wives, and Sipho, whose white mother and journalist father had to leave South Africa hurriedly, added new dimensions to our lives. A few years later when equal opportunities and ethnic records were burning issues at work I asked our teenage Susan and David how many black teachers there were at their school, Hampstead. They were bewildered. It wasn't just that they did not know; they didn't really understand the question. 'They're all just teachers to us,' was their enormously encouraging reply.

Margaret's uncanny success in job-hunting stayed with her in London. She turned down a post as Head of Science at South Kilburn, a new school with hardly any pupils which closed not long after, and was herself rejected as second deputy by the spinster head and deputy of a large girls' school who clearly doubted the commitment of a married woman with young children. The Inner London Education Authority had no such inhibitions and within a month or two of our arriving in London Margaret was appointed Head of Highbury Hill, a small grammar school in Islington. She busied herself with visits and training for the new responsibilities she was to assume six months later. Half way through her induction the Authority announced that her school and neighbouring girls' secondary school Shelburne were to merge. Rupert Prime, the newly appointed Head of Shelburne, was no more aware of this possibility than Margaret. She was even more surprised in due course to find herself Head Designate of the new school, Highbury Fields. 'The Fields' opened with twelve or thirteen hundred girls on four sites, and Margaret's major task in its early years was to manage a rapid reduction in numbers to about five hundred, with a matching reduction in staff numbers and consolidation on two sites. Before this process had ended the school was engulfed in the most damaging industrial action English teachers have ever undertaken. Margaret had to devise *ad hoc* timetables almost every day in response to teachers withdrawing for ten minutes, twenty minutes, half an

Culturally diverse, a Hindu wedding passes our front window.

hour, or half a day, as well as refusing to attend meetings out of school hours and refusing duties they thought inappropriate. Almost every day she had to make time to draft and send explanatory letters to parents. Very often she was outraged and near despair to find herself facing representatives who treated her as the personification of the despicable forces against whom they were struggling. When Her Majesty's Inspectors came to see how the school was coping after reorganization the HMI withdrew without joining battle. Few heads can have had to contend with such exceptional pressures over so long a period.

Working as I did in the fairly rarefied air of the Schools Council and the upper slopes of the education service in Harrow, it was helpful to be reminded constantly of what it was like trying to steer an inner city school. And perhaps it ought also to be a condition of appointment that everyone with some responsibility for running the public education system should have children at what are now called state schools. Susan and David were my unwitting secret agents for almost twenty years. When I asked Susan about moving up to the junior school she said the big difference was that when she was an infant she was allowed to go straight to her classroom to play or to work; now, however bitter the weather, she had to queue outside until someone in authority decided to admit the children. Though she had a milk allergy from birth, she was sharply told that no one had an allergy to custard. When she performed in the school concert Head Teacher Ron Singer refused to admit younger siblings 'because they make a noise'. When I expressed surprise that the classroom display board was adorned with many more black marks than gold stars, David's ten year old peers soon let me know that they no longer bothered about collecting the gold stars they had earned. Excellent though he was in many ways, Ron dangled a cigarette as he addressed a parents' meeting with children in the room. And when I went to consult him about a secondary school for Susan, Ron was nonplussed when I said we favoured a state school rather than one of London's famous independent girls' schools, and dumb-founded when I mentioned a personal preference for co-education rather than the prestigious Camden Girls' School. As I was to find a year or two later when David showed some aptitude for cricket and enrolled for coaching at Lord's some of Ron's fellow heads showed even less faith in state schools. As I chatted to other aspiring dads while our progeny sported in the nets I heard of junior school heads advising parents to transfer their children to private schools because they really couldn't stretch them, or advising against choosing a state secondary school. I was dismayed by their lack of loyalty to the system which gave them their livelihood and their *raison d'être*. My old friend Lester Roth, Professor of Education at California State and a great anglophile, was even more amazed to hear Jo Wagerman trashing the local authority which funded the Jewish Free School of which she was Head. Fresh from the Californian melting pot where community schools are an essential part of the socializing fabric he was astonished and repelled by such divisively English idiosyncrasies as publicly funded faith schools and parental choice. Twenty years on there are few things about our society which make me more uneasy than the educational apartheid which is endemic in London and the south-east.

Despite Margaret's commitment to her own girls' school we chose co-educational Hampstead as the most promising of three secondary schools roughly equidistant from home. Hampstead's first Head was Philip Halsey, now one of my principal sparring partners as one of the Department of Education and Science's senior representatives on the Schools Council. His successor Ted Field was a generation younger than my Colchester Head Jack Elam but of a similarly liberal outlook. He ran a school with few if any formal rules, no school uniform and no corporal punishment though it was still permissible and was common enough in a few London schools, including the one Prime Minister Blair was to choose for his own sons. We were to find later that Hampstead retained one sanction which struck me as a particularly cruel and unusual punishment. With my history I had to smile a little when the school forced our youngsters to write us little notes saying how sorry they were to have let us down by skipping a few lessons or taking part in an end-of-term flour and foam battle.

While we were thinking about secondary schools the local press reported that several Hampstead pupils had won places at Oxford or Cambridge. Here was a local school which seemed to combine academic achievement with social values with which I could empathize. Hampstead's vigorous new Head, Tamsyn Imison, renewed the school's vision but in the 1980s even she could not promote the range of out-of-school activities which enriched my own

A comical house on a stalk.

The River Spey, a hundred yards away.

Ben Macdui: a hard-earned break.

years as pupil and teacher. The three-sided dispute between teachers, employers and government caused a fair amount of collateral damage. London's sports centres, gym clubs, music groups, clubs, theatre groups, junior cricket teams and similar groups soon filled the void.

Riding a bicycle and self-government are very similar. The only way to become proficient is to get on and perhaps to fall off a few times. You can hardly expect people to behave responsibly as adults if they've had no previous practice in making their own decisions. The only inviolable rule at home was that regardless of gender our children were not to have their ears pierced until they reached eighteen and paid for the piercing themselves. From when they were about twelve or thirteen we gave Susan and David an inclusive monthly allowance to cover clothes, hairdressing, pocket money and other personal items, and when they were beginning their university courses we cashed an insurance policy and gave them each a lump sum to cover their outgoings for the following three years. They learned to drive as soon as they were old enough and must have had to hone their negotiating skills when as undergraduates two hundred miles apart they were offered the chance of sharing Margaret's old car.

Like every other parent we hoped we were striking the right balance between encouraging independence and being supportive at school and play. For four or five years two devoted young Brazilians, Elizabeth Hamer, a thoughtful young woman who was interested in history and language and philosophy, and Cecilia Gomez, an excitable frolicsome black kitten who went to New York when she left us and was shot dead by her policeman husband, held our household together while our youngsters enjoyed a varied diet of cricket, football, gymnastics, swimming, music, concerts, outings and holidays. We ventured into time-share with a comical house on a stalk dangerously near the middle of a small Scottish golf course. Cairn Gorm, Braeriach and Ben Macdui were there to challenge those with staying power, alongside family swimming, tennis, billiards and even golf. Ospreys and ptarmigan were at hand and not far away there were Flodden Field, the whisky trail, the Loch Ness Monster and a dozen Scottish castles. We enjoyed the mix well enough to try another week on the south coast where we could explore the New Forest, admire England's first nesting egrets on the saltings, and visit the Isle of Wight, evoking memories of Susan and David's school journeys and their work on Carisbrooke Castle, the Needles and Alum Chine. We acquired a taste for islands, explored Rhodes and Crete in the spring, and at New Year bathed outdoors in Reykjavik's hot springs while we sampled Iceland's frigid moonscape. When we ventured to Cairo and the Nile one Christmas holiday David was still young enough to be worried that Christmas might be cancelled altogether. And I was still young enough in 1987 to enjoy Disney World and the Universal Film Studios when we all went to California during a coast-to-coast tour of the USA. Another year we all marvelled at the strangely alien world of Tokyo and Kyoto and the oddly contrasting charms of bullet trains and Shinto temples. Our Japanese guides surprised us with their unexpected sense of irony, and the way young people laughed and chatted quietly in the streets would appeal to all the old codgers who pine 'disgustedly' for the good old days. Even the dogs behaved decorously. Their little vocal chords were cut, we heard, to stop them barking.

CHAPTER 16

To Stop the Council Barking

Red skies at dawn

THE CHALLENGE to the Council was not unexpected. When it adopted its new constitution the Council itself had talked of the need for an internal review, and Sir Leo Pliatsky had recommended generally that quangos be reviewed. The government's decision to review the Schools Council was taken in December 1980, and the appointment of Mrs Nancy Trenaman to undertake the review was announced in March 1981 just as we prepared to publish *The Practical Curriculum*. Mrs Trenaman was the Principal of St Anne's College, Oxford, a former civil servant who had worked mainly in the Board of Trade and had served also while Principal of St Anne's on the Committee on the Constitution which had reaffirmed the principle of devolution. She seemed calm, polite, detached and business-like, a person whose independence and integrity could not be doubted. She garnered a rich harvest of evidence. Organizations as varied and diverse as the CBI, the TUC, the local authority associations, the National Confederation of Parent-Teacher Associations, the Canadian High Commission and the teacher associations were at one in asserting the need for the Council and expressing broad approval for the way it worked.

The main dissenting voice was that of the Department of Education and Science. 'In the DES view,' according to the confidential *aide-mémoire* for their representatives, 'the Schools Council, if it continues, needs to be radically reorganized so that there is: (1) A proper management body, appointed by the Secretary of State…' This proposal amounted in Mrs Trenaman's view to the abolition of the Council and its replacement by a new body. Speaking for a moment perhaps as a member of the former Committee on the Constitution she thought that a nominated body 'was…consistent only with central control of the curriculum'. She concluded that 'the Schools Council should continue, and with its present functions,' and that it should not be made the subject of further external review for at least five years. There was indeed no further review because in April 1982 six months after receiving Mrs Trenaman's report the Secretary of State announced that he had decided to disband the Council.

Sir Keith Joseph was the fifth Secretary of State to have dealings with the Council in less than seven years. His predecessors were Mr Reg Prentice, Mr Fred Mulley, Mrs Shirley Williams and Mr Mark Carlisle. It was Reg Prentice who appointed Alex Smith as Chairman in 1975. Alex was a distinguished industrial engineer, a Scot, enticed from Rolls Royce to become Principal of the Manchester Polytechnic, a busy man who accepted the chairmanship of the Schools Council somewhat reluctantly only after Permanent Secretary Sir William Pile had assured him that he would have the Department's help and support. Alex succeeded two distinguished educators, Dame Muriel Stewart, a former President of the National Union of Teachers, and the unctuous Director of Education for Norfolk, Sir Lincoln Ralphs. Perhaps the decision to appoint an outsider with no previous links with English schools should have been seen as a portent, a sign that someone thought an outsider's view of the English school system would be timely. Alex Smith's career had odd similarities in that respect to that of James Hamilton, the fifty-three year old Scots aeronautical engineer who came from the Cabinet Office to succeed Pile as Permanent Secretary early in 1976. Once Director General of the gleaming white elephant Concorde project, Hamilton was obviously expected to bring an engineer's purposeful clarity to the Department. When he retired in 1984 the *Times Educational Supplement* entitled its valedictory 'The Unrepentant Centralist'. Perhaps Hamilton has a campaign medal for dispatching the Schools Council. At about the same time as Hamilton went to the DES Prime Minister Callaghan asked the Department for a memorandum on four salient issues. The Department's reply *School Education in England: Problems and Initiatives* was marked 'for official use only', was leaked almost immediately in July 1976 and was widely publicized as the *Yellow Book*. 'The Schools Council', it said,

> has performed moderately in commissioning development work in particular curricula areas; it has had little success in tackling examination problems…it has scarcely begun to tackle the problems of the curriculum as a whole…the overall performance of the Schools Council has in fact, both on curriculum and examination, been generally mediocre. Because of this and because the influence of the teachers unions has led to an increasingly political flavour – in the worst sense of the word – in its deliberations, the general reputation of the Schools Council has suffered a considerable decline over the last few years. In the light of this recent experience it is open to question whether the constitution of the Schools Council strikes the right balance of responsibility…There will have to be a review of its functions and constitution.

Alex Smith was outraged.

> If, I wondered, this is what they do when they support you, how do they behave when they dislike you? It was professional conduct of a kind that I was not accustomed to. The DES, after all, were members of the Schools Council. If the Council's performance in their judgment was mediocre, what efforts had they made as members to raise the standards of performance? What attempts had they made, as members, to express their criticisms within the Council? In my time I had seen none.

Alex Smith's assessment rings true. In my experience the Department remained at best a semi-detached member of the Council.

Alex persuaded Shirley Williams who was now Secretary of State to stay her hand and allow the Council to conduct an internal review. At the farewell party for Alex in 1978 Shirley Williams spoke of the importance of the new-style Council. When she and John Tomlinson spoke about remedying deficiencies revealed by local authorities' reports on their arrangements for the curriculum, she assured him, 'Don't worry. We haven't put you there to do nothing.' In the event, a change of government in 1979 meant that her assurances were worth no more than my supposedly 'permanent' appointment. By 1982 Sir Keith Joseph was ready to disband the Council, to end a unique experiment in participatory management. To what extent was this his own decision? Or was he merely articulating the impatient views of his official entourage?

The Trenaman enquiry revealed the extent to which the Department's views and values challenged those of many of its supposed partners. At the first meeting of Convocation in December 1979 the DES spokesman, Deputy Secretary John Hudson, had declared roundly that the NUT were propagating a heresy when they said that teachers had always seen their job as serving the interests of children and their parents, not an assumed national interest. Now in 1981 the DES submission to Trenaman categorically rejected the ideas of distributed power and participative consultation, they ignored what the Council and others had learned about the limitations of blockbuster projects, and they had, it seemed, a utilitarian view of education and a patronizing attitude to teachers. Deputy Secretary Walter Ulrich who had spent a couple of years in the Cabinet Office before coming to Education at the age of fifty now led the small Departmental team which gave oral evidence to Mrs Trenaman on 30 July and 3 August 1981. They thought the School Council's task with regard to curriculum development should be to know broadly what the present state of the curriculum is and what development work is going on, identify gaps in accordance with a strict assessment of national priorities, and take quick and efficient action to repair deficiencies. A good plumber would have done no less, I thought.

A small Council with ten members nominated by the Secretary of State would be enough to oversee the work of two small committees, one for primary and one for secondary education, with perhaps two or three sub-committees to which knowledgeable teachers might be appointed as individuals. This Council would act as a board of management determining policies and priorities and supervising the activities of staff.

As things were, 'the highly idiosyncratic constitution and organization of the Schools Council fails altogether to meet' the two requirements that it should 'be capable of rendering an account of its stewardship and of effectively discharging its functions'. The organization was certainly unusual, and it did not conform to the hierarchical structures Ulrich would have recognized from first-generation management texts, but he should have known of the sheer volume and high quality of the Council's contributions on curriculum and examinations. There is an admirable account of our stewardship in *Issues and Achievements*, the sharp sixteen-page pamphlet we published in 1982. But this complaint about the constitution was odd, in that three years earlier John Hudson, another Deputy Secretary, had said at the end of Alex Smith's constitutional review, 'The DES will support the proposals as they stand.' Now Ulrich complained that the internal nature of the review had precluded any radical proposals.

In any case, he said, things had moved on since then and it was generally accepted now that the Department could speak with authority on curriculum issues. Bizarrely, in view of this claim, Ulrich also complained that because Professional Committee sometimes failed to determine educational priorities DES officials in the Finance and Priorities Committee were in the invidious position of having to make decisions on curriculum issues for which they were ill equipped.

It was indeed the case that many DES officials were ill prepared for Schools Council committee work. This was partly because the Department had failed to come to terms with the Council's legal status as an independent body and a charity. The difficulty they had is well illustrated in a letter dated 2 July 1981 from Miss Jean Dawson saying, 'I understand that Mr Ulrich deliberately withheld DES approval' to the Council's annual report at Convocation. In reply I wrote saying, 'As I understand the constitutional position, it is for Convocation acting corporately to approve the annual report rather than the constituent members acting separately.' This letter was never acknowledged, but neither was my 1979 letter to the Permanent Secretary saying I hoped the Schools Council would be able to follow up some of the ideas I had heard him outline in a speech to the Society of Education Officers.

I often had the feeling that DES officials were not really at ease as full and equal members of an independent Council. Some seemed to find it incongruous and others frustrating that their reasoning sometimes failed to win assent. They would rather have been observers at the meetings of some dependent grant-aided body whose accountability to the DES was beyond doubt. One odd example of their inability to live with divergent views occurred when our Parents Liaison Committee decided that schools ought to publish more information than the Education Act 1980 required. To the evident annoyance of departmental officers the Liaison Committee's views were endorsed by Professional Committee and Convocation, and we published a list of the information the Council thought should be published together with a note of where to find the statutory requirements.

They had too a fairly unsophisticated view of how to work to a budget. Murphy's Law asserts that if things can go wrong they will, and delays in getting work done or having supplies delivered are much more likely than completion ahead of time. If you want to ensure that you spend every penny of your annual budget, you should launch projects and place orders worth 5 or 10 per cent more than your budget. Keep a close watch on progress and actual disbursements, and if the unexpected happens and everything comes in on time for the first nine or ten months of your financial year decelerate and if needs be apply the brakes. That way you've a fair chance of hitting the target instead of undershooting as government departments are prone to do. Unhappily, this creative approach to controlling a budget greatly disturbed Jean Dawson and her colleagues.

Another difficulty was that DES officials were unwilling or unable to speak freely for the Department whereas the senior councillors and chief officers who represented the local authorities and the general secretaries and leading executive members who represented the teachers' unions seemed to see themselves as plenipotentiaries. Only a Minister would have had that freedom to represent the DES. Ministers might also have been more at ease than DES officials in the Council's more robust debates. Most of the teachers and local authority people were used to mixing it in union meetings, council rooms and public meetings and NUT General Secretary Fred Jarvis was not the only one to introduce an overly political point to some of his contributions. The DES thought real debate was impossible in Convocation, and saw no room for any such gathering in their ideal Council. Mr Ulrich thought Alex Smith's comparison with Parliament showed 'a frightening ignorance of what Parliament is and does' whereas John Tomlinson believed that a national educational council in which the producers and consumers of education met on equal terms was an essential part of an open educational society.

Most of the teachers on the Council's main committees, though not those on the subject committees, were nominated by their unions. The DES recognized that the teachers' professional contribution was indispensable but thought some of the unions' representatives were ill equipped to make a professional contribution and were inclined to act as if they were union delegates.

> This tendency has unfortunately been the more damaging because the Secretary of the Council has acted throughout on the premise that it is more necessary to have regard to the views of the teachers (as expressed by their unions) than to those of all the other interests. In the DES view, this is both inappropriate...and unnecessary in practice. The great majority of working teachers are content to work within a system which is largely determined externally provided their own contribution, in curriculum development as in their other work, is acknowledged and humanely fostered.

It was of course a great relief to know that the DES thought teachers should be treated humanely, though as they said this only in giving confidential evidence it may still be an official secret. But I was surprised by the charge against the Secretary. In my early days at the Council I had to rebut in almost equal numbers the charges that I was a Departmental lackey or a union stooge. As long as the numbers were roughly equal I thought I was probably on the right course. No one from the Department ever mentioned their concern about my apparent regard for the views of teachers, but there is a grain of truth in the charge that I attached great importance to the views of teachers. Overwhelmingly the teacher members were committed to the Council. Many were long-standing and enthusiastic supporters of its work, and it's hard not to respond warmly to enthusiasm. By contrast the DES officials who attended committees were necessarily somewhat reserved. More important, I believed then as I had in Sheffield that, as Lawrence Stenhouse put it, 'it is the task of all educationists outside the classroom to serve the teachers.' The deal pupils get depends on their teachers, so in that sense no improvement is possible unless the teachers support it.

Mr Ulrich went on in his private sessions with Mrs Trenaman to level other criticisms against Council staff: 'Neither the Secretary nor his senior staff have created order out of or given direction to the multifarious activities of the Council in relation to curriculum development.' He clearly hoped for a tightly managed system whereas we saw ourselves more as gardeners or conservators in a vast ecological park. Above all, 'the Council required a competent, loyal and submissive staff… but now there seemed to be a serious danger of disorder through lack of control.' I was certainly conscious of the need for tighter control, but it had taken eighteen months to get DES approval to appoint a qualified accountant and two and a half years to get DES clearances to appoint all our management team. The full team did not assemble for the first time until shortly after Mrs Trenaman's appointment. It's true the staff were not all equally competent, but I've never worked with more enthusiastic people, every one a self-starter. The only one whose resignation I had to ask for had an overly casual view of what constituted out-of-pocket expenses. And who it was who failed to doff his or her cap submissively I do not know. All I remember of my one conversation with Walter Ulrich, over lunch during a Council meeting at a London hotel, was his asking provocatively whether a system of selective schools might be better than comprehensive schools. But then, he was a Wykehamist who had come fairly recently to a high-ranking post in the DES after a working life in government departments like Housing and Works. On a busy day this seemed a fairly dead issue and certainly one on which the Council had no vote. Perhaps it was I who lacked the gene of deference.

For Ulrich the central problem was that

the appointment of the Secretary had been constrained by the level of salary available, and hence an inadequate pool of applicants. With the right kind of management structure however the Secretary would have to conform to acceptable practice; at present there was no means of coercing him to do so.

No doubt Walter Ulrich was as surprised as I was to see the gist of his comments displayed for all the world to read in *The Times* on 3 December 1981. A decade or two later I might have sued, but the Council's lawyers said

Ulrich's 'evidence' had 'qualified privilege' and in any case I was really more surprised than hurt. After all, the DES vetted each Council post and determined its grade, Deputy Secretary John Hudson and Senior Chief Inspector Sheila Browne were members of the panel who had interviewed candidates for the Secretaryship and decided to make an appointment, and my grade was the one just below Ulrich's own grade. Did he really think my job was so onerous it should have been on the same grade as his, or even higher? Had he forgotten that in 1979 the *Times Educational Supplement* said there was a good team of candidates? Was he aware that not a single DES official had ever spoken to me about the Council or my role and duties?

Oddly enough his remarks might have been counter-productive. Finance and Priorities Committee, lacking its DES members who tactfully stayed away, were outraged and John Tomlinson was obliged to seek an immediate audience with Sir Keith Joseph, the new Secretary of State. And Christopher Price has recorded his impressions as Chairman of the Select Committee on Education Science and Arts. The Council had made a fairly good impression on the Committee when we went to give evidence. Our delegation included Jim Deboo of Baker Perkins and the CBI, Ron Cocking of the NAS/UWT, Alastair Lawton from the County Councils, Peter Horton from the Municipal Authorities, and Arnold Jennings, the Head of Ecclesfield School, once of the West Riding but for some years part of Sheffield. It was almost a Sheffield reunion for Christopher Price, Peter Horton, Arnold Jennings and myself. Arnold Jennings was our linchpin. In a rich and varied career he had taught classics and cross-country running to my good friend John Morris, employed Christopher Price and my brother Peter and sister-in-law Sheila as teachers at Ecclesfield, served on the Sheffield City Council, campaigned unsuccessfully for election to Parliament, and was said to have launched Christopher Price on his political career. Arnold was by far the fastest talker I've ever met, a friendly open man with an endless fund of anecdotes and immediate recall of any topic however casual the conversation. Having narrowly failed to become President of the National Union of Teachers he had become President of the Head Masters' Association. Through all this he was a committed Schools Council man for all its twenty years, chaired its Examinations Committee, and as Acting Chairman was to preside over its last rites. He was, said Price, the most plausible and impressive witness in our team, convincing the Select Committee that there was a job to do and that some reasonably independent body was necessary to do it.

Since Mrs Trenaman was thought to be a personal friend of the Prime Minister the Conservatives on the Select Committee rather assumed that when she blessed the Council the Prime Minister must have done so too. And when the minutes of the DES meeting with Mrs Trenaman were leaked to the Select Committee, according to Price even the most right-wing Conservatives warmed to the Council. The minutes made it clear that one of the DES officials had made some deeply damaging remarks about John Mann, the Council's Secretary, without chapter and verse to back them up and without, of course, John Mann having an opportunity to rebut them. Since the DES official who we deduced had been conducting the campaign against John Mann in private, had also made a thoroughly bad impression on the Select Committee when he appeared to give evidence before it, that also, ironically, raised the Council's status in Conservative eyes.

Writing four years later Christopher Price confessed that he thought the Trenaman Report would have settled the issue. But, 'I had underestimated the rapacious determination of the government to obtain ministerial control over the curriculum.'

By December 1981 however when Ulrich's private thoughts were publicized I had been three years in post and was accustomed to the Department's idiosyncratic approach to staffing matters. Apart from about a dozen people, including a handful of editors, one or two information officers and a few of the curriculum and research officers, the Council had no directly recruited or permanent staff until 1978. The secretarial and administrative staff came on secondment from the DES who seemed to move people as and when they chose with no regard for team-building, expertise in the Council's affairs, or the need to see things through to a successful conclusion. Three different officers headed our committee secretariat in just four years, and we lost a second finance officer only two years after I joined the Council. They were both capable men, but neither had any accountancy qualifications. For fifteen years the Department allowed the Council to develop a new support system for curriculum development involving complex contracts with many other academic and commercial bodies without ensuring that the Council had the capacity and the expertise to develop and run appropriate financial systems. Coming from a city education department with a qualified accountant to head the department which prepared our annual estimates and handled income and expenditure, and a second accountant to undertake the financial appraisal of all new schemes, I felt naked. It was I who had to press for a qualified accountant, and it was more than eighteen months before we were able to recruit Gerry Callen. His expertise would have been enormously helpful when we were planning the new programmes but he arrived only as they were starting.

Most urgent in 1978 was the need to introduce a pension scheme for the growing number of directly recruited staff. This depended on the findings of a Departmental inspection team that had to satisfy itself that the posts were appropriately graded. Between my appointment in June 1978 and starting work in October I made two special visits to London to discuss the inspection report. At the second meeting on 22 September I was told that the draft report would be ready in about six weeks and we discussed arrangements for consulting staff about the draft. We even discussed when and how to submit the report to Council committees. What actually happened was quite different.

We received no draft. The inspection team came to see me on 4 December 1978. They brought no draft but we were told to expect it in January. It did not arrive. An interim note with some key recommendations arrived too late for me to consult staff before submitting its recommendations to a January committee. As March 1979 approached it became clear that the report would not be ready for the Finance and Priorities Committee that month. The report eventually reached me on 7 March 1980, two years after the new Council came into being. Had the inspection team intended to undermine morale and sabotage the Council, what more could they have done?

By that time of course some points of detail had been settled and F.A. Harper, an officer at my own level and head of the relevant DES section, came to see me in February 1979 to explain with a meaningful tap on his nose that he and his closest colleague were in the fast stream and if there were any difficulties with his slower colleagues I had only to have a word and particular matters could be quickly sorted. That, to adapt Roger Sturge's phrase, was not an approach which would have occurred to me.

My experience of the inspection team was my first direct involvement with the Department. Instead of making rapid progress in creating a new management team the Council had to proceed piecemeal until a new team finally gathered during the course of the Trenaman review in 1981. I wasn't quite sure whether the inspection team were obstructive, incompetent or overworked. They certainly did nothing to make me or my Council colleagues feel that the Department was there to help.

Whether the Department had a consistent long-term agenda is a moot point. Schools and their teachers enjoyed increasing freedom from the 1920s to the 1960s or 1970s. In the 1920s the Board of Education stopped controlling elementary schools and in 1950 the examining boards lost control of the secondary school curriculum when the single-subject General Certificate of Education replaced the School Certificate. After a lengthy period of post-war austerity the 1960s were a time of relative prosperity, optimism and trust. In the 1960s teachers were trusted to control the new Certificate of Secondary Education, became equal partners in the Schools Council, and won seats on the governing bodies of colleges of education. As late as 1977 the Taylor Report recommended that teachers sit by right on all school governing bodies. But by then the counter-revolution was well advanced. Minister Sir David Eccles first talked of the 'secret garden' of the curriculum in 1960, and in 1961 an internal departmental memo suggested that Ministers should have policies with regard to teaching methods, subjects, curricula, examinations, the internal organiza-tion of schools and the use of staff. Any immediate attempt to develop and implement these policies was averted by the creation of the Schools Council. Before long, however, the Department was able to return to its centralist agenda. In the 1970s the oil crisis and trade deficits spelt financial constraint, and schools were blamed at least in part for the shortage of skilled workers, rising unemployment and the collapse of manufactures. The Department of Education was itself condemned, by both an OECD team and a House of Commons Select Committee, for its poor planning. In response to this critique the government brought in new management at the DES, Hamilton and Ulrich from the Cabinet Office and Stuart from the Prime Minister's Office, and the Department counter-attacked by asking local authorities to describe their arrangements for the curriculum. The gaps their replies revealed led the Department to say that it would issue a framework for the curriculum, and that in turn led the Council to publish *The Practical Curriculum*. It had a good press and may have influenced the evidence to Mrs Trenaman and her conclusions.

Mrs Trenaman had been appointed by Mark Carlisle, a liberal and fair-minded lawyer who had been a junior judge (a recorder) before he became Secretary of State. He fell in Mrs Thatcher's first major cabinet re-shuffle, and was succeeded on 14 September 1981 by Sir Keith Joseph, a former Fellow of All Souls College, Oxford, the most prestigious academic achievement open to new Oxford graduates. Sir Keith was one of the most brilliant and original Conservative political philosophers of his day, often credited with laying the foundations of Thatcherism. I once heard him wrestling privately with the problem of how to improve the country's schools. What instruments could a politician use? He discounted local authorities and their advisory staff, Her Majesty's Inspectors, the Schools Council and other agencies. The only levers which might effect change were money and parents. Others might question this monetarist and consumerist approach. I was more interested in his use of terms like instruments and levers. He seemed to see the education service in mechanical terms and his own role as that of an engineer, a mechanic or a builder. Perhaps that came from his own nurture and experience. The Joseph family made their money from Bovis, the building contractors, and Sir Keith had worked for the family firm. He and the aeronautical engineer Hamilton, and Ulrich, the man whose formative years in the civil service were in departments like Housing and Works, may have come to education in middle age with a shared taste for mechanical control systems.

Within a few weeks of taking office Sir Keith Joseph found the Trenaman Report on his desk. After allowing a decent interval for the furore over Ulrich's 'evidence' to die down he wrote on 22 April 1982 to the Council's Acting Chairman, Dr Peter Andrews, saying, 'We have weighed carefully the available evidence including of course Mrs Trenaman's Report.' Whatever that report may have said he was going to disband 'the Schools Council and replace it with two separate bodies, one for examinations, the other for curriculum development'. 'We must have some ritual bloodletting' said his junior Minister, Rhodes Boyson, with Lancastrian candour. And the Prime Minister herself bandied words with a former Joint Secretary, observing that 'the Schools Council always was a lousy organization'.

Obviously John Tomlinson and I had been licking the wrong boots all those years, if indeed either of us had been licking any boots at all. I sometimes wonder what would have happened if I'd responded differently when John aired the possibility of the Council acquiring a royal patron. He seemed to think the auguries were good, but I felt royal patronage would undermine the Council's democratic character and we took the matter no further. I wonder still how Sir Keith and his acolytes would have dealt with a Council with a royal president.

Announcing that the Department would stop funding the Council was one thing. But did this mean that Sir Keith was closing the Council? The Council was an independent body, an unincorporated association and a registered charity, with its own royalty income of some £250,000 a year. Though the Department never admitted they had lost the plot, it gradually became apparent that they had failed to grasp that the Council was an independent body whose existence no one else could terminate. We explored some intriguing futures for a free-standing Council. When the Department withdrew its grant perhaps the local authorities would continue to fund a smaller Council. If the local authorities also withdrew their grant, the royalties might be enough to fund a small Council with a few staff. Perhaps such a nucleus would attract additional funding from other charitable foundations.

Interest in these speculations waned a little when Council members began to understand for the first time that each of the individual members of an unincorporated association may be liable for all the association's debts. The Council's byzantine constitution made it hard to know exactly who the members of the Council were, but there did not seem much doubt that all the members of the four main committees were members of the association. If the grants dried up and the Council became liable for the cost of redundancy or forced retirement, individual members might have to foot the bill.

This would not have mattered very much when most of the staff were seconded from their regular employment on short-term assignments to the Council, but now most were on permanent appointments the Council's potential liabilities were much greater and individual members might have been ruined.

For once the Department and the Council were as one with a shared aim, to ratify the Council's pension scheme and agree redundancy terms. Only then would it be possible for the Council's life to end peacefully. The interminable staff review which was under way when I joined the Council had ended happily enough with agreement that Schools Council gradings were comparable with those in the Department and that Schools Council staff were therefore entitled to pensions similar to those of civil servants. Our staff could not join the civil service pension scheme itself, but they would enjoy all the same benefits in what was called a 'by-analogy' scheme. But things are rarely as simple as they seem. Some civil servants are regarded as 'mobile' and have somewhat different benefits from their immobile colleagues. Were we at the Schools Council to be regarded as mobile or not? Pensions and redundancy payments vary according to length of service, so were our years of service to be calculated from the introduction of the 'by-analogy' scheme, the day we joined the Schools Council, or the day we joined some other public service pension scheme? These and other fine details mattered enormously to my colleagues. One of our editors, an otherwise mild-mannered man named James Ryan who chaired our staff side, proved to have an incisive grasp of these matters. So too did the civil servants still working for the Council, and above all those at the Department who had to clear whatever was agreed with their Treasury colleagues. I never admired the civil service mind more than in observing the prompt and detailed analyses which went into winding up the Council's affairs.

Within a few days of Sir Keith's announcement Anthony Chamier, the Department's shrewd, fair-minded Director of Establishments, wrote to ask me to ensure that the Council entered into 'no new contractual obligation, whether for work, staff or premises, without our explicit permission'. Like the centralists in Sheffield a few years earlier the Department soon withdrew from this extreme position. They had no wish to control our day-to-day administration. We could buy things like Sellotape and instant coffee and modest supplies of headed paper, go on maintaining our computers and fax machines, engage agency staff on a week-by-week basis, transfer and promote existing staff, and go on making small grants. Longer-term contracts for new work or appointments were another matter, but our well-publicized fate meant there was little risk of anyone wanting to sign a new agreement with a prospective corpse.

We certainly needed the Department's blessing if we were to vacate our premises at Great Portland Street as the Property Services Agency wished and move to other accommodation. We had wanted for some time to move to less expensive accommodation to make our diminishing resources go further. We even considered places like Milton Keynes, Peterborough and Birmingham where rents and salaries were really low. We would have been happy to move to one of the outer London boroughs where rents were much lower than in central London. We found several promising buildings, each rejected by the Department largely it seemed because it lay outside London's magic Inner Circle and beyond Jean Dawson's mental horizon. Eventually, too late for the move to affect our budget significantly, we moved to Newcombe House at Notting Hill Gate.

Unravelling our existing engagements was rather more complicated. The Department had failed to grasp how extensive and how complex our activities were. Each activity was at a different stage in its life cycle, and we had differing kinds of commitment to many different partners. Fortunately the new School Curriculum Development Committee agreed to take on several major activities in mid-stream, including the Industry Project, the Secondary Science Curriculum Review, and our Guidelines for Review and Internal Development. Fortunately too the Council had planned only a three-year life for the five programmes launched in 1980, and several of the older large-scale projects also came to an end by 1983. Our minds wonderfully focused by the thought of execution, we worked flat-out to prepare and publish the results of all these activities. From 1982 to 1984 we held press conferences almost every week to announce an impressively varied selection of pamphlets, teachers' guides, pupils' books, reports and handbooks. Just a week or two before the Council shut its doors in 1984 the Secretary of State spoke at an international colloquium about the Mother Tongue Project, funded by the European Community and run by the Schools Council. Did Sir Keith realize, we wondered idly, that he was celebrating one of the achievements of the Council whose demise he had ordered? Was this the priceless 'power of holding two contradictory beliefs in one's mind simultaneously, and accepting both of them', which Orwell described as doublethink in *Nineteen Eighty-four?*

CHAPTER 17

Harrow on the Hill

Dialogues of the deaf

'YⁿOU'RE A BIT OLD for this sort of job, aren't you?' It was June 1983, and the Conservatives had just won the General Election. 'Perhaps, but I'm slightly below the *average* age of Mrs Thatcher's new Cabinet, so if some *much* older people are to be Cabinet ministers...'.

That answer may just have tipped the scale in my favour. After five years at the Schools Council and a gruelling safari lunch with Harrow councillors and chief officers I became the London Borough's Director of Education. The work would be varied and challenging and my journey to work still only half an hour. Our family income went up because long after Sir Keith Joseph decided to close the Schools Council his Department began to read the small print in our contracts and had to agree quite generous redundancy terms. Of all Mrs Thatcher's Ministers it was the arch-monetarist who took a leap into the dark without counting the cost. As Audit Commissioner John Banham once said 'you cannot be surcharged for wasting money' and by the time the last Council pensioner dies it will be too late to hand the final accounts to Sir Keith and his clever minions.

The London Borough includes three old villages with medieval roots, Pinner, Stanmore and Harrow on the Hill, and Wealdstone, a small industrial township which grew up round the Midland railway station on the London to Birmingham line. But modern Harrow is the heart of John Betjeman's beloved Metroland, an outer London suburb which grew in the 1920s and 1930s. Its four tube lines give ready access to central London, and a ready way out for city workers. More than 60 per cent of those employed still work outside Harrow and in return twenty or thirty thousand workers pour into Harrow every day. There was it seemed no matching flow of innovative practices to and from local schools. In that respect Harrow seemed further from the educational hub than Sheffield, or even Leeds.

Among the twentieth-century settlers in Harrow were waves of second- or third-generation Jewish and Irish families from East London, and from the 1960s Asians, mainly from East Africa or India, who were already about a quarter of the population. Harrow has exceptionally high proportions of home-owners, and of professional and managerial workers, high achievers with high ambitions for their children. One child in eight went to private schools, about twice the national average. If a school failed to satisfy them

Harrow parents were unusually quick to show their concern by taking their custom elsewhere, often from private to maintained schools, or vice versa.

It was a very different world from what I'd known in Sheffield, with one remarkable exception, the council's commitment to equal opportunities. Although Harrow's Council usually had a Conservative majority, its one Labour administration had revolutionized the borough's schools during their short lease of power from 1971 to 1974. Uniquely among English local authorities Harrow had a system of first, middle and high schools, with transfer at eight, twelve and sixteen years of age. For students over sixteen there were no sixth forms, only sixth form colleges and a college of further education. As far as possible both main parties tried to ensure that the schools serving each age group were about the same size as each other, had much the same accommodation and offered the same curriculum. There was in consequence no outstandingly successful school, nor any failing school. But taken as a whole in the mid 1980s Harrow's secondary schools were among the country's most successful.

Councillors feared that using a crude pupil–teacher ratio to determine the number of teachers at each school might lead to schools losing a teacher or two if the number of pupils changed, and that a school might then be forced to modify its curriculum or change its organization. A small change in numbers might force a first or middle school to introduce mixed-age classes, or a secondary school to drop a subject. My colleagues and I had to devise ways of distributing the teaching posts we could afford so as to protect every school's organization and curriculum. This kind of conundrum is among the most satisfying and creative tasks an administrator has to tackle.

Even with the most refined staffing formulae Harrow's high schools were too small to offer a wide choice of subjects. There was certainly no demand for the pre-vocational courses which some Leeds schools had offered in the 1960s, but in a compact borough like Harrow, no more than four or five miles from side to side or end to end, some specialization among the schools might have widened choice across the whole borough. One school might have offered Latin, another Spanish, a third Music, and so on. But these modest suggestions made no headway in Conservatively egalitarian Harrow in the 1980s. Two decades later it took a Labour government to invent 'specialist' schools.

In the meantime I enjoyed a soft landing in Harrow. To ensure a smooth handover my new masters arranged for me to start work two months before my predecessor retired. There was time and space to meet new colleagues and find my way round Harrow and its schools and colleges. I had time to see Michael Johnson sitting defensively in a corner behind his desk so that it protected him from any possible assault, physical or verbal. Not that assault was likely. Any visitor had first to pass the inquisitorial eye of gatekeeper Maggie Hickey in the next room. Not even Barry Turner ever presumed to use the other door straight from the corridor. Barry was a retired railway engineer, kindly, bluff and cheery, magistrate and councillor, Chair of the Schools Sub-Committee, and married to one of Harrow's primary school head teachers. Once she went off to work in the morning he liked nothing better than to drop into the office to chew the cud with the Director and have a coffee before going on to one of his many other meetings. If by chance the Director was not available Barry would work his way along the corridor from one Assistant Education Officer's room to the next. Michael Johnson might chunter about losing half the morning to desultory gossip but he had been trapped in this routine a long time ago. Sitting in on a dozen or two of these *conversazione* gave me a lot of useful background, but it might be better, I thought, if I was not to be found at my desk at 9.30 every single morning.

Maggie controlled the access to my deputy's room as well as mine. Michael Sansome had twice applied for the Directorship and having been rejected twice had not risked a third rejection when Johnson retired. Michael was a private person, friendly, neat, clean-cut, almost officer-like in manner and bearing, very proud of his talented sons, amused and pleased to share a Pinner garden fence and even an occasional security officer with the great Minister Dr Rhodes Boyson. He kept of course a clean and tidy office, modestly furnished with a small book-case and a few pristine texts.

Michael's clear table and uncluttered desk mystified visiting delegates from India, raised as they had been in the Victorian high-stool, quill-pen bureau-cracy which Britain left as a legacy to the sub-continent. 'Where are your files?' they demanded inquisitorially. Even Michael himself was amused. Michael had a great talent for seeming both business-like and busy as he oversaw our building projects and it was some time before I realized that a crisp manner and the ability to bring matters to a successful conclusion do not always go hand in hand.

It took me even longer to grasp that my friendly colleagues had expectations which I could not meet. When they were doubtful about what to do with regard to some administrative matter or a head teacher's or a parent's request they expected the Director to know precisely which existing rule should be applied. Being totally unaware of these local rules I caused great confusion by propounding principles which I hope were liberal but which happened all too often to be at variance with the unwritten house rules. Confused, my colleagues naturally took to referring more and more specific questions to me personally, while I became increasingly dismayed by their apparent reluctance to decide fairly low-level matters for themselves. Without knowing it I had moved from a value-led and structured department in Sheffield via a less structured but even more value-led Schools Council to a rule-led department in Harrow. I and my new colleagues would be more comfortable with each other once we had agreed which values fired our department.

Fortunately the Local Government Training Board came to our rescue. They were ready to help arrange and fund their first management development seminar for an education department. Our party of twenty-four included the heads of the advisory, careers, library and psychological services, the education specialists from the council's finance, law and personnel departments, and career administrators as well as education officers. We were the senior managers of a public service enterprise with capital assets of £200 or £300 million, about 4,000 paid employees and 30,000 clients. Some met each other for the first time at this seminar. We had no printed programme, and no planned talks.

Instead we met first in groups to identify the Department's problems, then shared our thoughts with other groups, considered the most serious problems in detail, and worked out how to tackle them. Ten minutes with paper and pencil and a quick brainstorming session showed how much scope there was for in-house as well as off-the-job training. By the final session we had fashioned a sturdy platform on which to build: we were committed to agreeing values and developing mutual trust, and we understood that we could all contribute to developing our Department.

Then the whole Department joined in discussions about what we contributed to the education service in Harrow, what objectives we should set ourselves for the following year, which officers should be responsible for achieving each objective and how the Department should be structured to make its contribution as effective as possible. Within six months or so the council agreed proposals for restructuring, and three years after my move to Harrow the new management team held a second residential seminar when we agreed that providing 'a service which puts the consumer first and gives access to educational opportunities to all' was our key value. This agreement cloaked the Damascene revelation which came to me during one of our group meetings: one of my senior colleagues and I held such conflicting values there was hardly room for both of us in the same organization. Fortunately a timely escape route appeared when long-standing physical problems forced my colleague to retire early.

At the same seminar we also agreed five key objectives: improving our own *Efficiency*, improving our *Relations with Others*, promoting *Equal Opportunities*, setting up a system of *Tertiary Colleges* and developing Harrow's services for *Children with Special Needs*. The first three may sound like pious aspirations. Not so. Managers at every level were challenged to identify tasks which would contribute to achieving our objectives and to show every three months what their team had done to meet the objectives. Each of the functional branches: Personnel, Client Services, Premises, Finance and Supplies, and Committee and Office Services set up computer databases, and we could soon report better systems for dealing with many routine tasks such as recovering costs from other local authorities, paying invoices, allocating school places, controlling expenditure, assessing and paying student awards, and assessing our own training needs.

Some of our attempts to meet these needs broke new ground. We could not use Fred Cooper, Ralph Coverdale and Esso as I had in Sheffield, but my friend Professor Keith Jackson of Bulmershe College had developed a similar systematic approach to *Getting Results and Solving Problems* when there are obstacles to be overcome. To help promote a sense of common purpose Keith ran a series of training sessions for mixed groups of head teachers and people from the Education Department. Reviewing their experience a few months later several heads said it was the best help they ever had from the Department and one said it had helped her revive the torpid run-down primary school she had just inherited.

From time to time I made space to continue my own professional development. Industry Year 1986 gave me an opportunity to strengthen my own links with local firms and foster closer links between our schools and local firms. Rank-Xerox contributed an industrial perspective on management for a dozen education officers and a student shadowed me for a week as part of her work experience. It was a full week. I chaired departmental meetings where relations were hierarchical and other meetings of volunteers. I met union secretaries, my chairman, my chief executive, a bank manager whose help I needed with Industry Year, a journalist who interviewed me about Industry Year, a university teacher to discuss training for education officers, a head who came to discuss the pressures to which a group of Asian parents were subjecting him and his school, and a head of department who thought her head teacher was undermining an excellent department. We went to a degree-giving ceremony at the College of Higher Education, heard Jeremy Isaacs talk to the graduates, and ate strawberries. My shadow paid her way by making a detailed analysis of how I spent my time. Once or twice in my life I've summoned enough energy to note for a week or two exactly what I was doing every ten minutes. It's much easier when someone else does this for you. I was surprised how much I got out of being shadowed. I was suddenly much more aware of the many different kinds of relationship my work involves, much more aware of other people's sensitivities and the kinds of confidence being given and expected in my varied transactions. Without exception those I met responded well to my being shadowed; after a moment's hesitation they extended to both me and my shadow the trust I was giving my shadow. The need to explain each new encounter to an outsider reminded me how many had a previous history. The presence of an outsider who had to be briefed and debriefed seemed to make many of these encounters more purposeful and more productive than usual.

A week with the Grubb Institute exploring tasks and roles in education management was more demanding. Even before the course began I had to find ten people to say how they would characterize my leadership and management style, how in my work I usually came across to them, and how they would characterize their working relationships with me. Chairman, chief executive, college principal, head teacher, personal assistant, union secretary, chief adviser and three departmental managers offered snapshots from many different angles. 'Willing to measure sacred cows for slaughter' the chief executive observed enigmatically. No wonder others sometimes found me guarded and hard to read. Mostly however Dr Jekyll seemed friendly, good humoured, tolerant and open-minded in one-to-one relations. Mr Hyde was impatient and directive, prone to take decisions without seeking the best advice, and somewhat authoritarian. Both Jekyll and Hyde appear in the mirror each time I shave, each growing more pronounced with advancing age.

These experiences were certainly enjoyable and stimulating. They may also have helped to make the Department more efficient and improve our relations with others. They certainly did not distract me or my colleagues from our two biggest tasks, effecting radical changes in Harrow's provision for students over sixteen, and improving the services for students with special needs.

When the Committee reorganized their schools in 1974 they created four sixth form colleges and planned a fifth. Plans for the fifth college were soon abandoned when the expected upsurge in student numbers failed to materialize, and the frailest of the four colleges was closed when it became clear that in Harrow the number of young people between sixteen and nineteen would fall by 30 per cent in the 1980s. At the same time the Committee realized that they would have to replace the antiquated and inadequate premises of the former Commercial Travellers' School which masqueraded as Harrow's College of Further Education. With astonishing boldness they decided to merge all their sixth form and further education courses in a new tertiary system. There was no significant opposition. The secondary high schools had already lost their sixth forms, so their main concern was the quality of the links between the high schools and the post-sixteen system. The fundamental question was whether there should be one large college on a single site, one large college using several sites, or several colleges on their own sites. Broadly speaking the further education people favoured one large college and the sixth form and schools people small colleges. The Education Committee tended to prefer small and equal schools, so it was no great surprise that they decided in favour of three colleges of about the same size and standing as each other. Each college would provide the same range of academic, general and business courses, each would offer some of the less popular academic subjects and have one major vocational specialism such as catering or travel and tourism, and each would contribute to Harrow's extensive adult education programme. The funds released by selling two redundant sites would cover much of the cost of huge extensions at the three remaining sixth form college sites.

Secretary of State Sir Keith Joseph was sufficiently intrigued by these radical notions to summon the Chairman and other councillors to explain them. He wondered whether the Education Committee had been bewitched by card-carrying officers. No one could have presented Harrow's case more persuasively than Chairman Brian Clark. Scientist by training, Kodak manager by profession, and lately Leader of the Council, numerate, moderate and reasonable, Brian had a thorough grasp of the political, financial and educational issues. I only saw him discomfitted once, when I drove him and Barry Turner to Newcastle to the annual conference of metropolitan authorities. After a convivial conference dinner Brian showed his appreciation of the expert Durham sword dancers who had entertained us by tossing money into their collecting box. Too late, his Tory colleagues soon let him know he'd contributed generously to Arthur Scargill's fund for the miners' war against Mrs Thatcher.

Sir Keith's approval reached Harrow as a timely accolade for Michael Johnson in his last few weeks as Director. 'Going tertiary' was to be one of my main preoccupations for the next four years. The Committee were much exercised about the management structure for the new colleges. Liaison with industry and commerce and with other colleges and schools seemed so important that they entrusted this responsibility to the two vice-principals in each college. Instead of the great baronial faculties to be found in some further education colleges, the Committee favoured a flatter structure in which the directors of studies, student services, staff development, adult education and information technology were principal lecturers on the same grade as the heads of the major teaching programmes.

They were also much exercised about admission policies. In line with their commitment to equal opportunities they wanted to provide suitable courses for everyone in Harrow who wanted to go on studying beyond sixteen. The emphasis switched from trying to select the most promising students for scarce places on A-level courses to counselling young people and trying to find or devise a course which would help each of them. The Committee insisted that the colleges co-operate in a joint campaign to publicize and promote the much-extended opportunities now available for education beyond sixteen. This approach was remarkably successful in attracting students. Within a few years the colleges had twice as many students as the 2,600 we expected.

As the overall aims were clarified, we thought increasingly of Fred Cooper and Keith Jackson and their systematic approach. What obstacles had to be overcome before the colleges could open? What had to be done and who had to do it? Much of 1983 went in identifying ninety-seven different tasks which had to be completed, assigning these tasks to specialist groups drawn from the Department and the colleges, and agreeing a provisional timetable which took account of the need for the Education Committee to be informed and to take certain critical decisions. Our tasks included drafting Instruments and Articles of Government for the Colleges and securing the Secretary of State's approval for them, drafting any local financial rules which might be needed, and ensuring that extensions and adaptations worth £7 million were ready on time and the buildings properly equipped and furnished.

Naming the new colleges was among the most contentious issues. The teachers at Stanmore, suffering from low self-esteem because their sixth form college had been established for youngsters from secondary modern schools, wanted a change of name to mark their new standing as one of three equal colleges. On the other side former Home Secretary Merlyn Rees, once a pupil and then a teacher at Harrow Weald Grammar School, was perhaps the best-known of the vocal band who mounted the barricades to guard famous names like Harrow Weald. A happy compromise saw Elm Park rise from Stanmore's ashes, Lowlands renamed Greenhill, and Harrow Weald reborn as Weald by much the same process as Merlyn Rees became Lord Merlyn Merlyn-Rees.

Another stirring issue was that of union recognition. The union for teachers in further and higher education claimed exclusive negotiating rights even though most of the staff in the new colleges were to come from sixth form colleges and were members of school teachers' unions. My enquiry to other local authorities about their attitude to this question elicited an amazing 90 per cent response within three weeks. The further authorities were from reorganization the more inclined they were to say they would consult everyone, negotiate with everyone and recognize every union. The few who had already reorganized had reluctantly applied the national agreements which gave exclusive negotiating rights to the National Association for Further and Higher Education. In Harrow we tried to safeguard the interests of the schoolteachers' unions by devising local arrangements for consulting all the unions before NATFHE was asked to ratify any agreement formally.

This did something to allay the fears of sixth form teachers, many of whom were uninformed and apprehensive about their impending transfer from schools to what were legally colleges of further education. We had to tell whole staffs and many individuals about the tertiary system and the nationally agreed conditions of service. My own contribution included speaking to whole staff meetings at each of the sixth form colleges and meeting many of their staff individually.

Then came the more arduous process of selecting people for posts in the new colleges. This meant re-deploying more than 500 people. Once principals and vice-principals had been appointed they and a group of officers and advisers interviewed ninety of the 120 applicants for the twenty-seven principal lecturer posts. We met every day for two weeks and each candidate was seen by three panels of three or more people. The three principals designate, the adviser for post-sixteen education and I saw all the candidates, though other members of the panels saw only some of the candidates. Our twice-daily meetings for briefing and debriefing and our corporate sandwich lunches were of great value in ensuring that the complex interview arrangements worked smoothly and that the interviewers remained on pretty well the same wavelength. Among the incidental benefits one was that the senior people in each college got to know each other and the Authority's officers very well so that a strong tertiary management team was created, and similarly, within each college, the principals and vice-principals met together very much more than they had done previously. A final session when we agreed who was to be appointed to each college was surprisingly harmonious.

One factor we had not considered was the scale of disappointment when the results were announced. In some areas like Information Technology and Art and Design there were comparatively few strong candidates, and some fairly inexperienced and junior people were appointed. In other areas such as Student Services and Staff Development there were many interested and comparatively well-qualified candidates, and a number of well-qualified and mature people were not appointed. In some of the sixth form colleges, perhaps Harrow Weald especially, several experienced heads of department were dismayed when they did not achieve promotion to third-tier posts in the new colleges.

Some of the comments made when the appointments were announced showed how febrile college staffrooms were. I was asked whether I knew how many further education people had been appointed, whether I knew how many members of the Assistant Masters and Mistresses Association had been appointed and whether there were enough women. In fact, without striving for equality and certainly without ever appointing a second-choice candidate to achieve some sort of quota, the appointing group felt that the outcome was reasonably fair as between the further education and school sectors, the various colleges and the two sexes.

Our helicopter view of the situation gave little comfort to people who were worried about their assimilation to different salary scales and the small print in their future job descriptions. We had at this point to abandon our intended timetable and spend a month in detailed discussions between officers and principals, officers and unions, officers, principals and unions, officers, principals, unions and councillors. These discussions were of considerable value in developing a shared understanding and the habit of collaboration. As a result we were able to reach general agreement with the unions on matters like safeguarding, assimilation and the timetable for appointments.

The principals were surprised by their central role in this debate. They came as observers to the Tertiary Education Sub-Committee and were invited to speak, and, even more surprisingly, sitting in the gallery at the full Education Committee on 17 June 1985 they were also invited to speak. Their contribution to these discussions was an interesting extension of democratic processes because there was no doubt that in talking about the plans for each college, which already reflected the managerial experience and thinking of their principals, the principals were able to speak a great deal more authoritatively than any of the officers could have done.

During these discussions someone suggested that it would be very helpful if the staff of the existing colleges had the opportunity of meeting the principals to hear their thinking about the new colleges. One suggestion was closing the colleges for half a day so that we could have a mass meeting at the Leisure Centre. This idea did not appeal. Another suggestion was closing each college for half a day and the three principals appearing together on one platform. Again, this did not seem the best way of effecting a meeting of minds. What was decided was that the principals should try to go separately to each college to meet the staff, outline their thinking, answer questions and exchange views. The main difficulty was that the staff at Harrow Weald insisted that any meetings ought to be held in normal working hours, not after hours. An extended lunch hour or an early closure for such a purpose seemed entirely justified and was unlikely to interfere with the normal work of the colleges at that time of year. On that basis the principals met the staff of each of the existing colleges in June and July 1985. They spent much of the following year filling the remaining vacancies at their colleges, while we helped by securing funds from the Manpower Services Commission for in-service training and team-building. The funds covered the cost of intensive management courses for most of the newly appointed senior people and a residential conference for the principals and vice-principals, secondary school heads and their deputies, advisers and officers. This broadly based group gathered to consider the implications of tertiary reorganization for the education service. The first such conference in Harrow, it proved most helpful in developing a shared sense of purpose.

If the tertiary colleges started well it was at least partly because Sir Keith Joseph allowed a generous three and a half years between his formal approval and the launch in 1987. With the principals and their senior managers designated two years in advance, and most of the remaining staff appointed a year ahead, we in the Education Department were less and less involved in detailed preparations.

This left us with more space to think about improving our services for people with special needs. The Warnock Report on Special Educational Needs had emphasized that educational need is a continuum. Most of the children with special needs are already in mainstream schools, and only a small proportion need a statement saying in some detail what special provision must be made for them. Wherever possible this special provision should be in ordinary schools. The Education Act of 1981 embodied these principles, but the government's follow-up circular on assessments and statements of need was not published until shortly before the Act came into effect on 1 April 1983.

This prompted Harrow to take a fresh look at its arrangements for children with special needs. Many of the children with statements went to day schools in other parts of London or to boarding schools. We were spending almost half our £3.5M special needs budget on sending 200 children to schools outside the borough. No other authority was spending a higher proportion of its budget on places at private schools. If we could only make other satisfactory arrangements the potential savings were enormous, and the money saved could be used with advantage to enable some of Harrow's primary and secondary schools to educate many more children with special needs. My experience in Sheffield and what I had seen in Sweden and the USA convinced me that this was what we could and should be doing.

Fortunately there were several heads like Stella Chapple and Christine Gilbert who shared this belief and were ready for their own schools to play a part. When retirement gave me the opportunity to appoint a new Principal Psychologist I was delighted to find Tony Kerr who had cut his professional teeth in the Sheffield service and shared the broad view we had there of the role of education psychologists. I cherry-picked a small working party on Learning Difficulties and we put together the first of a number of suggestions for improving the educational opportunities of many low achievers. We encouraged teachers to attend a course run by the Dyslexia Association, and supported three on one-term courses, a step towards ensuring that a good proportion of our specialist teachers had formal training in special education. The following year a group of thirty people from primary, secondary and special schools and the psychological service took an Open University course in special needs, a shared experience which did much to foster mutual understanding and good relations. In September 1985 the Committee approved a four-year programme to strengthen a primary school unit for children with hearing loss, and to establish support units at four mainstream schools, one for children with emotional and behavioural difficulties and three for children with physical disabilities. A year later the Committee agreed to consult widely on various strategies to enable mainstream schools to provide for special needs. In June 1987 they took the decisive step of agreeing that for three years the special needs budget be updated annually in line with inflation and that funds voted for out-borough day or residential places might be used to provide staff, equipment or other resources to enable a child who would otherwise attend a special school to go to an ordinary school. Following earlier improvements at various primary and secondary schools this was a decisive step towards integration. With a scheme to support the parents of young children under five whose development was delayed, another project at Greenhill College for adults with severe learning difficulties, and a new local college course leading to the teachers' Diploma in Special Learning Difficulties, we were fast developing a coherent system of support and education for people with special needs. I was delighted that Harrow was chosen as one of the three local education authorities in a study of how the 1981 Education Act was working.

In many respects Harrow was one of the country's outstandingly successful education authorities in the late 1970s and early 1980s. No other area had a higher proportion of its pupils doing well at O-level. Only Barnet had more of its sixteen to nineteen year olds in full-time education, and only Richmond and Barnet were slightly ahead at A-level. Only four London boroughs and two other authorities were giving more new student awards for higher education.

Harrow people were naturally pleased to be sitting on top of the league tables. In this position many head teachers believed that the status quo was the way forward. An HMI warned me that some of Harrow's schools might seem a little self-satisfied and stuffy; 'dull competence' was, he thought, the borough's hallmark, a judgement confirmed by Harrow's chief adviser. The schools and the Education Committee were inclined to take credit for Harrow's high place in the league tables without pausing to ask whether it might be linked to the Borough's social and ethnic mix. I found myself wondering whether it was also attributable in part to Harrow having fairly small schools and to the high schools having a precisely defined task compared with secondary schools elsewhere which covered the whole span from eleven or twelve to eighteen.

In any case there was still much to be done. I reminded the Education Committee that even Harrow's results fell some way short of the targets Sir Keith Joseph had set in his Sheffield speech a few days after I arrived in Harrow. Harrow's middle and high schools lacked adequate accommodation for science and technology and Her Majesty's Inspectors said there was a statistically significant relation between the quality of accommodation and equipment in schools and their performance. Brian Clark was particularly concerned by this evidence, and under his leadership the Committee approved a £5 million programme to upgrade the schools' facilities for science, design education, craft and technology. Financing the programme would depend on the Committee's ability to cut the number of spare places in its secondary schools.

By this time Sir Keith Joseph and his ministerial colleagues had taken control of virtually all the money available for new developments in schools. Government intervention now went far beyond the long-established Home Office pump-priming grants for teaching English as a second language and the Department of Trade and Industry's Micros in Schools scheme. The Department of Education and Science funded training for the new General Certificate of Secondary Education and also gave Education Support Grants, which in Harrow paid for drugs education, computer equipment, and five much-needed advisory teachers for Mathematics and Science. The Manpower Services Commission launched its Technical and Vocational Education Initiative, funded tertiary college staff-training, and used its grants to take effective control of further education. Many of these schemes required matching contributions from the local authority. Running the rest of the service within a constrained budget grew more and more difficult.

From the time of the oil crisis in the mid 1970s councils had been preoccupied with the search for their own El Dorado, value for money. Alongside the latest rounds of grant applications my colleagues had to devote more and more time to making economies in catering, cleaning, energy consumption, lettings, advertising and other aspects of the service. The pressure redoubled when hard-line conservatives displaced the moderates who had held office in Harrow for several years. Early in 1985 the Council demanded 10 per cent savings over the following four years. By 1987 the Education Committee had fallen behind and were asked to save £2M from the £47 they needed to maintain existing services. Luckily I was able to convince the Education Committee that they could not save more than £1M without serious damage to the service. The Policy and Resources Committee reluctantly agreed and added the shortfall to the next year's target.

By this time we in the education party were clutching at straws. In a desperate effort to show we were leaving no stone unturned I suggested that secondary school governors might consider adopting a continental day. This would save a little on heating and support staff wages, and the schools would keep some of the savings for themselves. If the Christmas holiday was extended by a week or two with compensatory cuts in the summer holiday, we might save £10,000 a day on fuel. Such heterodoxy was cold-shouldered by heads and governors.

They were more at ease with my next proposals. Although Harrow was high in the league tables, about one in six of the secondary school pupils were going to schools outside Harrow. Some parents evidently chose a church school because there was no comparable school in Harrow, and some chose the most accessible school even though it was in another borough. Others preferred a more conventional school system in which children went to their secondary school at eleven not twelve and stayed at the same school for their sixth form course instead of going to a college. Some parents feared too that transfer at twelve meant that their children would lose the opportunity of going at eleven to their second-choice school in a neighbouring borough. To meet some of these concerns the Committee decided to offer secondary school places more than a year before children were due to change schools at twelve.

Whatever the reasons, the financial consequences of these individual choices to go outside Harrow were calamitous. We had to pay our neighbours the nationally agreed fee for every Harrow pupil in their schools, even though this was £600 a year more than the cost of educating each extra pupil in one of our own schools. Our own schools were only three-quarters full, and would soon be only two-thirds full. We could easily accommodate the 1,600 young people who were going to schools outside Harrow: if only a thousand came to Harrow schools instead of going elsewhere we could save £600,000 a year. Further long-term savings of some £400,000 a year were possible if the council insisted that the school meals service break even.

I expected the council to welcome this blue-skies thinking and challenge me and my colleagues to deliver results over the next few years. I did not anticipate the avidity with which Councillor Ron Grant would seize on the possibility of large-scale saving. But at that time I hardly knew him. Ron Grant was an accountant by trade, with a mini-mansion and a Roller as palpable evidence of worldly success. A hawk by inclination, following a right-wing *coup* Ron became Chair of Policy and Resources and aide-de-camp to Major Donald Abbott, the Leader of the Council. Donald Abbott was a smart little man who made much of his title and the vicarious knowledge of education he acquired through his wife's ownership of a small school. He reminded us constantly that she had bought usable secondhand chairs from one of our schools for next to nothing. This manifest profligacy in the education system called, he thought, for a firm hand. I must have been a grave disappointment to him. Vague complaints about one Head's day-to-day management of his school led him and Ron Grant to demand that I should 'discipline' the Head. They could not understand that in England's system of distributed powers no one in the Harrow Education Department was the Head's line manager, and that it was not possible for me to do what they wanted. Of course, if they already had an inkling of the more serious breaches of trust which led that Head to leave the area abruptly a few years later, I might have been justified in suspending him while the charges were investigated.

Donald Abbott was curiously impatient of the protocols of local government. Following a direct approach from the Sail Training Association he became a great enthusiast for their character-building courses. He thought we ought to meet the cost of sending suitable young people on these courses. Our youth and community officers demurred: this would be possible only if we diverted funds from other activities which they thought were more valuable for more young people. Donald persisted. We pointed out that only the Committee could abort an activity they had already approved. Given the council's calendar of meetings this would take some weeks. By that time, as Donald pointed out tartly, it would be too late to take places for the current sailing season. He obviously thought I ought to instruct my colleagues to do as he wished.

Ron Grant proved even more demanding when he succeeded Abbott as Leader. As an accountant he had a thirst for quantitative data and he had taken to heart the importance of persuading parents to send their children to Harrow schools. I found it hard to slake his thirst.

- *How many Harrow children were attending schools outside the borough?* We did not know. Parents were not required to tell us when they accepted places at out-borough schools or when they moved their children from maintained to private schools or vice versa.

- *Had the Education Committee's decision to stop paying the travelling expenses of children going to church schools outside Harrow affected the numbers going to those schools?* We did not know, because when other boroughs sent their claims they gave only total numbers with no breakdown for each school. (Readers may wonder how our auditors checked the claims. I don't know.)

- *Could we not telephone the schools themselves to find out how many Harrow children they had on their registers?* No. Local authority protocols were clear. We could not telephone schools in another area to ask for this kind of information.

- *Could we make dottographs showing the areas from which children were going to out-borough schools? Why did it take so long to supply simple information?* To keep within budget we had to keep one post in eight vacant and my colleagues were working flat-out.

- *Was it really true that the O-level league tables putting Harrow comfortably ahead of other authorities and so widely publicized in 1987 were based not on the latest examination results but on those for 1981, 1982 and 1983?* Yes indeed, so the tables were history rather than news. And they may have favoured Harrow because they included a standard weighting for children from non-white ethnic groups which took no account of the fact that many of Harrow's black people were ambitious, well-educated Gujerati from East Africa whose children probably enhanced the schools' results rather than depressing them.

- *Could we refute alarmist newspaper articles about the standard of repair and maintenance of school buildings?* The state of Harrow's schools bore comparison with other areas. But Ron was clearly unaware of a series of committee reports on freezing outside toilets, leaking flat roofs, inadequate heating systems, unusable swimming pools, sub-standard playing fields, inadequate facilities for practical subjects, and constant delays in effecting repairs and carrying out maintenance. He did not acknowledge the news that Her Majesty's Inspectors now rated Harrow among the two in three local authorities where decoration, repairs and maintenance were less than satisfactory.

Since the messages were unpalatable it was clearly time to think of shooting the messenger. But it's not every messenger who naively makes and loads the weapon for his own execution. Towards the end of 1987 the Audit Commission were looking for an education officer to join their investigative team. I had at least a nodding acquaintance with most aspects of an Education Department's work and a fair knowledge of making and controlling budgets, and I'd been a member of working parties on esoteric topics like management information, computer timetabling and the relation between inputs and outputs in education. This seemed a useful basis for work with the Commission, so I made some tentative enquiries and ascertained that what they really wanted was a serving officer whose employers would be prepared to second him half time. I had a word with Brian Clark who seemed interested and sympathetic. After a day or two he suggested that I speak to Ron Grant. 'Most interested in your aspirations,' said Ron, 'very happy to release you to work *full time* for the Audit Commission.' 'Oh! no,' said the Commission, 'we want someone who is still a serving officer with his feet firmly on the ground.' 'Oh! no,' said Ron, 'We insist. You must go.' 'Oh! no,' said I, 'the Audit

Commission don't want me now, you've queered the pitch by insisting that I go full time.' 'Ah! ha,' said Ron, 'we'd like you to go anyway.' 'Oh! no,' said I, 'I have a wife and young children, and expected to go on working for another seven or eight years…Unless, by chance, you were thinking of paying me seven years' salary…?'

I spent a day or two sticking pins in plasticine Ron Grants. This had no evident effect, so I dusted my notes on Getting Results and Solving Problems and began to make a list of all the options I could think of.

CHAPTER 18

Power without Responsibility

In fair round belly with good capon lined

I BECAME A CONSULTANT. The old joke about lawyers applies even more to consultants. Researchers prefer consultants to rats because there are more of them, you don't get fond of them, and they have no scruples. Like the consultant who stopped to put on running shoes when a big brown bear chased him and a civil servant in Yellowstone Park. 'Why on earth are you doing that?' said his companion. 'You'll never be able to out-run the bear.' 'No, but I'll be able to out-run you.'

1988 was a good time to start this new venture. The Inner London Education Authority was being abolished and thirty London boroughs found an enormous cuckoo in their nest, an education service which dwarfed all their other responsibilities. I was invited to help Camden, a famously left-wing authority with a good deal of political baggage. I persuaded my old colleague Harold Taylor to join me. Harold had been the chief adviser in Harrow, once an *Observer* Debating Mace winner, an indefatigable worker with an unrivalled talent for punning and a wide knowledge of education. He always suspected me of an unduly mechanistic approach, but we shared an upbringing in Methodism and an interest in history and architecture, and I knew he was totally reliable. The third member of our team was Paul Corrigan, a splendidly articulate generalizer wished on us by Camden's Labour leaders. Paul went on to some ill-defined advisory role at the Labour headquarters in Walworth Road and later became the *éminence gris* behind Hilary Armstrong, Chief Whip and Minister under Tony Blair. He was a most engaging, stimulating colleague who took in good part my and Harold's attempts to turn his philosophizing drafts into committee speak.

We were all part-timers, though as team leader I put in more time than Paul or Harold. Until Peter Mitchell became Director of Education a year or two later I was *de facto* Camden's Mr Education, and virtually every thing to do with schools or colleges came my way. I was most surprised to hear one day that no less a personage than Sir Keith Joseph would like to meet me, and even more amazingly would come to Camden to see me. I had no office so I booked a Town Hall Committee room. On the appointed day the list of Council meetings displayed for all the world to read, 'COMMITTEE ROOM 3 – Mr MANN and Sir KEITH JOSEPH.' For a few hours my credit in left-wing Camden was zilch. In fact Sir Keith's concerns were personal and apolitical. A physicist professor friend of his had mentioned the lack of science teachers at Hampstead School where his children were. Since the school was in Camden Sir Keith thought I might be able to help. Our own children were at the same school so I could empathize but I had to explain that I and Camden were powerless because the Inner London Authority was still in charge.

When we came to appoint Camden's first education officers I soon realized how much Sheffield and Harrow had still to learn about full-blooded equality, red in tooth and claw. Camden had specialist equal opportunities officers for women, disabled people and ethnic minorities. Jabbering like Macbeth's three witches these officers would materialize mysteriously at every interview, observing the proceedings with baleful eye, ready to overturn them at the first suspicion of any deviation from the opportunities code. Once Peter Mitchell and some of his senior colleagues were in post we consultants gradually withdrew. But I left them two useful legacies, a detailed description of Camden's many and varied services for young people with special needs and suggestions as to how those might be improved, and one other suggestion. Camden certainly needed a vision of its role, it needed high aspirations for community schools and equal opportunities; but its immediate reputation as a new education authority would depend much more on such banausic matters as making sure that its home-to-school transport could be relied on and all the part-time teachers in its colleges and adult institutes were promptly paid. In the short run, 'whate'er is best administer'd is best.' I like to believe this advice was partly responsible for Camden's rating a couple of years later as one of the best of the new London authorities.

The demise of the Inner London Education Authority left a number of their talented officers high and dry. Under Alan Groves' inspirational leadership a few of us began to think about setting up a new society of education consultants. We did the usual things, listed all the people we thought might be interested, roughed out some ideas for a meeting or two and began to think about a draft constitution. Sir Peter Newsam, then Director of the Institute of Education after holding many other leading posts, gave all the help he could. Among the first wave of members were many retired Chief Education Officers, HM Inspectors, civil servants, professors, and other eminent people. In the early days we met regularly with speakers like Sir Christopher Ball, former Warden of Keble College and now a free-lance consultant on higher education, Sir John Cassels, once Director of the National Economic Development Council and now running the National Commission on Education, John Hedger, a Deputy Secretary at the Department for Education, and Brian Oakley Smith, founder of Cambridge Education Associates. The Society's meetings were high-level seminars for people who wanted to stay near the leading edge of educational thinking. We borrowed freely from other professions in developing our own code of practice and standards of performance. 'You think you have problems? Wait till you see our solutions.'

As the society's honorary secretary for the first four or five years I was at the hub of this new world of educational consultancy and happy, as a sideline, to put consultants and prospective clients in touch with each other. We soon recruited waves of new members, often younger men and women forced into early retirement and much more dependent on making a living from their work as consultants. I was a little less enthusiastic about giving my own services freely to help other mercenaries make a living.

I was also busy with my own work. Other invitations soon followed Camden's. KPMG, Price Waterhouse, Capita and other leading firms of accountants and management consultants were anxious to strengthen their education teams and like other former education officers I soon found myself preparing bids, running seminars and helping to compose newsletters. Articles on the latest legislation and its implications were in great demand, and book reviews too. My friend Ron Glatter at the Open University asked for a chapter on how institutions manage their boundaries with their local authority and Christine Gilbert for one on local management, Secretary of State Baker's nostrum for school improvement. For some years John Fielden of KPMG and I wrote the education chapter in *The Public Services Yearbook*, another OU handbook.

Most satisfying was my work for one of the teachers' unions. I had been a fairly active member of the Assistant Masters' Association, branch chairman and mover of resolutions at its annual conferences. When conference supported my call for Oxford and Cambridge to drop compulsory Latin from their admission requirements and the press mentioned my connection with CRGS, Jack Elam seemed to take the resolution as a personal affront. Later on, the Association merged with the Assistant Mistresses and in due course the new body became the Association of Teachers and Lecturers. For all sorts of reasons more and more members needed support in competency proceedings, disciplinary proceedings, ill health and breakdown, redundancy and early retirement. My work for the Association's support team took me to scores of schools of every kind, counselling our members, negotiating on their behalf, and sometimes representing them in formal hearings. Almost all were victims, some of their own ill health or incapacity, some of impersonal budgetary forces, some of their superiors' abuse of power. Looking after their interests, securing the best possible deals for them, and in some cases helping them to come to terms with what they felt was a personal disaster, seems still to have been the most moral job I ever did.

From time to time the consultant enjoys icing on his cake. The British Council, short-handed perhaps, invited me to be one of two UK representatives at a Latin American conference in Mexico. We enjoyed the platform by-play between the ever so, ever so susceptible President and his ravishing Minister of Education. There was time also to visit the Aztec Temple where by happenstance I bumped into Irene, my gifted Schools Council assistant and

Conference at the Aztec Templo Mayor, Mexico: Alvaro, Maria (my Mexican mentors), John, Irene, Ray.

her husband Ray, to enjoy the Ballets Folklorico, buy Margaret some handsome silver, and become acquainted with tequila and *mole poblano*, the spicy chocolate sauce Mexicans like with their chicken. Best of all was the reception in a seventeenth-century palace where Mexico's teachers entertained us royally with the distinctive music and dancing of their own regions. Each of the foreign delegates was given a handsome Metepec Tree of Life as a souvenir. But the most valuable lessons I took away from the conference were never ever to agree to be the fifth of seven plenary speakers at an afternoon session, and never again to rely on simultaneous translators to relay my best jokes.

In the course of consultancy I met the port wine community in Oporto and enjoyed their best vintages, played a few holes at one of the Algarve's most prestigious golfing hotels with Andrew Stuart, once our man in Helsinki, met the ghosts of Agatha Christie and the spy Cicero in Istanbul's Perla Palace hotel, visited the Blue Mosque and the Topkapi Palace in driving snow, admired the versatility of the Macedonian education adviser who ran a first-class winery in his spare time and sat in his snug till the small hours listening to melancholy folk songs about chaps going off to the wars and leaving their girls behind. With an armed soldier in attendance I swore eternal loyalty to the Stars and Stripes in return for US Social Security number 624 – 26 – 1221 and a small honorarium.

At the Chilean Ministry of Education I exchange fond embraces with a

The consultant plays a solo trumpet on the Danube.

dozen charming senior inspectors and civil servants not once but sometimes several times a day. Claiming the oldest democracy in Latin America, Chileans feel the British are their soul mates even if they do find us a bit obsessive about punctuality; everyone smiles when you arrange to meet 'British time'. Generations of British traders and engineers and freedom fighters like Admiral Cochrane have left their mark. There are Santiago 'tea shops' where you can still eat cake and sip tea at 4 o'clock. An incompetent jack of all trades will always be a 'gas fitter' in Chile. The middle classes have a small bedroom for their Indian live-in maid, and another Indian to sweep the pavement outside the house and tend the garden; they live well. Other things seem to work less well. At their national institute for educational development the director has to ask his secretary for the key if his guests need a loo.

On our first evening I and my colleague, Scottish HMI David McNicoll, are amazed to see so many youngsters wearing the same blue uniform; there must be an enormous school close to our hotel. But no, throughout the country every child wears essentially the same uniform, with only minor variations in the pocket badge and the quality of the cloth to distinguish one school from another. Since most of the schools in Santiago work shifts you feel as if their pupils are patrolling the streets from early morning until mid-evening. It's a curiously illuminating experience. In Britain school uniform is about celebrating the differences between one school and its neighbours. In Chile it's about what all young people have in common.

Chileans are the warmest, most affectionate people you could wish to meet. Whole classes of ten year olds line up to shake hands (the boys) or embrace (the girls) when you visit their schools. And you're bowled over when a beautiful seventeen year old head girl welcomes you to her school with an embrace and an affectionate kiss. But it's a country of dramatic contrasts. I visit Santiago's most prestigious boys' school, a highly selective school whose entrance hall is festooned with the portraits of former Chilean Presidents who were alumni of this one school. In every classroom the boys bombard me with probing questions. A few miles from the city there's a tiny village school with hardly a book or a pencil to its name, where each child has a stony two or three square foot patch of soil and a stick to scratch the surface with which to learn the bare essentials of subsistence gardening.

The young people are open and friendly but it's only a year or two after Pinochet was toppled and many of their teachers are harassed and edgy. Teachers' wages are so low that many take advantage of the shift system to work in two schools and earn two salaries. And they cannot easily adjust to a change of government. Like Cromwell's major-generals, Pinochet's soldiers ruled the country. They had the right to enter schools and inspect classes. The slightest note of humour at the regime's expense could lead to a tap on the shoulder. Promotion went only to those whose records were squeaky clean; and not all the head teachers who survived Pinochet's fall are trusted by their colleagues.

I was out and about a lot as a consultant but it was good to be based at home. If deadlines threatened I could work fourteen or sixteen hours a day. Or my working day could be a three- or four-decker sandwich, spells of work interspersed with personal correspondence, household shopping, light gardening, and time for the daily paper. But it's fiendishly hard for a lone worker to keep up to date without the sustaining nourishment of all the information which pours into a large organization, and I'd never really expected an unlimited shelf life. After four or five years I no longer knew instinctively who to invite to speak at a seminar, or what to say in a leading-edge article. It was time to withdraw from activities like those.

That left more space in my portfolio for voluntary activities. Margaret has a remarkable talent for devising beguiling little tasks for other people, and she suggested that any residual skills I had as historian and educator might be usefully deployed in writing the story of her own school, Highbury Fields, the one formed by merging Shelburne and Highbury Hill. Its history was a rich tapestry illustrating many aspects of education from the 1830s to the present. On the Shelburne side the school's history could be traced through the London County Council's secondary modern school to an earlier merger between the Holloway Free and Ragged School and the St Barnabas National School. On the Highbury side its history went back beyond the LCC's Highbury Hill High School to a whole family of schools established by the

Home and Colonial Society. Setting out to train infant teachers in premises in Gray's Inn Road, the Society were soon running a complete range of model and practising schools grant-aided by the government. By 1882 they could claim that one in nine of the country's trained women teachers was Home and Colonial trained and for many years the Home and Colonial were at or near the top of the inter-college league tables published by the government. Though pleased with this success, the Society disliked the system. As they said in 1885, 'it cannot be denied…that the pernicious fashion of late years, in schools of every grade, has been to set up Examination rather than Education as the end and aim of school life.' It's a fashion which seems destined to surface every century or so.

The Society's non-government department was even more remarkable, running in-service courses for serving teachers and providing opportunities for training and professional development for intending missionaries and others working overseas. Many of its graduates were to be found all over the world, from India and China, New Zealand and Australia, to Canada and the USA where Home and Colonial methods were adopted in New York and California. One unusual client was the War Department, for whom the Home and Colonial ran courses for the women employed in the army's schools for soldiers' children. Another surprising client was Mrs R.W. Buss of Camden who asked the Society to run a course for governesses and kindergarten teachers. Many of those who took this course went on to work for families or to teach in secondary schools. Among them Mrs Buss's daughter Frances Mary was to found both Camden School for Girls and the North London Collegiate School. Twenty years later Miss Buss used to require all her kindergarten teachers to take the Home and Colonial course. The Society was the first to provide any kind of training for secondary school teachers.

Very early in their life the Society decided to diversify. There was a demand for junior as well as infant teachers, and in 1844 the Society opened a Model Juvenile School. This later became a Middle Class School for boys and girls. and was then renamed the Mayo High School. In 1884 it became a girls' secondary school with a few little boys. Ten years later it was this school which moved to Highbury Hill where it survived only by seeking refuge with the LCC as one of the new grammar schools created under the 1902 Education Act. Eighty years later Margaret effected Highbury Hill's merger with Shelburne to create Highbury Fields, Islington's most successful comprehensive school.

Researching and writing this story took much of my playtime for two or three years. Another labour of love also took more and more of my disposable time. I happened to spot an advertisement in Hampstead's famous local paper, the Ham and High. My local Brent Samaritans were looking for volunteers. Here was a chance of contributing to my own community. I'd been aware of the Samaritans for many years, and felt that in our increasingly atomized society more and more people had a need for a listening ear. That was something I could offer, so I applied, braving the possibility of rejection at interview or failure on the preparatory course. Starting with a single telephone line at the Reverend Chad Varah's church, St Stephen Walbrook, the Samaritans had grown rapidly to some 200 branches with more than 20,000 volunteers waiting for calls from despairing or suicidal callers. An annual rally sustained their enthusiasm, but even to stand still, what the true believers liked to call a movement needed to recruit and train several thousand new volunteers each year to compensate for a 20 per cent turnover. To maintain some sort of consistency the volunteers were obliged like legionnaires to observe a strict code, complete confidentiality for every caller however reprehensible his actions, never to reveal their own name to callers, never to mention their being Samaritans to any outsider, never to offer advice, always to ask callers to talk about their feelings, and in every conversation to ask whether the caller had ever considered suicide. I sometimes wonder why a congenital Nonconformist like myself should have joined such a rule-bound organiza- tion. Was it always a good idea to encourage callers to talk about their feelings? Some seemed more in need of help in conceiving possible solutions to their problems. In spite of these doubts I soon found a niche. Most of the volunteers wanted above all to support our troubled callers and had no great interest in mundane business matters like applying for council grants, paying bills, keeping accounts, finding new premises or running the committee in an orderly way. Within a year or two I was branch committee chair and soon after that branch treasurer as well. For three or four years I was happily busy, liaising with a supportive local council, drafting a large and successful bid for lottery funding to refurbish new premises, working with architects and builders and keeping an eye on our high street shop. That and sometimes helping out as a shop assistant allowed me to claim a new life as a high street trader. We had some astonishing gifts, uncut books and unwrapped clothes among them. Perhaps the most spectacular came from clearing a house whose doctor owner had been generously rewarded by his patients over many years; in a couple of private garage sales I sold innumerable bottles of spirits, Grand Marnier, Benedictine, Cherry Brandy and the like, and numerous cases of fine wine. Our funds benefited by many hundreds of pounds. Whenever the newspapers said high street trade was brisk or sluggish so too were our own takings. When the bottom fell out of the German recycling industry, we could no longer get a price for the clothes and fabrics we could not sell in the shop. I imagined somehow that charity shops would buck the normal trends. But I guess my commercial antennae, momentarily sensitive in my air force life, must have atrophied some years ago. With my talented, charismatic friend Alastair de Watteville I bought for resale expensive signed prints only days, it seemed, before the print market peaked and slid into a prolonged trough.

The annual Samaritan Walk was open to every branch, a fun tramp along

Brent's Samaritans ready to tackle the Malvern Hills: John, Dan, Penny, Ian, Julie, Zarine.

the Malvern Hills, the South Downs, the North York Moors or somewhere similar. It was a great fund-raiser but finding sponsors was much more demanding than the thirty-mile hike. Three or four years on the trot I managed to complete a personal 'ton', miles walked plus age in years equalled a hundred, or more. What I wondered was the optimum age for doing this? One barbed critic said all he hoped was to walk one mile when he was 99.

In the 1990s Samaritans suffered like other groups from a shortage of volunteers. Our national HQ decreed that we must not open unless we had at least two volunteers on duty That made it even harder to provide a round-the-clock service so we sometimes had to divert calls to other branches. Nationally Samaritans moved into e-mail and set up a central sorting office to receive and distribute messages. We were it seemed no longer one of a bundle of support services for our own locality, but increasingly part of a huge call centre. These developments strengthened the movement's latent authoritarianism. It was time, I thought, for a change of air.

After fifteen arduous years of headship Margaret was allowed in 1994 to retire early. Her influence lingered. One of her deputies was Head of Highbury Grove boys school for a while, and another succeeded her at Highbury Fields to be followed a decade later by the first teacher Margaret appointed when she went to Highbury. Margaret herself remains a governor, an elder whose unthreatening contributions are still valued.

CHAPTER 19

Spacious Days

Hedge-crickets sing

A SEPTEMBER HOLIDAY, a Thursday matinee, a weekday at leisure. For roughly sixty years these were unknown pleasures. Throughout these years the school day and the academic year constituted some sort of framework for me and my family. With Margaret's retirement the last remnants of this structure fell apart. Suddenly we felt hugely privileged, with vast expanses of time at our disposal and enough resources to enjoy ourselves. Leisure, Lin Yutang once observed, is in time like unoccupied floor space in a house; I seemed to be living luxuriously in a spacious mansion.

Its many rooms were soon furnished, at least partly. We knew some parts of Britain quite well. Could we manage to set aside a week to explore each of the counties we did not know? Even a week in each would be ridiculously inadequate. But we set out on a long-term odyssey and still have the greater part of this voyage to complete.

We began too to explore London, greatly helped by the London Society and the London Appreciation Society. Founded a century ago as a campaigning body to preserve and enhance London's architectural heritage the London Society also arranges a richly varied programme of visits and lectures. This programme is dwarfed, at least in number of events, by that of the London Appreciation Society, a society launched half a century ago by eccentric genius Dr Bryant Peers, geography teacher turned travel agent, who began organizing low-cost visits and talks as an offshoot of his travel business. From Roman London to Mayor Livingstone's new offices, from Queen Elizabeth's Hunting Lodge to Vavasour's Ham House, and Walpole's Strawberry Hill to Bazalgette's Sewage Pumping Stations, we have looked in on almost every aspect of London life and culture. In one notable week we visited both the Palace of Westminster, to see Lord Chancellor Irvine's elaborate wallpaper, and No. 10 Downing Street, where the Prime Minister's wife said 'hello' in the hall as she clutched a bottle of lemonade.

And we walk. Up the highest Cairngorm peaks because they're there, for the Ramblers Association to safeguard local footpaths, sometimes to look in detail at London's architectural and historic heritage, sometimes to explore green London. Last year Margaret and I tackled the London Loop, a 150-mile trail along canal and riverside, through field, forest and park, all inside London's orbital motorway, the M25. This year we're leading a group of

Margaret faces retirement with a smile…

…and soon learns to relax.

Margaret's city haven.

kindred spirits round the Green London Way. By easy stages we're following a 90-mile trail all within five or six miles of Trafalgar Square. We marvel at the courage and vision of countless ordinary folk who campaigned, fought and were sometimes imprisoned to preserve some of London's ancient commons from rapacious landlords and developers. From the sandy ridges north and south of the Thames we can see that the Great Wen is still largely contained in a huge green-rimmed saucer across which the Thames winds.

A week for each of the London boroughs perhaps? A week each to begin to get to know London's major galleries and museum? As 'friends' of this and that we are just beginning to dip our toes in the great pools of riches which London offers. There's more than enough material to sustain lifelong education. A little group of local enthusiasts is examining our own patch microscopically. 'Mapesbury' derives its name from Walter Map, one of those all-purpose courtier clerics, a prebendary of St Paul's Cathedral who served Henry II as itinerant justice, diplomat and special envoy to the Vatican, a life which gave him plenty of material for satirical lampoons on life at court. When the enormous parish of Willesden was carved up Walter Map was one of the beneficiaries, though he was abroad with the king so much and had so many other duties he can hardly have spent much time here. For hundreds of years the area had one substantial manor house and not a great deal more. Railways cut through Mapesbury in the 1860s and 1870s, the church sold its lands, and for three or four decades this was the fastest-growing part of London, its leafy boulevards flanked by handsome villas. Since few modern households need a Victorian or Edwardian villa for themselves, multi-occupancy and redevelopment are constant threats. Conservationists fight continually on both fronts.

I forget when I first heard Margaret described locally as 'the geranium lady', a tribute to the wonderful pots of pelargoniums which used to fill our front patio every summer. In retirement she's had more time to develop and indulge a latent talent for creative horticulture. Our own urban garden is too small to satisfy an almost maternal passion for nurturing young seedlings. Year after year she contributes hundreds of burgeoning plants to a summer garden sale in aid of local charities. From time to time our own garden is one of a dozen or fifteen open to local residents as part of the slow process of developing a sense of community in an urban enclave.

My own contribution to this enterprise is modestly unskilled, barbering hedges, shrubs and lawn, humping pots and scattering compost. I like activities which are hot and sweaty, so one year I dig an enormous hole in our London clay, line it, make a 'natural' surround with spare blocks of York stone, and hey presto we have a large pond. I install an electric pump and eventually learn how to operate my new toy. We are now the proud owners of a baby waterfall. It's a mystery how all the creepy crawlies and flying insects find these new facilities, but find them they do. We introduce fish and frogs, and predatory herons take to looking in. One year a pair of mallards treat the place like a boarding house, dropping in two or three times a day and tapping impatiently on our patio door if there's no meal ready. Droppings from our bird table attract scavenging pigeons who themselves provide a fast food option for passing sparrowhawks. Squirrels chase up and down our one surviving apple tree and urban fox cubs from the nearby railway embankment gambol on the lawn.

Her rare combination of energy, enjoyment, expertise and a little time made it impossible for Margaret to avoid becoming the animatrice of a small group of gardening enthusiasts. Like me, and I daresay many others, she finds it hard to resist a direct plea. She's become an added governor at two more schools, and is chair of one of these, as well as being the active treasurer and outside pillar of the local branch of Victim Support. My own thirst for committee work was pretty well sated by three decades of public service, though I've found a new role as independent chair of the local council's Standards Committee. But in the lush undergrowth of community activities there are plenty of little tasks to be done, as organizer, tour leader, treasurer, report writer, proposer of votes of thanks or working-party chair. Don't mind if your working party's recommendations seem like red revolution to a torpid committee. Don't fret if you feel you're being hassled by an over-zealous chairman. As a volunteer you are always free to walk away if the kitchen begins to feel a little warm.

Escaping is easy enough. On any comparative scale we're extraordinarily

The day of the dead: Purepacha Indians come to life after an all-night vigil in the graveyard.

privileged. Britain's productivity may limp along, but for all that Margaret and I are moderately comfortable citizens of one of the richest societies the world has ever known. Along with others like us we're free to travel the world. We see something of what we in the West like to call the Ancient World, at Mycenae and Athens, in Sicily and Rome. We begin to discover the Moslem world, travel a little way along the Silk Trail to visit Khiva, Samarkand and Tashkent, catch glimpses of the Moghul Empire in Delhi and Agra, visit Bursa, Edirne and Istanbul, the ancient capitals of the Ottoman Empire, and marvel at Cordoba's Mesquita and Granada's Alhambra. Visits to Venice and Vienna remind us that they too, like Malta and Granada, epitomize the long struggle between the Western Christian world and the Moslem world whose science and arts we are just beginning to appreciate. An excursion to Sagres and Cape St Vincent reminds us of Henry the Navigator, the Portuguese explorers, and the exquisite Manueline architecture of Lisbon's Jeronimos and Belem Tower. Madrid and Seville recall the Spanish Kings, Ferdinand and Isabella, and the amazing way in which a few Spanish adventurers overthrew subtle and sophisticated peoples like the Aztecs, the Mayans and the Incas. We fly over the Nasca lines and follow the Inca trail to Machu Picchu, marvelling at the administrative skill which enabled the Incas to rule their extensive empire without any written language.

Our daughter Susan's move to Mexico gives us every reason to get to know the Latin American people. Annual visits for six or seven years have been occasions to travel widely in Mexico, surprised that one country should embrace almost all the world's main climatic regions, amazed at what the Olmecs, Toltecs, Aztecs and Mayans achieved, fascinated by what remains of Indian culture like the Day of the Dead, and delighted by the charm and splendour of Spanish colonial cities like San Miguel de Allende, Cuernevaca, Guanajuato, Zacatecas and many others. Mexican people are friendly and

All together for David and Valerie's wedding: sister-in-law Sheila, John, Valerie, David, Margaret, brother Peter, Susan, mother-in-law Marjorie.

pleasantly laid back, the result perhaps of their mixed ancestry. Most impressive is the way in which Mexico seems to have set aside centuries of strife and is now building a sense of nationhood. Scores of public buildings from the President's Palace to the Ministry of Education and many more display the works of muralists like Diego Rivera and David Siqueiros portraying key events in Mexico's history, all freely accessible to Mexicans and visitors alike. Countless mariarchi bands enliven the restaurants and streets, but we've also heard Jesus Christ Superstar blaring out in an almost deserted silver mining village and Pomp and Circumstance as the grand finale in a state band concert. We've looked in terror at wrecked railway engines hundreds of feet below our own train as it huffed and puffed on its way through the Copper Canyon. And as I tumbled head over heels down the rocky lumps of lava on a volcano some twenty years younger then myself I realized that my skull looks rather like an eggshell. Would it shatter if it hit a rock, I wondered?

From time to time we catch glimpses of another more sombre world. Cubans seem healthy and well schooled but they keep their heads down in Castro's world. The old eastern bloc countries seem drab, as enticing as Stockton-on-Tees on a wet Friday in the 1950s. In Ronda we see the gorge into which Republicans and Nationalists tossed their opponents. In Madrid we see Picasso's Guernica, in Beirut a shattered city, from Krakow we go to Auschwitz.

Which grandfather sold coal?

Which grandfather campaigned?

It's a chilling contrast to the cossetted life I've enjoyed, a salutary reminder of how lucky I've been. A secure childhood and a famous university are a good start to life. In Margaret I was lucky enough to find a talented and amazingly selfless wife. Our grown-up children are fun to be with and David's marriage to the stylish lovely Valerie makes us honorary members of a lively French clan.

I was lucky too in my working life. I've had half a dozen challenging, satisfying, stimulating jobs. For five glorious years at the Schools Council I was at the centre of a creative web of participative professional development which has had no equal anywhere in the world. The phrase 'Thank God it's Friday' bewildered me when I first heard it. Such a thought had never crossed my mind. I never wanted to bunk school or work. Perhaps I had too little imagination to envisage an alternative. A boisterous class or a bolshie committee were a challenge, not a crisis. Awkward colleagues were problems not insurmountable obstacles. Nil illegitimi. If I happened to lose one round, I started planning the *revanche*.

In the 1950s grammar school teachers enjoyed enormous freedom, con- strained only lightly by the General Certificate of Education. And in the 1960s teachers and schools were trusted, there were more funds than there had been, and local education officers had enormous scope for creative initiatives. It was perhaps the best of times to be a young education officer. My own small 1930 age group had better prospects than most because many not much older than us had lost their lives in the 1939–45 war. My own college lost in effect a whole year group and this may well be typical of all universities. My generation had too the good fortune to enjoy grants for our university courses and final salary pensions, index-linked.

It was all a far cry from the old nursery rhyme which encapsulates my own family's history:

> Tinker, tailor, soldier, sailor
> Rich man, poor man, beggarman, thief.

I carry the genes of a couple of tinsmiths, a pair of tailors, two soldiers, two fishermen sailors, a fellmonger who made money and lost it several times, two bankrupts and a needy Methodist minister. So far I haven't identified a thief. One grandfather was a railway apprentice turned campaigning lecturer, the other a farrier who became a fairly prosperous coal merchant and an Alderman. They would all be astonished at the lives we live. My next task is to get to know them all a little better.

Postscript

As Huck Finn said, 'There ain't no more to write about and I'm rotten glad of it because if I'd a' knowed what a trouble it was to make a book I wouldn't a' tackled it.'

Index

Books and Authors mentioned in the text